D0146425

Gloria Naylor

In Search of Sanctuary

Twayne's United States Authors Series

Frank Day, Editor

Clemson University

TUSAS 660

GLORIA NAYLOR
Marion Ettlinger

Gloria Naylor
In Search of Sanctuary

Virginia C. Fowler
Virginia Tech

Twayne Publishers
An Imprint of Simon & Schuster Macmillan
New York

Prentice Hall International
London • Mexico City • New Delhi • Singapore • Sydney • Toronto

Twayne's United States Authors Series No. 660

Gloria Naylor: In Search of Sanctuary
Virginia C. Fowler

Library of Congress Cataloging-in-Publication Data

Fowler, Virginia C., 1948–
    Gloria Naylor : in search of sanctuary / by Virginia C. Fowler.
        p. cm. — (Twayne's United States authors series ; no. 660.)
    Includes bibliographical references and index
    ISBN 0-8057-4025-2 (alk. paper)
    1. Naylor, Gloria—Criticsm and interpretation. 2. Afro-American women in litera-
ture. I. Title. II. Series: Twayne's United States authors series ; TUSAS 660.
PS3564.A895Z67 1996
813'.54—dc20   95-21069
                                                                                CIP

10 9 8 7 6 5 4 3 2 1 (hc)

Printed in the United States of America

Contents

Preface

In the relatively short period of time since Gloria Naylor published *The Women of Brewster Place* (1982) to wide acclaim, she has established herself as a significant contemporary writer. A self-avowed feminist and black cultural nationalist, Naylor has produced a body of work that resists easy classification. Through her four novels published to date, she enters a dialogue with a wide assortment of earlier writers, from Shakespeare and Dante to Zora Neale Hurston and Toni Morrison.

My study of Naylor attempts to situate her novels within the context of African American women writers since the late sixties, whose works she discovered, in a sense, all at once. When Naylor's involvement with the Jehovah's Witnesses ended when she was 25 years old, she had to re-create herself entirely, she has said. This re-creation led to her simultaneous pursuit of a college education, her discovery of African American women writers, and her resolution to become a serious writer herself.

My study tries to suggest some of the ways in which Naylor's artistic sensibility has been shaped by her personal and religious background as well as by her strong identification with feminism. Before offering a close analysis of each of Naylor's novels, I thus devote considerable attention to two important aspects of Naylor's life: the defining features of the Jehovah's Witness religion, and the emergence in the early 1970s of a new generation of black women writers and scholars.

Naylor's work has received selective attention from other critics. In my own discussions, I attempt to avoid repeating the work they have accomplished and to focus instead on aspects of the texts that have received little previous attention. Some of the most valuable work to date has addressed Naylor's uses of Shakespeare, but this aspect of her fiction still needs considerable exploration, especially in light of her statement that Shakespeare figures prominently in the novel she is currently writing (*Sapphira Wade*). Other areas of her work that surely need extensive scholarly attention include her use of the Bible, her extensive reliance on colors as a strategy for developing characters and themes, and her proclivity for creating elaborate, symbolic settings. I draw attention to and comment on these areas, but exhaustive treatment of them lies beyond the scope of my study.

Naylor's fiction is in many ways uniquely suited for transference to other media, as was evident early on in the success of Oprah Winfrey's television production of *The Women of Brewster Place*. For the past several years, Naylor's own production company, One Way Productions, has been working to fund a film version of her third novel, *Mama Day*. Most recently, Naylor has written a playscript for *Bailey's Cafe*, which had its world premiere in April 1994 by the Hartford Stage Company. The stage version differs considerably from the novel, and a study of Naylor's work in another genre would open interesting and potentially fruitful avenues of discussion. Because the playscript is still something of a work-in-progress, however, I made the decision to exclude it from this study.

My study has benefited greatly from Gloria Naylor's generous cooperation. Not only has she answered numerous questions, but she has talked with me at length about her family and her life; the biographical section of the study would have been sketchy indeed without her assistance. She also agreed to a lengthy interview (see appendix), which has also been of enormous value to me. I am grateful to Ms. Naylor for her cooperation and generosity.

Acknowledgments

Special thanks are due to my friend and colleague Nikki Giovanni, who read and talked with me about the manuscript, generously shared her ideas, and provided encouragement and support. I am also grateful to several classes of students whose lively discussions helped me in my thinking about these texts; I should like to mention in particular my spring 1994 graduate class and my fall 1994 honors colloquium and senior seminar.

Kim Euell, the director of new play development at the Hartford Stage Company, very kindly provided me a copy of the playscript for *Bailey's Cafe*, as well as an audiotape of the interview workshop of Gloria Naylor and Novella Nelson; for her generous assistance, I am greatly appreciative.

Many fine people at Twayne have contributed significantly to the successful completion of this project. In particular, I would like to express my appreciation to my very fine and very supportive editor, Mark Zadrozny, and to Cindy Buck, copy editor *par excellence.*

Completion of the book was made possible in part by a 1994 Summer Humanities Stipend from Virginia Tech's Center for Programs in the Humanities. The Department of English at Virginia Tech has also provided funding for travel and research materials. For these forms of institutional support, I am most grateful.

Permission to use the photograph for the frontispiece was granted by the photographer, Marion Ettlinger.

Permission to quote at length from the following material protected by copyright has been granted by Gloria Naylor: *Bailey's Cafe* (Harcourt, Brace, Jovanovich, 1992), *Linden Hills* (Ticknor & Fields, 1985), *Mama Day* (Ticknor & Fields, 1988), and *The Women of Brewster Place* (Viking, 1982).

Chronology

1950   Gloria Naylor born in New York City on 25 January, first child of Roosevelt and Alberta McAlpin Naylor. Father drafted into armed forces in November.

1951   Birth of sister Fanny Bernice.

1952   Father discharged from service.

1954   Birth of sister Carolyn. Family moves to housing project in upper Bronx. Father becomes a master framer in a custom frame shop.

1957   Death of maternal grandfather, Evans McAlpin.

1960   Family moves to apartment buildings, on West 119th Street in Harlem, owned by maternal grandmother, Luecelia McAlpin.

1963   Family moves to Queens.

1963–64   Mother joins the Jehovah's Witnesses.

1964   Death of paternal grandfather, Henry Naylor. Paternal grandmother, Callie Canada Naylor, moves to Chicago.

1967   Apartment buildings owned by maternal grandmother destroyed.

1968   Naylor graduates from high school and is baptized as a Jehovah's Witness, thus becoming a minister. Father leaves framing business to become a transit worker. Death of paternal grandmother.

1968–74   Naylor works as a switchboard operator in various places in New York to support her work as a Jehovah's Witness minister. Continues to live with parents.

1974   Moves to Dunn, North Carolina, and then to Jacksonville, Florida, preaching as a "pioneer" (a full-time worker) for the Jehovah's Witnesses. Supports herself through jobs as a switchboard operator and in fast-food restaurants.

1975   Leaves the Jehovah's Witnesses. Moves back to parents'
        home. Has a nervous breakdown. Begins college, first
        studying nursing at Medgar Evers College, then trans-
        ferring to Brooklyn College of CUNY to study English.

1976   Moves out of parents' home.

1977   Reads Toni Morrison's *The Bluest Eye* (1969), her first
        encounter with a novel by a black woman. Death of
        maternal grandmother.

1979   In November, receives encouragement from Marcia
        Gillespie of *Essence* magazine to pursue her writing.

1980   Marries.

1981   Receives bachelor of arts degree in English from
        Brooklyn College. Completes *The Women of Brewster
        Place*. Divorces. Travels to Spain and Tangiers during
        summer. Begins *Linden Hills* while in Tangiers. Begins
        graduate work in Afro-American Studies at Yale
        University.

1982   Publishes *The Women of Brewster Place*. Works on *Linden
        Hills*.

1983   Receives master of arts degree in Afro-American stud-
        ies from Yale University. Receives American Book
        Award for Best First Novel. Writer-in-residence at
        Cummington Community of the Arts and a visiting
        lecturer at George Washington University. Receives
        Distinguished Writer Award, Mid-Atlantic Writers
        Association. Travels to Guadalajara, Mexico. Begins
        work on *Mama Day*. Finds "key" to structure of *Mama
        Day* from reading Faulkner's *As I Lay Dying* (1930) in
        the American consulate.

1985   Publishes *Linden Hills*, which had been her master's
        thesis at Yale. Receives National Endowment for the
        Arts fellowship. Cultural exchange lecturer in India for
        the United States Information Agency for three weeks.

1986   Receives Candance Award of the National Coalition of
        One Hundred Black Women. Scholar-in-residence at
        the University of Pennsylvania; visiting professor at
        New York University; and visiting lecturer at Princeton
        University. Works on *Mama Day*.

1987   Visiting professor at Boston University. Works on *Mama Day*.

1988   Publishes *Mama Day*. Receives Guggenheim fellowship. Fanny Hurst visiting professor at Brandeis University and senior fellow in Society for Humanities, Cornell University. Becomes a member of Book-of-the-Month Club selection committee.

1989   Receives Lillian Smith Award. Begins work on *Bailey's Cafe*.

1990   Establishes One Way Productions, her own multimedia production company. Her nephew Roger moves in with her.

1992   Publishes *Bailey's Cafe*. Visiting writer at University of Kent, Great Britain, under the auspices of the British Arts Council.

1993   Travels in Seregambian region of Africa, lecturing and doing research for next novel. Father dies on 17 September. Travels to Oslo to do research for next novel. Stage reading of *Bailey's Cafe* at Lincoln Center.

1994   Stage production of *Bailey's Cafe* by Hartford Stage Company, 28 March–30 April.

Chapter One

Writing as Witnessing: An Introduction to the Life of Gloria Naylor

Although Gloria Naylor is a native New Yorker, her roots, like those of many African Americans of her generation, are in the South. Her personal history takes on an almost mythic quality, in fact, because she was conceived in the South but born in the North, grew up in the largest urban center in the United States but had instilled in her the values associated with rural America.

Robinsonville, Mississippi

As Naylor has recently written, she "had two grandmothers for the price of one heritage: my parents grew up next to each other in a small settlement of sharecroppers in Robinsonville, Mississippi."[1] Just 29 miles from Memphis and even closer to the Arkansas line, Robinsonville lies on historic Route 61, which leads, some 50 miles further south, to Clarksdale, often considered the birthplace of the blues because Muddy Waters was born on a plantation near it. Naylor's family history, stories of which she listened to as a child, resembles that of many southern blacks whose ancestors experienced the outrages of slavery and for whom the conditions of the postslavery South were little better.

Naylor's parents, Alberta McAlpin and Roosevelt Naylor, were both members of large sharecropping families on the Leatherman cotton plantation. Her maternal grandparents were Luecelia and Evans McAlpin, who also migrated to Harlem and whose home there was central to Naylor's childhood years. Luecelia was one of four daughters born to Fanny Johnson, a slave who was just twelve years old when freedom came. Fanny's first daughter, Maggie, was the offspring of Fanny's white master, while her other three daughters—Mae, Sadie Mae, and Luecelia—were the fruit of her marriage to Samuel Johnson. Stories of these great-aunts and their exploits helped shape Naylor's sense of unusual possibilities for female independence and autonomy. Her Aunt Sadie, for example, worked in vaudeville, while her Aunt Mae was a successful bootlegger whose acquisition of real estate in Harlem made it possible for her youngest sister, Luecelia, to migrate north. Naylor has commented that the character of Etta Mae in *The Women of Brewster Place* (1982) embodies or evokes the spirit of Aunt Mae.[2]

Naylor's grandmother Luecelia was in fact the only one of her siblings to live a traditional life as a wife and mother, even though these roles were not actually congenial to her. Born in Memphis, Luecelia Johnson married Evans McAlpin, son of Oliver and Fanny McAlpin. Because Evans suffered from a nervous condition, he and his young wife moved from Memphis to Robinsonville; there, as sharecroppers on the Leatherman plantation, they eventually met Callie and Henry Naylor, and the two women became close friends.

Callie Canada, Naylor's paternal grandmother, was born in Arkansas, the daughter of a farmer who lost his land because he was illiterate. She eventually married Henry Naylor, an orphan, a wanderer, and a blues man. Henry Naylor settled down after his marriage to Callie, although family legend has it that on more than one occasion Callie took a shotgun after Henry and an anonymous young girl ("Telling," 60). Naylor's father, Roosevelt, was nine years old when the Naylors moved to Robinsonville and became sharecroppers on the Leatherman plantation.

If Callie Canada was jealous in her love of Henry Naylor, Luecelia Johnson, or so the family stories suggest, was thought to have betrayed her husband with the blacksmith, whose frequent visits to the McAlpin home were mysterious given that the McAlpins owned no horses.

As sharecroppers, the Naylors and the McAlpins and their children put in 12-hour days, "from can't see to can't see," working in the fields.[3] The writer's parents, Alberta and Roosevelt, were each one of eight siblings; as Naylor has stated, "large families were an asset because the additional child meant that in less than ten years there would be an extra pair of hands to add to the collective earnings. Children worked beside their parents, at first using short-handled hoes to chop away the weeds, then gleaning behind the pickers, until finally graduating to 'pulling their own hundred-weight sacks' of cotton" ("Reflections," 68). The 12-hour days put in by the entire family would yield, on an average, $600 a year.

Something of the spirit of Naylor's great-aunts Mae and Sadie must have been passed on to her mother, for even as a child Alberta was determined to transport herself away from this physically exhausting life through the magic of books. It is to her mother that Naylor has repeatedly attributed her own love of reading. As she recently wrote, "We heard her story so often it became the stuff of family legend."[4] That story relates the determination of the young Alberta to acquire books even though her parents were too poor to buy them and even though, as a black child in Mississippi, she was denied access to the public library. So she used Saturday, her one day off from sharecropping, to hire herself out to work someone else's field—"and she got a sum total of fifty cents a day for doing that. At the end of the month, though, she had two dollars. And she could take that two dollars and she would send away to book clubs, and that's how she was able to feed her love of learning."[5]

Given the close friendship between Callie Canada Naylor and Luecelia Johnson McAlpin, it is perhaps not surprising that their children would share close bonds, although the only marriage between the two sets of children was that of the writer's parents. Alberta McAlpin and Roosevelt Naylor married in June 1949, on Alberta's family's front porch. Just as she had found a way to acquire books, Alberta was also to find a way out of Mississippi. She had exacted a promise from Roosevelt, before they were married, that "if they had children, those children would not be born in Mississippi" (Bellinelli). It was, in fact, a stipulation she had presented to every young man who wanted to marry her. As she later explained her reasoning to her daughter, "I had always promised myself that if I had children, I would not raise them in Mississippi. Because it used to gall me to see that we had to work, we had no schooling if the kids wanted to go on to school. And my parents were too poor to send me away and pay for me to go somewhere else. . . . I figured a whole new world would open up for you because here you had freedom" ("Reflections," 68–69). And so Alberta and Roosevelt boarded the train from Memphis to New York in December 1949, and a month later their first child, Gloria, was born.

Early Childhood

Like countless African American people before them, Alberta and Roosevelt quickly discovered that in New York "there was as much segregation as in the South, but it was more subtle" (Bellinelli). Still, there were schools and libraries, and these were to Alberta "the key to your dreams and the key to any kind of advancement" (Bellinelli). Roosevelt Naylor first found work at a doll factory but was soon drafted by the army and spent two years in combat training, though he was never sent to Korea. After his discharge from the service in 1952, the young couple and their two daughters, Gloria and Fanny Bernice, moved into a housing project in the upper Bronx. In 1954 the third and final child was born, also a daughter, Carolyn. During these years, Roosevelt worked as a master framer in a custom frame shop.

Naylor's mother played a crucial and frequently acknowledged role in the young girl's life; only since the death of her father in 1993, in fact, has the writer begun to explore in print what her father's experiences and feelings may have been. Theirs was a southern home, with southern food, southern language, southern values, southern codes of behavior. The young Gloria, always quiet and shy, grew up hearing her parents talk about their lives in Robinsonville, about "fishing and going to the woods and picking berries."[6] Although Gloria and Bernice were playmates who dressed alike when they were small, Gloria "didn't really pal around" with her sisters.[7] The family was close-knit, but it consisted of distinctly different personalities. Gloria's mother Alberta was very close to her own mother and sisters.

Through the help of Aunt Mae, Luecelia and Evans McAlpin had moved to Harlem just a few months before Alberta and Roosevelt's move in 1949 and had bought two apartment buildings on West 119th Street. Unlike many southern blacks who migrated north, Naylor's maternal grandparents were able to buy property, an asset that greatly benefited their family. The various members of Naylor's extended family lived in these apartments at some point or another, and the ground-floor apartment where Gloria's grandparents lived reverberates in the memory of the novelist: it was "a weekend mecca for my immediate family, along with countless aunts, uncles and cousins who brought along assorted friends. It was a bustling and open house with assorted neighbors and tenants popping in and out to exchange bits of gossip, pick up an old quarrel or referee the ongoing checkers game in which my grandmother cheated shamelessly. They were all there to let down their hair and put up their feet after a week of labor in the factories, laundries and shipyards of New York."[8] So important was her grandmother's home in her imagination that Naylor has written that it was "a recurrent setting in my dreams when I was a child," and later she was to use the street numbers of the apartment buildings, 314 and 316, in *The Women of Brewster Place*.[9]

In 1960, Alberta, Roosevelt, and their three young daughters moved into an apartment in one of these buildings in order to save money to buy a home of their own. The location of that future home was one of many subjects upon which Alberta and Roosevelt disagreed; as with the move north, Alberta's vision prevailed. Roosevelt had wanted to live in the upper Bronx, an area that was familiar to him, while Alberta wanted to buy in Queens, which in those years represented suburbia. As the novelist was later to write, "Their disagreement over the location for their home was only a continuum in the friction that often developed from their distinctly different personalities and visions. My mother tends to be more withdrawn, while my father loves a crowd. Yet the inverse always seemed true of their approach to a goal; she was impulsive, the visionary who urged along a cautious plodder more comfortable with the known than the unknown" ("Reflections," 71).

Naylor has spoken and written often of the conflict between her parents, conflict that arose from their being almost polar opposites. A handsome, gregarious man, Roosevelt Naylor loved music, especially jazz and blues. Alberta, by contrast, was timid, quiet, and shy—a homebody. Although the novelist looks like her father, she has repeatedly stated that in her personality and even the way she talks she closely resembles her mother. She has also observed that her parents' different personalities might have "led each to feel that their individual lives would have been happier apart" ("Reflections," 71), but they shared a strong belief in a united family and a desire to make a better life for their children.

The year the Naylors moved into their new home in Queens— 1963—was a critical year not only in their personal lives but in the life of America itself. One of the most significant years in the civil rights movement, 1963 witnessed the assassination of Medgar Evers, the August March on Washington, the bombing of the 16th Street Baptist Church in Birmingham, and the assassination of President John F. Kennedy in November. Although Naylor's parents were not actively involved in the tumultuous events of the time—she has referred to her father as an " 'armchair' activist" ("Reflections," 70)—both they and she, always an avid reader, were certainly aware of the turmoil. The double confusion engendered by the upheaval in the larger world and by the upheaval brought about by puberty within the adolescent Naylor had in fact led Alberta a year or two earlier to give her daughter a diary in which to write about her feelings. The move from her grandmother's apartment building in Harlem to the more middle-class borough of Queens when Gloria was 13 precipitated her increased awareness of racism in America: "That's when I first began to understand that I was different and that that difference meant something negative" (Bellinelli). In retrospect, Naylor has written, she understands that her parents "were trying to protect us from pain, and they took us up to Queens . . . to put us into a good school system."[10]

If the move to Queens jolted the young girl into a new awareness of the "negative" difference of race, it also prompted her parents to teach their children to look within for their sense of self-validation. Although her father had hoped for sons, he recognized that he had to give his daughters the same kind of independence and self-confidence he would have instilled in sons. He was "sort of quasi-feminist, if you will. These are my girls, and no one's going to treat my girls badly, and I'm going to equip them to go out in the world."[11] He and Alberta instilled in their three daughters the idea that "you don't look to the outside world for your validity, you must look within. You can do whatever you want. You set your own limits for yourself" (Bellinelli). The turning inward served to counteract the hatred projected by a racist white world that was desperately fighting in 1963 to maintain the privileges made possible by its hegemony. It also led the young Gloria to turn to writing in her diary as "a way of making order out of internal chaos, making sense out of things" (Bonetti), which remains for her the primary function of her art.

Yet another significant event coinciding with the family's move to Queens was Alberta Naylor's conversion to the faith of the Jehovah's Witnesses. Naylor's mother had throughout her life been interested in all kinds of religions. As a child in Mississippi, she had been a Methodist, and then, when Gloria was about nine years old, Alberta and Luecelia both joined the Baptist church. But Alberta, who "had a great respect for religion" (Bonetti), continued to explore until, in 1963, she joined the Jehovah's Witnesses. Her daughters all studied the religion, and although Bernice eventually became a Jehovah's Witness also, and remains one today, Gloria was the one most attracted to it initially, in part perhaps because she "liked to be different."[12] Five years later, following her graduation from high school, she would abandon her plan to attend Hunter College, be baptized as a Jehovah's Witness, and spend the next seven years of her life devoted to its ministry.

Overviews of Naylor's life nearly always acknowledge her work with the Jehovah's Witnesses, and she has herself talked about her attraction to it, but to date no one has looked seriously at the possible influence this religion had on the shaping of Naylor's identity or on the directions taken by her art. I believe such an influence not only exists but is profound. The features unique to this Christian sect play an important role in Naylor's vision of the world.

The Jehovah's Witnesses

The common image of the Jehovah's Witnesses held by people unfamil-iar with the actual beliefs of the sect is of a contemporary Ancient Mariner determined to tell you his—or more likely, her—story. Such an image is not far from the reality: since Jehovah's Witnesses believe their most important mission in life is "to witness," every Jehovah's Witness is a "minister." Every minister in the Jehovah's Witnesses spends hours each week going door to door to preach the truth, and that "preaching consists primarily of placing publications with members of the public."[13] These publications are all written and produced by the Watch Tower Bible and Tract Society, *The Watch Tower* magazine being the best known. Each issue of *The Watch Tower* is produced in print runs "in excess of ten million copies," making it "one of the most widely circulated magazines of any kind in existence" (Botting and Botting, xxxiv). The Witnesses' belief in the power of the written word (setting aside for the moment the particular substance of that written word) would have obvious impor-tance in the developing mind of a future writer.

The Jehovah's Witnesses claim to "have no creed" but simply to "follow the Bible."[14] Their interpretation of the Bible, however, yields a "fundamentalist, apocalyptic, prophetic religion"; adherents proclaim that the prophecies set forth in the Bible are being fulfilled in the twen-tieth century.[15] The most important of these prophecies is the immi-nent end of the world. Since 1914, when Christ took power in Heaven and cast Satan out of it, we have been "living in what Jehovah's Witnesses call 'the Time of the End'—a period of unparalleled deca-dence" (Botting and Botting, 3). When Armageddon comes, "God will destroy the entire wicked system of things, and then the Devil himself will be completely put out of action" (Henschel, 133). After Armageddon, "earth will be made a paradise" and "those in the graves will be resurrected, with the opportunity of living forever if they prove themselves obedient to God" (134). Although eternal life in an earthly paradise will be available to all who are righteous, only a chosen few will receive "the reward of spiritual life with Jesus Christ in heaven," the number of those chosen few being, according to Revelation 7:4, "exactly 144,000" (134).

The theocratic vision of the Jehovah's Witnesses dictates some of the behavior that has gained public attention, including their refusal to salute the flag or to fight in wars. In fact, their persistence in taking cases of conscientious objection to military service to the U.S. Supreme

Court has resulted in important broadening of the meaning of the First and Fourteenth Amendments: "It is impossible to speak of the history of civil liberties in this country without speaking of them" (Harrison, 186).

The images used in the Witnesses' literature juxtapose the Witnesses to the world, just as the history of the world has to them been the story of clashes between Christ and Satan. Because the world is seen as an evil place, its destruction is to be yearned and prayed for; hence, violent images of "rampant destruction" are relished by the Witnesses, who see themselves as set apart from that destruction in images of ideal community (Botting and Botting, 105, 101). The evil of the world, which can easily corrupt, is to be avoided in every way: Witnesses are discouraged from reading anything other than publications by the Watch Tower Bible and Tract Society; they are discouraged from seeking postsecondary education (although this may be changing) and are taught to value primarily practical training, by which they can earn the money necessary to support their volunteer ministry; and they are cautioned to avoid the companionship of those outside the Witnesses. Children in particular are trained in ways designed "to ensure that [they] will remain misfits in relation to the larger cultural world. . . . 'The World' becomes a most unpleasant and alien place. As a misfit in the broader society, the child *must* seek companionship within his family and religious community" (Botting and Botting, 118).

Within that community, however, the Jehovah's Witness finds friendship and fellowship. Questions of moral and ethical conduct have definite answers. Events in the world have assigned meanings. Persecution from the world is not only explainable but evidence of one's favor with God. In short, the uncertainties, isolation, and injustices that often characterize modern lives are answered for those who join the "only true faith" (Henschel, 141). As explained by Barbara Grizzuti Harrison, who was a member for 12 years, the Jehovah's Witnesses'

> religion allows them to believe that the world is terrible, but that life is not hopeless. Because it rigidly controls all aspects of their behavior, it gives them the illusion of moral superiority, and of safety. It delivers people who have no tolerance for ambiguity from having to make ethical choices. It allows self-loathers to project their hatred onto the world. It translates the allure of the world into Satanic temptation, so that those who fear its enticements are armed against seduction. It provides ego balm for the lowly, an identification with The Chosen. (217)

Not surprisingly perhaps, the majority of Jehovah's Witnesses today are people of color, and female adherents continue to outnumber male adherents. It is not, in fact, unusual for families to be divided; most often the wife and children become members while the husband remains an unbeliever. Such was the case in Gloria Naylor's family: although she says that her parents did not argue about religion, her father never joined the Jehovah's Witnesses. Perhaps because the Jehovah's Witnesses support the idea of the nuclear family and promote traditional roles within the family, Naylor's own experience may not be unusual. For even when, as is most frequently the case, the man in a marriage is an unbeliever, the woman is counseled by her religion to "accept his headship" in the marriage in all matters other than religion: "She is to defer to him in all other matters, but not to permit his indifference or opposition to deter her from going to religious meetings, proselytizing, or instructing her children in the faith" (Harrison, 82).

Women may find through their witnessing a significance and value not accorded them by the world: "Their religion allows their voices . . . to emerge. As female Witnesses preach from door to door, instructing people in their homes, they experience a multiplication of their personalities. People *listen* to them; they are valuable, bearers of a life-giving message" (Harrison, 82). Similarly, for African Americans and other people of color, the religion provides an explanation for and a defense against the destructive experience of racism. Racial prejudice and hatred are interpreted as further evidence of a corrupt world in need of destruction, an interpretation that protects the self from the psychically damaging impact of racism. In this regard, the religion of Jehovah's Witnesses is somewhat consistent with the historical functions of religion in African American life. "The spiritual legacy of black life in America," states Kimberly Rae Connor, "is one of creating a sacred world in the midst of a world that denied meaningful forms of personal integration, thereby providing the opportunity for the attainment of a status, a self."[16] Not surprisingly, the Jehovah's Witnesses sect seems to appeal most to individuals who, like African Americans, have been marginalized and oppressed.

Individual Jehovah's Witnesses believe that they will witness Armageddon in their lifetime, but the actual date of the holocaust has had to be altered more than once. Originally scheduled to arrive in 1972, the date was subsequently changed to September 1975—the year Gloria Naylor left the sect.

The Role of the Jehovah's Witnesses in Naylor's Life

Although Naylor began to study the tenets of the Jehovah's Witnesses when her mother joined in 1963, she was not baptized into the faith until 1968, when she was 18 years old, baptism being reserved for adults. As we have seen, Alberta Naylor joined the sect at a time of great national turmoil as well as of great personal changes (with the family's move to Queens). Gloria Naylor was originally supposed to attend Hunter College following her graduation from high school in 1968, but she abandoned that plan and decided to commit herself to being a Witness. Naylor has written and spoken about her days with the Jehovah's Witnesses in various places and in various terms. For example, she has sometimes spoken of her involvement as her way of being "a sort of radical" (Carabi, 37) and of trying "to work for a better world" (Bonetti), statements that seem somewhat ironic in light of the fact that the Jehovah's Witnesses do not work to change the world but simply await its destruction.

Repeatedly, however, Naylor has tied her ministry in the Jehovah's Witnesses to two conditions, one public and the other personal. Like many Americans, she was devastated by the assassination of Martin Luther King, Jr., on 4 April 1968. Coming as it did at the end of a decade of violence against African Americans, and followed as it was in November by the election of Richard M. Nixon, King's assassination made 1968 a year of infamy to many in this country. Naylor has stated that after that tragedy, "I just felt there was absolutely no hope in this system, in this country, for any real change. . . . I thought, if they'd kill a voice that is this moderate, where's the hope?" (Bonetti). The Jehovah's Witnesses prophesied the destruction of this evil world, followed by a theocracy in which "there'd be a world government ruled by God, and then that would alleviate all of the inequities, all over the entire planet" (Bonetti). Naylor also ties her decision to become a Jehovah's Witness to her "budding sexuality" (Bonetti). Because the Jehovah's Witnesses allow only marriage or celibacy, and because she knew with certainty that she did not want to marry, she thought it would be "marvelous to remain celibate," thus avoiding the insecurities brought about by her awakening sexuality; she would be provided "a safe way of moving among men" (Bonetti).

By nature, Naylor had always been painfully shy and so unwilling to talk about her feelings that, as mentioned earlier, her mother encouraged her to write about them in a diary. Joining the Jehovah's Witnesses required her to encounter strangers and try to persuade them to let her talk to them, in their own homes, about "the truth"—in short, it brought her out of her shyness and gave her a cause (Bonetti). Despite her parents' efforts to instill in their children a sense of self-worth, Naylor seems to have suffered an extreme lack of self-esteem, which was made manifest in her shyness. It is easy to understand how being obliged by her religion to speak to others, and knowing that what she had to say was God's truth, would indeed help strengthen her sense of self-worth and self-esteem.

Being in the Jehovah's Witnesses also gave her a community and opportunities to travel. Throughout most of her years as a Witness (1968–75), she continued to live in her parents' home. She also worked as a switchboard operator in various hotels in New York to earn the money to support her "real" work—that of witnessing. In the final year of this period, she became a "pioneer," or full-time preacher, for the Jehovah's Witnesses and moved first to Dunn, North Carolina, and then to Jacksonville, Florida.

In 1975, the year Armageddon was to arrive, Naylor left the Jehovah's Witnesses "because Armageddon hadn't come; things weren't better but worse" (Bonetti). Other factors also influenced her decision. As the years had gone by, the girlfriends she enjoyed traveling with in order to witness had slowly begun to marry and enter a different kind of reality. An extraordinarily intelligent young woman, she also began "to feel dis-eased" because she was not using her mind.[17] There had sometimes been friction between her and Jehovah's Witnesses officials because she was a questioner, and questioning was not allowed: it was considered "an affront to God whose ways are higher than our ways" (Harrison, 92). She had always had a desire to learn, and learning was likewise not allowed. Although she does not remember it herself, people she knew then say that she talked about being a writer someday, though what she actually wrote then was theocratic poetry.

Interestingly, Naylor recently remarked about the fact that during her teens and early twenties (the years she was involved in the Jehovah's Witnesses) she would "have daydreams where one dream would leave off and then the next night I would pick it up and take it someplace else. The dreams would be in segments, like a soap opera. I was always the star. It was always me, five years later, or older, in some situation I thought pleasing. . . . They'd sometimes last a week, sometimes a month, it would depend on how interested I was in that particular fantasy. These daydreams would deal with either career aspirations or

romantic aspirations. I'd ultimately finish one off and start a new fantasy" (*Dreaming*, 168). The control over her life and behavior exerted by
the Jehovah's Witnesses at least seems to have had the salutary effect of
encouraging an already active imagination. In ways one can only speculate about, Naylor's years with the Jehovah's Witnesses clearly functioned as a period of gestation for her artistic sensibility. As we will see
throughout this study of her work, many characteristics of her writing,
as well as her conception of art, can be traced to her experience with the
Jehovah's Witnesses. The language with which she speaks about her art
is especially revealing. She has described her first novel, for example, as
having functioned to "exorcise" some of her "demons" (Carabi, 42). She
speaks of being a writer as "sort of like a calling";[18] arguing that literary
art offers "a form of language" that readers do not find "in secular texts,"
she refers to the world of the arts as "cloistered" (Bonetti). She acknowledges the dangers of her reliance on "cataclysmic events" in her writing
(see appendix). And just as she worked a "secular" job to earn the money
to support her "real" work as a Jehovah's Witness, she now regards her
writing as her "real work," something that exists "apart from the
world"[19] and is "sacred territory" (see appendix).

Leaving the Jehovah's Witnesses, though clearly necessary to her
development as a human being, let alone her development into the
writer she is today, was extremely traumatic for Naylor; it led to a nervous breakdown (although not her first). As she remarks frequently, control is crucial to her, and being a Jehovah's Witness undoubtedly gave
her, as it seems to give all its adherents, "the illusion of total control"
(Harrison, 242). Moreover, because membership in the Jehovah's
Witnesses places an individual in a closed society limited to other
Witnesses, to leave the religion is to leave one's friends, one's support
system: "The punishment most commonly meted out to Jehovah's
Witnesses who reject or challenge the fundamental doctrines of the
Watch Tower Society—or who ignore Watch Tower taboos such as those
against smoking or oral sex—is 'disfellowshipping,' a form of social and
spiritual ostracism the effects of which are legendary" (Botting and
Botting, 90).

It is little wonder that Naylor suffered extreme mental and emotional
distress upon leaving the Jehovah's Witnesses, for in addition to enduring the experience of "disfellowshipping" she had to begin the even more
difficult work of "rebuilding from the ground up a value system for" herself.[20] It took her many years, she has said, to come to see herself as a
good person.

That process was undoubtedly aided by the support and love she received from her parents, whose home she returned to in 1975, and by her decision to go to college. Initially, she enrolled in Medgar Evers College to study nursing, a smart, quick, practical course of study, so that "just in case this paradise was still coming, the New World, I'd have a good vocation" (Bonetti). In a very short time she realized, however, that she was spending more time studying for her English classes than she was for the science classes that constituted her nursing curriculum. She transferred to Brooklyn College, where she was to find some of the resources necessary to rebuild and reshape her identity.

Years of Transformation

The six years (1975–81) Naylor spent pursuing her undergraduate degree were years of enormous growth and change for her. She worked full-time as a switchboard operator, attended classes, and pursued her writing. At Brooklyn College she discovered both feminism and African American literature, and both discoveries were revitalizing, providing her with new ways to think about and define herself as a black woman. "I had never thought about who I was—I had other identities: I was Roosevelt and Alberta's daughter, and then I was a Christian, and then I was a switchboard operator; but I never knew, really and truly, what it meant to be a black woman" (Pearlman and Henderson, 30–31). She discovered writers like Nikki Giovanni and Ntozake Shange, whom she identified "as black feminist voices [who] . . . helped me just with establishing a separate entity in my mind as the black woman. Because . . . I built from nothing in the late seventies, I literally built from nothing" (see appendix). The extent to which Naylor's sojourn with the Jehovah's Witnesses had isolated her from her own culture is touchingly revealed by the fact that she was a 27-year-old sophomore in college when, in 1977, she encountered her first novel written by an African American woman, Toni Morrison's *The Bluest Eye*. To take the full measure of the impact of the Jehovah's Witnesses on her life, consider as one example the fact that Naylor, who had been a voracious reader as a child, was living in New York City during the early years of Morrison's writing career—during years, in fact, of an incredible explosion of black literature—and that by 1977 Morrison had published *The Bluest Eye* (1969), *Sula* (1973), and *Song of Solomon* (1977). And yet Naylor had never read a novel by a black woman until 1977.

Her encounter with *The Bluest Eye* was transformative, as was her subsequent attendance at a reading Morrison gave in New York. The novel gave her courage, as "a young poet, struggling to break into prose," to take that leap, and its story "said to a young black woman, struggling to find a mirror of her worth in this society, not only is your story worth telling but it can be told in words so painstakingly eloquent that it becomes a song" ("Conversation," 567). And when Naylor actually saw Morrison, she was struck by Morrison's physical resemblance to one of her own cousins: "I knew without a doubt that Jessie and I shared the same blood. And so that meant, somehow, the writer who could create a *Bluest Eye* was just like me" ("Conversation," 569).

And so Naylor began writing fiction, eventually submitting a story to *Essence* magazine, whose editor, Marcia Gillespie, set up a lunch date, in November 1979, to encourage Naylor to "keep writing" ("Conversation," 570). Although writing had been a lifelong dream, Gillespie's encouragement was at once exhilarating and terrifying to Naylor. Thus, when shortly after that encounter she received a proposal of marriage, she accepted, because "marrying somebody—anybody—was very traveled terrain, because I grew up feeling somehow that that was how you made your definition" ("Conversation," 570). Her writing, however, rather than her marriage, is what ultimately flourished.[21] By her final year at Brooklyn College, she was attending classes, completing *The Women of Brewster Place* on her days off, and working full-time as a switchboard operator on the midnight shift, using the quiet, early-morning hours to edit what she had written during the day. She completed her undergraduate education and *The Women of Brewster Place* in the same month, thus launching herself as one of the most important new writers in the country.

"This Bridge Called My Back"

Between 1977, when Naylor initially discovered a novel written by a black woman, and 1981, when she finished simultaneously her undergraduate degree program and her debut novel, she read voraciously, discovering a rich history of black writers, especially women writers. She later reflected that there was a remarkable irony in the fact that she was born the same year Gwendolyn Brooks won the Pulitzer Prize and yet, until age 27, had no knowledge that a Gwendolyn Brooks existed (Bonetti). But once she read *The Bluest Eye*, "it was like a floodgate had opened" (Bonetti); she began not only to seek and absorb the African

American literature that could "teach me about my reality" (Carabi, 37) but also to gain the courage "to presume" to tell her own story ("Conversation," 567). By 1977 there were increasing numbers of black women writing fiction, as well as numerous projects under way to make available earlier writers whose work had been long out of print. As a result both of the black arts and black nationalist movements of the late 1960s and early 1970s and of the concomitant women's movement, "black Americans and women found their way into the [educational] institutions" and "started to change our vision of American literature" (Carabi, 37). Naylor personally may have felt that her discovery of black women writers was late in coming, but that moment of discovery was in fact propitious, coinciding as it did with a relative wealth of newly available literature and with new academic programs. The result, Henry Louis Gates, Jr., has recently claimed, was that, "in the history of the African-American literary tradition, perhaps no author has been more immersed in the formal history of that tradition than Gloria Naylor."[22]

Many black feminist critics would agree with Naylor's own assertion that "the idea of art as a disembodied, autonomous entity is entirely false. Yes, the *process* behind the work of art has no race or gender. When I am actually within a work I am not black, I am not a woman, and I contend that I am not even a human being. . . . But the *product* of that force is always rooted in a specific body politic, both personal and historical."[23] Previously, I established some of the personal contexts in which Naylor's work is rooted; in the following section, I suggest some of the literary and historical contexts in which that work has been produced.

Naylor's childhood and adolescence coincided with the civil rights movement of the 1950s and 1960s, out of which sprang the black power and black arts movements of the 1960s and early 1970s. The writers who grew to prominence during this "new renaissance" of African American literature differed significantly from their predecessors. Their art, which was conceived as the cultural counterpart of political black nationalism, directed itself to a black, not a white, audience. Their art did not ignore white racism, but it offered more than protest: it celebrated black identity and black culture.

Many of the important leaders of the black arts movement were male (like their counterparts in the black power movement), and the rhetoric of both movements was antifemale. Nonetheless, important women writers emerged: Nikki Giovanni, Sonia Sanchez, and Audre Lorde, to name only a few. By the early seventies, a new women's movement was gathering strength; like earlier women's movements in this country, its impetus came from the struggle for civil rights. Just as the black nationalist movement generated an aesthetic counterpart, so too did the women's movement. Deborah McDowell observes, "Similar in spirit and methodology to the largely male-dominated black aesthetic movement, feminist critics likewise repudiated and subverted what they considered alien, male-created literary standards, and began to describe and analyze a female aesthetic which reflected women's unique culture." McDowell concludes that "these two modes of critical inquiry must be credited with opening up unprecedented possibilities for black and women writers. In isolating and affirming the particulars of black and female experience, they inspired and authorized writers from those cultures to sing in their different voices and to imagine an audience that could hear the song."[24]

The black women who began to publish fiction at the intersection of these different movements generated a new activity among black feminist scholars and critics (Mary Helen Washington and Barbara Christian come most immediately to mind), who began reclaiming earlier women writers whose books had long been out of print. Once these texts became more widely available, their possible connections to contemporary writers began to be explored. Christian, for example, traces a tradition initiated, she believes, by Gwendolyn Brooks's *Maud Martha* (1953), which marked "a definite shift in the fiction of Afro-American women," a shift by which greater emphasis was placed "on reflecting the process of self-definition."[25] Brooks's novel, which went out of print almost immediately after it was published, was a significant influence on Paule Marshall; Marshall's *Browngirl, Brownstones* (1959) is aptly described by Christian as "a definite touchstone in contemporary Afro-American women's fiction" ("Trajectories," 238). Marshall's second novel, *The Chosen Place, The Timeless People* (1969), was likewise destined to be influential on the novelists who began publishing in the seventies.

Margaret Walker's *Jubilee* (1965) was also published in the sixties, and its influence would ultimately be manifest in a novel like Morrison's *Beloved* (1987) some 20 years later. Reaching further back to reclaim women whose work had been lost, black feminist scholars, prompted in part by the efforts of Alice Walker, found Zora Neale Hurston's *Their Eyes Were Watching God* (1937), which became "an underground phenomenon, surfacing here and there, wherever there was a growing interest in African-American studies—and a black woman teacher."[26]

The women who began publishing novels in the seventies enjoyed a climate in which earlier novelists were being rediscovered and in which delineations of black experience and of female experience would find, as McDowell states, an audience. The difficulty, of course, lay in combining "black" and "female." When Toni Cade (Bambara) put together the first multigenre anthology of writings by black women in 1970, she did so, she states in the preface, out of a sense of frustration and impatience with both the black arts movement and the women's movement:

> The "experts" are still men, Black or white. And the images of the woman are still derived from their needs, their fantasies, their second-hand knowledge, their agreement with the other "experts." . . . And the question for us arises: how relevant are the truths, the experiences, the findings of white women to Black women? Are women after all simply women? I don't know that our priorities are the same, that our concerns and methods are the same, or even similar enough so that we can afford to depend on this new field of experts (white, female).[27]

Today, some 25 years after the pioneering efforts of Cade, Washington, and others, black feminist critics challenge the notion of "such unitary concepts" as the black woman: "'Black womanhood,' 'black female identity,' 'black experience' can no longer be viewed as unchanging essences."[28] The conception and structure of Naylor's own first novel were based on a similar resistance to reductive, unitary notions of black female experience.

Such notions, however, were (and are) more likely to underpin black feminist theory and criticism than the fiction itself. Like the flowering of the "new black poetry" of the 1960s, an explosion of black women's fiction occurred in the 1970s; the wide range of black female experience began to be inscribed by such writers as Toni Morrison, Alice Walker, Paule Marshall, Gayle Jones, and Ntozake Shange. But in their delineations of black worlds inhabited and experienced by black women, their work was often treated dismissively by white women and frequently attacked by black men. For example, in a review of Morrison's *Sula* (1974), the white critic Sarah Blackburn argued that "Toni Morrison is far too talented to remain only a marvelous recorder of the black side of provincial American life" and urged Morrison to take the steps necessary to "transcend that early and unintentionally limiting classification, 'black woman writer.'"[29] Similarly, black women novelists were castigated by black men for a perceived betrayal of their race and an ostensible corruption by the white women's movement.

Widespread success seems to have been responsible for the attacks made on Ntozake Shange's choreopoem *for colored girls who have considered suicide/when the rainbow is enuf*, which opened on Broadway to rave reviews in September 1976. McDowell usefully summarizes the furor created by Shange's work, which, along with Michele Wallace's *Black Macho and the Myth of the Superwoman* (1980), became "the subject of widespread and acrimonious debate from many sectors of the black community."[30] By far the most damaging and most famous criticism came from Robert Staples, "The Myth of Black Macho: A Response to Angry Black Feminists." Staples attacked Wallace and Shange in personal terms reminiscent of the attacks made on Nikki Giovanni earlier in the seventies, attributing their rage to their sexual need for a man.[31] He argued that, rather than supporting black men—who had historically been denied power and control—Shange and Wallace, succumbing to the influence of white feminists, were encouraging black women's "collective appetite for black male blood."[32]

The publication of Alice Walker's *The Color Purple* (1982), and even more, Steven Spielberg's 1985 film adaptation of that novel, renewed the attacks on black women writers. In a 1986 article in the *New York Times Book Review*, Mel Watkins summarized the complaints of men against "such notable writers as Toni Morrison, Alice Walker, Gayle Jones, Toni Cade Bambara and Gloria Naylor," whose novels "have, among other things, candidly focused on the perilous, sometimes embittered and brutal relationship between black men and women. Whereas the primary concern in the fiction of their male predecessors was the oppressive nature of American society—this concern remains paramount among contemporary male authors—many female writers have been equally concerned with the oppression women experience in their personal lives at the hands of men. This harmless expansion of the black writer's concerns, however, has had serious ramifications." Among the most "serious" of these "ramifications," Watkins argued, was that "those black women writers who have chosen black men as targets have set themselves outside a tradition that is nearly as old as black American literature itself. They have, in effect, put themselves at odds with what seems to be an unspoken but almost universally accepted covenant among black writers." This covenant "has been the commitment to rectify the antiblack stereotypes and propagandistic images created by non-black writers" and "to present positive images of blacks."[33]

Watkins articulated one side of an argument with deep historical roots but failed to acknowledge that the artistic responsibility for "racial uplift" had been intensely debated at least since the Harlem Renaissance. He conveniently forgot male writers who challenged the very "covenant" he invoked, most notably Langston Hughes. In his classic "The Negro Artist and the Racial Mountain" (1926) Hughes claimed the African American artist's right "to express our individual dark-skinned selves without fear or shame. If white people are pleased we are glad. If they are not, it doesn't matter. We know we are beautiful. And ugly too. The tom-tom cries and the tom-tom laughs. If colored people are pleased, we are glad. If they are not, their displeasure doesn't matter either."[34] The "covenant" to which Watkins alluded has not been "almost universally accepted," as he claimed. Nevertheless, Watkins went on to argue that some black women had broken this "covenant," and "in deciding that sexism is more oppressive than racism they can reasonably expect their writing will provoke different antagonists" (36). In a final shot reminiscent of Staples, Watkins urged black male writers to recognize that, however unfortunately, the issues addressed by black women writers "seem clearly to be of more interest to the reading and film-going public than those issues addressed by black male writers," perhaps, he speculated, because white people are fascinated by "tales of depravity and violence in the black community" (36). McDowell correctly observes that the crux of the issue, then, is not how black women depict black men; on the contrary, "what lies behind this smoke screen is an unacknowledged jostling for space in the literary marketplace" ("Reading," 83).

Watkins excluded Naylor's second novel, *Linden Hills* (1985), from the women's novels he found so troubling, but the widely held, long-fermenting sentiments to which his essay gave expression were clearly troubling to Naylor and to other women writers. Naylor has repeatedly felt the need to state that in *The Women of Brewster Place* she was celebrating women, not denigrating men, but that she "worried about whether or not the problems that were being caused by the men in the women's lives would be interpreted as some bitter statement I had to make about black men" ("Conversation," 579). Naylor's own 1988 essay "Love and Sex in the Afro-American Novel," which is in part a response to Watkins's article, protests the fact that "the black woman's novels . . . are held accountable for 'proving' that the Afro-American community contains harmonious and loving couples" (26).

Thus, contending forces have insisted, and continue to insist, that black women writers choose between gender and race, forces reflected in the aptly titled 1982 anthology *All the Women Are White, All the Blacks Are Men, but Some of Us Are Brave*. Black female identity—which is multiple—cannot be conceptualized as a function simply of race, gender, or, especially for Naylor, class. Instead, Barbara Smith reminds us, "a Black feminist approach to literature that embodies the realization that the politics of sex as well as the politics of race and class are crucially inter- locking factors in the works of Black women writers is an absolute neces- sity."[35] These are indeed the "crucially interlocking factors" and categories of analysis by which we will be examining Naylor's fiction.

Chapter Two
"Ebony Phoenixes": *The Women of Brewster Place*

"Celebrating Common Lives"

Naylor stated in an interview that *The Women of Brewster Place* is "the first thing that I began and finished" (Bonetti); it symbolized to her that she did in fact possess a staying power she felt she had previously lacked.[1] More important, the novel was something she had done exclusively for herself: "I wasn't living for anyone else or through anyone else; it was Gloria making a statement for Gloria" (Bonetti). Although *The Women of Brewster Place* is Naylor's first novel, it remains perhaps her most widely known. Published in 1982, it received strong initial reviews, and after winning the American Book Award for Best First Novel (1983), it captured and has retained the attention of scholars and critics. The made-for-television film version, produced by and starring Oprah Winfrey, aired to a huge audience, bringing the novel even greater popular recognition.[2]

Because *The Women of Brewster Place* is, as its subtitle indicates, *A Novel in Seven Stories*, each story about a different female character, critical attention has often focused on questions of form and unity. Other areas of critical interest include the formal and thematic functions of the novel's setting, the conception and presentation of the novel's characters, the feminist politics underlying the novel, and the relation of the novel to earlier texts, especially Morrison's *The Bluest Eye*, Jean Toomer's *Cane* (1923), and Ann Petry's *The Street* (1946).[3]

Naylor has repeatedly stated that "you should celebrate and celebrate voraciously that which is yours" (Bellinelli), and she insists that in *The Women of Brewster Place* she was "trying to celebrate common lives and common love" (see appendix). This celebration is at once generic and yet personal and specific to Naylor herself; in the novel, she says, she not only "had to get rid of some demons" but also was impelled "to confront what it meant to be a black woman and to celebrate it" (Carabi, 42). It thus seems significant that *The Women of Brewster Place* contains, like the quilt in *Mama Day*, numerous pieces of Naylor's personal and familial past in the form of names, places, and even stories. Naylor herself has highlighted some of the autobiographical elements. She has mentioned, for example, the fact that the house numbers of the apartment buildings in Brewster Place are the same as those of the apartment buildings in Harlem owned by her grandparents; she has also stated that she was evoking the spirit of her great-aunt Mae through the character of Etta Mae Johnson.[4] But the autobiographical connections extend even further. Brewster Place itself seems to be modeled after the section of West 119th Street in Harlem where her grandparents' apartment building was located and where Naylor and her immediate family lived for three years. During the time they lived there, Alberta Naylor took her daughters to Morningside Park, just two blocks away, to see "Shakespeare in the Park." Naylor and her sisters saw *A Midsummer Night's Dream*, the same play she sends some of the characters in her novel to see. Canaan Baptist Church, which Naylor's mother and grandmother joined in the late 1950s, is an important setting in the story "Etta Mae Johnson."

Naylor has stated that her "grandmother's old apartment building, which is no longer standing," "used to be a recurrent setting in my dreams" (*Dreaming*, 176). She also compares the women in her novel to the women she knew as a child, "poor women" who worked hard and dreamed "of the day that the children would go to college and they would not have to work so hard. And there was laughter in all that. They had good times. I saw more people depressed in graduate school than in Harlem!" (Carabi, 40). Naylor also speaks with considerable regret of the differences between the Harlem of her childhood and today's Harlem: "When I walk the streets of Harlem, I think about the people with whom I grew up and about the people who are there now. They are very different. . . . There was more community. I think that what is lacking is hope" (Carabi, 41).

Etta Mae Johnson in *The Women of Brewster Place* not only evokes the spirit of Naylor's great-aunt Mae but carries the same last name. Other family names also surface in the novel: for example, Mattie Michael's parents are named Fanny and Samuel, the names of Naylor's maternal great-grandparents. Lucielia Louise Turner bears the same first name (with a different spelling) as Naylor's maternal grandmother. Miss Eva, the old, wise woman who befriends, nurtures, and provides financial security to Mattie Michael, shares a name with both the original mother of the Old Testament and a friend of Naylor's grandmother, Eva

McKinney, who was a healer and midwife in Robinsonville and whom the novelist visited in the course of her research for *Mama Day*.

Like Naylor's own family, several of the characters in *The Women of Brewster Place* have moved to the North from the South. Mattie Michael and Etta Mae Johnson are both from Rock Vale, Tennessee; Lucielia Louise Turner, granddaughter of Miss Eva, grows up in North Carolina and Tennessee; Theresa, one of the lesbian characters in "The Two," is from Georgia; and Ben, the janitor, has likewise come to Brewster Place from the South, possibly Tennessee.

The accumulation of these biographical details in the novel has, I believe, important implications for our critical interpretations. They point to more positive and hopeful readings of *The Women of Brewster Place* than scholars have sometimes given. They help account for the tenderness that often emanates from the novel's pages, especially from its prologue and epilogue. And they suggest a somewhat different understanding of the significance of female bonding and of the efficacy of community than critical interpretations of the novel have often posited.

The Novel's Structure

"Dawn"

The seven stories comprising *The Women of Brewster Place* are framed by a prologue and an epilogue, entitled "Dawn" and "Dusk," which respectively describe the birth and the imminent—though not yet completed—death of the dead-end street known as Brewster Place. Serving as epigraph to the whole novel, the classic lines from Langston Hughes's *Montage of a Dream Deferred* (1951) pose a question central to the novel: "What happens to a dream deferred?" Each story in the novel, Naylor has stated, is "about a dream deferred in some way, which means that it gets pretty brutal. However, the women still continue to dream" (see appendix).

The novel's prologue serves to establish the kind of urban space to which America typically relegates its poor citizens, especially its African American citizens. Originally "the bastard child" of local government's liaison with business,[5] Brewster Place consists of "four double-housing units on some worthless land" built just in time to house the "patriotic boys who were on the way home from the Great War."[6] At the time of its construction, "there was a sense of promise in the street and in the times," but Brewster Place's potential for prosperity is destroyed when it is made

into a dead-end street "in order to control traffic" on the adjacent boule-
vard (*BP*, 2). The thwarting of the residents' hopes is made material and
visible by a brick wall that is erected at the end of the street because "the
neighborhood was now filled with people who had no political influence;
people who were dark haired and mellow-skinned" (*BP*, 2).

Naylor deftly sketches the typical evolution of the modern urban
ghetto in her description of the street, originally built to appease the
Irish community, which had been upset by the removal of the police
chief. After the street is walled off, its few remaining original inhabitants
move elsewhere in pursuit of the American dream of upward mobility.
Just as Brewster Place's second generation of "dark haired and mellow-
skinned" mediterraneans prompts the flight of its first generation of Irish
people, so too does its third generation of African Americans cause "the
exodus of the remaining Mediterraneans" (*BP*, 4). But Brewster Place is
not the transitional stopover for its third generation that it had been for
its earlier generations: "Brewster Place knew that unlike its other children, the few who would leave forever were to be the exception rather
than the rule, since they came because they had no choice and would
remain for the same reason" (*BP*, 4).

Naylor's description of Brewster Place in this prologue is striking for
the caring, nurturing qualities she attributes to the street itself.
Without question, the prologue establishes the poverty and decay of the
street and emphasizes that it is both literally and symbolically a dead
end, separated from the possibilities of the rest of the city by the wall.
But this is no typical description of urban blight and hopelessness.
Instead, Naylor personifies the street, which, though it may be a "bastard child" (*BP*, 1), is nonetheless human, eventually becoming a mother to its three generations of children. Kathryn Palumbo, discussing the
female imagery in the novel, points to the way the dead-end street
"becomes the womb in which the female characters nurture each
other."[7] The depiction of the street is also consistent with what Toni
Morrison has called the "affection of Black writers" for "the village"
within the city.[8] Brewster Place, the narrator tells us, "did what it could
for" the "children . . . of its middle years," and "cut off from the central
activities of the city, the street developed a personality of its own" (*BP*,
2). Like the mothers whose sons never returned from the Second World
War, Brewster Place "mourned . . . because it had lost children also—to
the call of a more comfortable life and to the fear of these present children who were once strange but were now all it had" (*BP*, 3). After
"integration came to Brewster Place on the rounded shoulders of a

short, brown-skinned man who had been hired as janitor and handy-
man for the buildings," the street welcomed its final generation of children: it "rejoiced in these multi-colored 'Afric' children of its old age"
and "became especially fond of its colored daughters" (*BP*, 4).

Naylor's delineation of the street's history suggests that it has been
victimized by the (white) male brokers of wealth and power in ways similar to the victimization of the black women who now reside on it. A further parallel is suggested by Brewster Place's illegitimate status as a
"bastard child": the very diversity of the women's skin tones points to
one of the more brutal historical realities of slavery. Both the street and
its African American daughters persist, however, in the face of efforts to
erase and negate them. The women, despite having reached what seem
to be the dead ends of their lives, continue to dream and to nurture each
other; similarly, Brewster Place, neglected and even eventually condemned by the city, nurtures those who find themselves in its run-down,
dilapidated, vermin-infested buildings. Ironically, then, Naylor celebrates the very space that she presents as a dead end for her characters,
precisely because it is and has been the locus of so much human desire,
human pain, and human hope.

The concluding paragraphs of the prologue, like Brewster Place itself,
rejoice in the African American daughters of the street's old age, who are
described as "hard-edged, soft-centered, brutally demanding, and easily
pleased. . . . They came, they went, they grew up, and grew old beyond
their years. Like an ebony phoenix, each in her own time and with her
own season had a story" (*BP*, 5). The final sentence of the passage
emphasizes the diversity of these women, the fact that each has her own
unique story. In attempting to present a microcosm of the black female
experience, Naylor states, she knew that "one character, one female protagonist, could not even attempt to represent the riches and diversity of
the black female experience"; thus, she created seven women of different
ages, different backgrounds, different skin colors (Bonetti). Despite their
differences, all the women share the experience of racism and sexism,
which, Naylor says, was "the reason for the wall" (Bonetti). They also
share, however, a resilient spirit that refuses, like the phoenix, to be
destroyed.

Naylor's belief that one female character could not "represent the
riches and diversity of the black female experience" and her decision to
write a novel featuring seven different women constitute a break with
the novelistic tradition of centering on a single protagonist.[9] The privi-
leging of community over the single individual suggested by the novel's

narration of a series of stories about the different women who find
themselves in Brewster Place is consistent with Naylor's belief that individual identity is shaped within the matrix of a community "that
birthed you and laid you away when you died. Community is what I
know and what I feel most comfortable with" (Carabi, 38). The novel's
structure also owes something perhaps to Ntozake Shange's *for colored
girls who have considered suicide/when the rainbow is enuf*, which likewise
presents a cast of seven women, each identified by the color of her
clothing.

"Mattie Michael"

The first story in *The Women of Brewster Place*, "Mattie Michael," introduces us to the moral center both of the novel and of Brewster Place
itself. The title character originated in the first story Naylor actually
wrote, a piece that eventually became "Lucielia Louise Turner." In that
story, the character of Mattie Michael functions as a kind of Earth
Mother; Naylor has said that when she wrote the piece she was experi-
encing a great deal of personal pain, and the writing served as a catharsis
(Bonetti). She wrote what she yearned for, namely, an "Earth Mother
who would come through my door, come sit down on my couch, and
just rock me out of my pain" (Bonetti).

Although Mattie Michael functions in just this way in Lucielia Louise
Turner's story, in Mattie's own story Naylor provides her character with
complexity and three-dimensionality. Naylor has stated that in going
back to her original writing and working to develop the character of
Mattie Michael, she deliberately "wrote against" William Faulkner's
character Dilsey from *The Sound and the Fury* (1929): "I created an Earth
Mother, and I wanted an anti–Earth Mother in that regard, so by the
time Mattie serves her Dilsey function on Brewster Place, she's been
given the things Faulkner never gave his Dilsey. She's been given a sexuality, she's been given a sort of ulterior motive for mothering, and it's
selfishness on her part" (see appendix).

The narrative of "Mattie Michael" consists of a long flashback detail-
ing Mattie's life, which is framed by her arrival, on a snowy winter
evening, in Brewster Place. Mattie's is "the last building on the block,"
and the forbidding wall stands "only six feet from her building" (*BP*,
7). The first three paragraphs of the story are replete with images suggestive of death and dying, culminating in the third paragraph with
Mattie's realization that her second-floor apartment will not provide

the sustenance necessary to the life of either her "beautiful plants" or herself:

> Mattie saw that the wall reached just above the second-floor apartments, which meant the northern light would be blocked from her plants. All the beautiful plants that once had an entire sun porch for themselves in the home she had exchanged thirty years of her life to pay for would now have to fight for light on a crowded windowsill. The sigh turned into a knot of pity for the ones she knew would die. She pitied them because she refused to pity herself and to think that she, too, would have to die here on this crowded street because there just wasn't enough life left for her to do it all again. (*BP*, 7)

Mattie's identification throughout the story with plants and vegetation is consistent with her role as a nurturer of life; we learn that the sun porch of Miss Eva's house, which Mattie inherited, had been the room Mattie "loved . . . above all others—a place to see things grow" (*BP*, 43). But the sun porch and the life it nourished cannot be found in Brewster Place, although Mattie believes for a moment that she can smell "freshly cut sugar cane" coming from the first-floor apartment of her building; she realizes, however, that "there was no sugar cane on Brewster. No, that had been in Tennessee, in a summer that lay under the graves of thirty-one years that could only be opened again in the mind" (*BP*, 8).

The precipitous change that Mattie's life has undergone is established in the five short paragraphs of the opening frame through a series of contrasts: between the cold, snowy winter of the present and the summer of the past; between the life-giving house Mattie once cherished and the dark, life-threatening apartment she now confronts; between northern, urban Brewster and southern, rural Tennessee. The remainder of the narrative provides the chronicle of Mattie's life, the details "of her long, winding journey to Brewster" (*BP*, 8).

The primary elements of Mattie's story are simple and all too familiar: a single sexual encounter leads to pregnancy, resulting in expulsion from her parents' home and a subsequent life as a single mother. The early moments of Mattie's seduction by the "cinnamon-red" Butch Fuller (*BP*, 8) recall both Cholly Breedlove's first encounter with Pauline in Morrison's *The Bluest Eye* and Tea Cake Woods's wooing of Janie Crawford in *Their Eyes Were Watching God*. The scene is also one of the most sensual of any in Naylor's work. It takes place among sugar cane stalks, dogwood, basil, and wild thyme. Although Butch Fuller is regarded by Mattie's father and the entire churchgoing community of Rock Vale, Tennessee, as a worthless but attractive womanizer, he is associated with positive images from the natural world: his laugh is "like the edges of an April sunset" (*BP*, 9), and he smells "like a mixture of clean sweat, raw syrup, and topsoil" (*BP*, 14).

Butch's appeal to Mattie is not simply sensual: he represents a freer and more open way of being in and looking at the world than Mattie experiences in her home. Mattie's official suitor is the "deadpan Fred Watson," whose company Mattie finds "boring" but who is "the only man in the church that her father thought good enough for her" (*BP*, 13–14). Mattie's life before her encounter with Butch has been lived within strict and conventional guidelines. Her future and her sexuality are in the control of her father, "an old man with set and exacting ways"; she is "the only child of his autumn years" (*BP*, 19). Although Butch Fuller clearly employs arguments he thinks will appeal to Mattie, making her more susceptible to his seduction, her interlude with him is one of the freest and most pleasurable, physically and spiritually, she has known. Susan Meisenhelder argues that Butch's "seize the day" philosophy, expressed through his description of the right way to eat cane, is "gender specific" in suggesting that women, like sugar cane, are to be disposed of once their sweetness has been enjoyed.[10] Several elements in the text suggest, however, a different and more positive reading of Butch's character.

Mattie is not discarded by Butch, because neither of them ever regards their encounter as the beginning of a lasting relationship. For Mattie, the encounter results in pregnancy, but neither she nor her mother considers that pregnancy a sin. As her mother says to her, "The sin is fornicatin', and that's over and done with. God done forgave you of that a long time ago, and what's going on in your belly now ain't nothin' to hang your head about" (*BP*, 20). Mattie herself reflects that "she didn't care about Butch Fuller, and they had hardly spoken since that day, but this baby didn't really belong to him. It belonged to something out there in the heat of an August day and the smell of sugar cane and mossy herbs" (*BP*, 22). Mattie's pregnancy belongs, in short, to her one experience of freedom, just as it constitutes the single exception to "her unquestioning obedience" to her father (*BP*, 21–22).

Samuel Michael is the only member of the household for whom Mattie's pregnancy represents dishonor and shame; as the patriarch of the family, he and only he has the power to decide to whom Mattie's sexuality will belong. Her refusal to name the father of her baby represents a betrayal of him: "She had chosen this man's side against him, and in his fury, he tried to stamp out what had hurt him the most and was now brazenly taunting him—her disobedience" (*BP*, 23). Naylor stated in an interview that, to Samuel Michael, "love equals obedience" (Carabi, 41); clearly, however, such obedience constitutes total submission to his control, and it is against this that Mattie has rebelled.

What Mattie ultimately loses as a result of her afternoon of freedom and pleasure in the woods is not Butch Fuller at all, but her home and her parents. The price of claiming her right to her own body is the severance of all the ties that have created and sustained her, the very ground of her being. As she rides the Greyhound bus out of Rock Vale, she finds this loss so painful that she will not allow herself to think of "the home that had been lost to her, or her mother's parting tears, or the painful breach with her father." Instead, "she forced herself to think only of the back road to the house, the feel of summer, the taste of sugar cane, and the smell of wild herbs. And when her son was born five months later, she named him Basil" (*BP*, 25). So disastrous are the consequences of her one sexual experience that she is never to allow herself another. And though the intense pleasure of her afternoon with Butch remains the focus of her memories of the past, she never attempts to re-create such pleasure; instead, she spends her life trying to capture it and eternally hold onto it through her relationship with her son, whose name symbolizes it.

Mattie's absorption with her child begins almost immediately after his birth; despite gentle warnings from her friend Etta, Mattie insists that she has no need of the larger world because she has "everything I need right here [in Basil]" (*BP*, 26). Even after her financial and child care problems are solved through the generosity and love of Miss Eva, Mattie continues to define herself completely through Basil, refusing to go out with men and allowing Basil to sleep in her bed long after he is an infant. When she tells Miss Eva that Basil sleeps with her because he is afraid of the dark, Miss Eva challenges her by asking, "You sure it's Basil who don't want to sleep alone?" (*BP*, 38). Mattie acknowledges to herself, if only briefly, the truth behind the old woman's question: "Her body had hungered at moments, had felt the need for a filling and caressing of inner spaces. But in those restless moments she had turned toward her manchild and let the soft, sleeping flesh and the thought of all that he was and would be draw those yearnings onto the edge of her lips and the tips of her fingers" (*BP*, 38). Instead of allowing this recognition to develop into self-knowledge, however, Mattie almost immediately projects her shame onto Miss Eva. In one of several instances in the novel of ordinarily passive and gentle characters fantasizing violent actions, Mattie imagines herself destroying the old woman's blue eyes, which have been able to see her "secrets": "She wanted to get up from the table and spit into those eyes, beat them sightless—those that had befriended her, kept her baby from sharp objects and steep stairs while she worked, wept with her over the death of her parents—she wanted them crushed under her fists for daring to make her ashamed of loving her son" (*BP*, 39).

These passages of Naylor's text are rarely noted in analyses of Mattie's character. While critics have generally acknowledged the dependency Mattie instills in Basil, their primary focus has tended to be on Mattie's role in saving Lucielia Turner. But the text itself clearly points to a much more complex character; the Earth Mother figure that Mattie becomes for others, especially Ciel, seems to require a distortion and repression of desire and a self-denial for which Mattie ultimately pays a high price. That price includes her loss of both her son and her home. The house Miss Eva leaves Mattie is more than a house: it is a symbol of nurturance and warmth and love and life, of Mattie's magical second chance for another home. Mattie understands that Miss Eva "had wanted her spirit to remain in this house through the memory of someone who was capable of loving it as she had" (*BP*, 40). When Basil skips bail, forcing the forfeiture of the house, Mattie has betrayed Miss Eva's spirit just as surely as Basil has betrayed his mother's.

The dependency Mattie has taught Basil eventually makes her "the refuge when he ran from school to school, job to job" (*BP*, 43); she has taught him that he need never confront the consequences of his behavior. She has asked nothing of him for herself but his presence, and as she finally realizes, she has succeeded in stunting him entirely: "Whatever was lacking within him that made it impossible to confront the difficulties of life could not be supplied with words. She saw it now. There was a void in his being that had been padded and cushioned over the years, and now that covering had grown impregnable. She bit on her bottom lip and swallowed back a sob. God had given her what she prayed for—a little boy who would always need her" (*BP*, 52).

Mattie's desire to protect unchanged her one moment of happiness with Butch by keeping the fruit of their moment an eternal child results not only in her crippling of Basil but in his abandonment of her. Butch's words to her about the sugar cane expressed a truth that Mattie was never able to absorb, just as she was unable to accept the truth of Miss

Eva's words to her about her mothering of Basil. It is thus not surprising that, in the dream she has just before Basil calls her from jail, the figures of Miss Eva and Butch are conflated. During Mattie's idyllic afternoon with Butch, we recall, he had urged her to understand that "eating cane is like living life. You gotta know when to stop chewing—when to stop trying to wrench every last bit of sweetness out of a wedge—or you find yourself with a jawful of coarse straw that irritates your gums and the roof of your mouth" (*BP*, 18). In the dream, Mattie is

> running and hiding from something among tall bamboo stalks and monstrously tangled weeds. She was terribly hungry and mysteriously frightened of the invisible thing that was searching for her. She had a piece of sugar cane in her hand, and she wedged it into her mouth and chewed, trying to stop the burning hunger in her stomach. She was desperately trying to chew the cane before this stalking thing found her. She sensed it coming closer through the tall grass, its heavy footsteps pounding in her ears, timed with the beating of her heart. She screamed as it parted the grass that was covering her. It was Butch. He was smiling and glowing, and his eyes were blue and spinning crazily in their sockets. He tried to pry open her mouth and scrape out the mashed wad of sugar cane. He grabbed her by the throat to keep the saliva from being swallowed, and she opened her mouth and screamed and screamed—shrill notes that vibrated in her ears and sent terrible pains shooting into her head. (*BP*, 44)

The fact that Butch's eyes in Mattie's dream are blue, the color of Miss Eva's, points to the similar truth each of them tries to teach Mattie about her relationship with her son. As her dream suggests, Mattie has run from adult relationships, but her "terrible" hunger cannot be assuaged by Basil; if she will not relinquish him—allow him to mature and become an independent person—she is destined to get not "sweetness" from him but only "a jawful of coarse straw." Despite the warnings her unconscious mind tries to give her, however, Mattie persists in giving everything she can to Basil and in trying to protect him from the consequences of his own behavior. The result, of course, is that she loses "a lifetime of work lying in the bricks of her home" (*BP*, 53) and finds herself on Brewster Place.

Mattie's use of mothering as a way of defining and anchoring herself as a woman is paralleled later in the novel by the character of Cora Lee. Cora Lee is obsessed with having babies, who lose their appeal once they grow beyond infancy. Significantly, what she likes about babies is that

they can "be fed from her body," and that "she alone could be their substance and their world" (*BP*, 112). Although there are certainly many
differences between Mattie as we see her in Brewster Place and Cora Lee,
Mattie's relationship to Basil seems to have been based on needs and
desires somewhat similar to those that prompt Cora Lee's obsession with
babies.

"Etta Mae Johnson"

The second story in the novel centers on Mattie Michael's childhood
friend, Etta Mae Johnson; the two women "had taken totally different
roads that with all of their deceptive winding had both ended up on
Brewster Place" (*BP*, 60–61). Not only have their "different roads" in
life brought them to the same destination, but they are polar opposites
in almost every way, suggesting that their race and their gender are the
primary factors that have led them to the dead end of a Brewster
Place.[11] While Mattie has spent her life devoted to her child, has had no
relationships with men after Butch, and is a faithful churchgoer, Etta is
a childless woman who has spent her life hooking "herself to any promising rising black star, and when he burnt out, she found another" (*BP*,
60). Unlike Mattie, who grew up being obedient and conventional, Etta
"spent her teenage years in constant trouble. Rock Vale had no place for
a black woman who was not only unwilling to play by the rules, but
whose spirit challenged the very right of the game to exist" (*BP*, 59).
The "rules" include a submissive attitude toward whites and a chaste
desire to marry and become a wife and mother. Because "Etta soon
found out that America wasn't ready for her yet—not in 1937 . . . she
took her talents to the street" (*BP*, 60).

Etta is consistently associated with the blues, and particularly with
Billie Holiday, whom she heard sing one evening and "*never forgot. The
music, the woman, the words*" (*BP*, 55). She brings splashes of color to drab
Brewster Place, arriving at Mattie's one August afternoon in an "apple-
green Cadillac" and wearing a "willow-green sundress" (*BP*, 60); later
she changes into a "red sundress" when she goes to church with Mattie
(*BP*, 65). Although the other residents of Brewster Place disapprove of
her, welcome her failures, and are disappointed by her successes—all in
silence or inaudible undertones—she has "learned to tread through these
alien undercurrents so well that to a casual observer she had mastered
the ancient secret of walking on water" (*BP*, 57). Naylor's narrative skill
is at its finest in her portrayal of Etta Mae Johnson, forcing readers to
question our assumptions about concepts such as "whore" and "hustler."

The text elicits our tenderness for this character, whose life so closely resembles the blues music she loves.

The central episode of Etta's story is clearly representative and typical of countless experiences in her life. Recognizing that her age will not allow her many more years of hustling for her survival, Etta agrees to go to church with Mattie, who claims there are "a few settle-minded men in our church, some widowers and such" (*BP*, 61). In some of the most devastating satire in the novel, Naylor creates in this scene a vivid portrait of the church, its congregation, and its leaders.

Even the physical structure of the church is forbidding. Described as "a brooding, ashen giant," Canaan Baptist has "multi-colored, dome-shaped eyes" that "glowered into the darkness" (*BP*, 62). As Mattie and Etta approach this monster, "fierce clapping and thunderous organ chords came barreling out of its mouth," for Canaan's congregation is made up of poor people who "still worshipped God loudly" (*BP*, 62). The congregation and choir are singing the slave spiritual "Go Down, Moses," a song with words "as ancient as the origin of their misery. . . . They were now sung with the frantic determination of a people who realized that the world was swiftly changing but for some mystic, complex reason their burden had not" (*BP*, 63).

The church no longer has the power to comfort Etta, though the music drags her memory "back past the cold ashes of her innocence to a time when pain could be castrated on the sharp edges of iron-studded faith" (*BP*, 63–64). Mattie, in contrast, is transformed by the music, which smooths the lines in her face so that they "almost totally vanished. She had left Etta in just that moment for a place where she was free. Sadly, Etta looked at her, at them all, and was very envious. . . . Could there have been another way?" (*BP*, 64). Etta envies the solace that Mattie and the rest of the congregation derive from the music and the church, a solace unavailable to her, she suddenly realizes, because of the life she has chosen. Her desire for such spiritual comfort, as much as her desire for material security, seems to prompt her fantasy of being a respectable wife of a church official. So compelling is this fantasy that Etta suppresses all that her knowledge and experience have taught her and convinces herself that the visiting minister, Reverend Moreland T. Woods, might actually want to marry her rather than simply enjoy a brief, sexual interlude with her.

In spinning her fantasy, Etta does not ignore the fact that Reverend Woods exercises with the congregation a "talent" that Etta has seen "in poolrooms, nightclubs, grimy second-floor insurance offices, numbers dens, and on a dozen street corners" (*BP*, 66). What he offers the congregation, for which they would be willing to "give over half of their little to keep this man in comfort" (*BP*, 66), is a temporary release, described in sexual terms, from the pain and misery they find in "that great big world out there that exacts such a strange penalty for . . . being born black" (*BP*, 65). The fact that Reverend Woods is a con artist and a hustler who offers the congregation a "fix" that differs little from the fix of dope or gambling does not diminish his power to "move [Etta] up to the front of the church, ahead of the deacons' wives and Ladies' Auxiliary, off of Brewster Place for good" (*BP*, 66). What Etta does not recognize, of course, is that he not only knows her game but can play it better than she.

The narrative suggests that Etta's demoralizing experience with Reverend Woods is simply a variation on the pattern of her life: central to Etta's conception of herself as a woman is the belief that only by attaching "herself to any promising rising black star" can she shine. The narrator makes this point clear: "Even if someone had bothered to stop and tell her that the universe had expanded for her, just an inch, she wouldn't have known how to shine alone" (*BP*, 60). Because she does not know "how to shine alone," Etta spins a fantasy around Reverend Moreland T. Woods, and only "his last floundering thrusts into her body" shatter the fantasy "to bring her back to reality" (*BP*, 72). Once she realizes that Reverend Woods is no different from the countless other men who have outconned her, she knows without looking the features of the cheap motel room she has gone to with him: "She didn't try to visualize what the name would be. It didn't matter. They were all the same, all meshed together into one lump that rested like an iron ball on her chest" (*BP*, 72).

Although the downward arc of Etta's experience with Reverend Woods is familiar, its impact on her, the narrative suggests, is uniquely devastating. The residents of Brewster Place would not have recognized Etta when she walks down the street after her evening with Reverend Woods, for although they have seen her arrive in many conditions, "never had she walked among them with a broken spirit. This middle-aged woman in the wrinkled dress and wilted straw hat would have been a stranger to them" (*BP*, 74).

Richly ironic, the narrative of Etta Mae Johnson's experience with Reverend Moreland T. Woods counterpoints the previous narrative of Mattie Michael in numerous ways. Like Mattie's encounter with Butch

Fuller, Etta's experience occurs in August; despite the promise of Reverend Moreland T. Woods's name, however, there is nothing natural or transcendent about their mating, as had been the case in Mattie's encounter with Butch. The wall on Brewster Place, which had seemed somehow welcoming when Etta arrived in the afternoon, takes on a different, more realistic appearance when she sees it in the early morning hours, after Reverend Woods leaves her: "It had looked so different then, with the August sun highlighting the browns and reds of the bricks and the young children bouncing their rubber balls against its side. Now it crouched there in the thin predawn light, like a pulsating mouth awaiting her arrival" (*BP*, 73).

Mattie's dream had been to make her son—the symbol of her glorious afternoon with Butch Fuller—into a man who would never leave her.[12] Similarly, Etta's dream is to find self-definition and security from a man; she has spent her life using her body as a bargaining chip, in every instance believing that somehow the outcome would be different. Only after she loses it does Mattie realize the value of the gift Miss Eva had bestowed in providing her a spiritual and material home. But it is a similar gift she offers Etta, who does, the story's ending suggests, recognize its value. As Etta, her spirit all but broken, walks up to the stoop of Mattie's building, she suddenly hears music coming from the window and realizes that, completely uncharacteristically, Mattie is playing Etta's Billie Holiday records. But what is most important, Etta realizes, is that "someone was waiting up for her. Someone who would deny fiercely that there had been any concern—just a little indigestion from them fried onions that kept me from sleeping" (*BP*, 74). Etta's story ends on a note of hope for both women, the last sentence suggesting that they will build their lives around the love and support they find in each other: "Etta laughed softly to herself as she climbed the steps toward the light and the love and the comfort that awaited her" (*BP*, 74). With these words, the novel makes one of its most explicit statements of its central theme.

These first two stories are a sort of interlocking pair, Mattie and Etta counterpointing and complementing each other in important ways. These two characters are also the oldest of the principal female characters in the novel, and their friendship is rooted in their shared childhood in the South. For both of them, Brewster Place represents a dead end, as is suggested by their proximity to the wall. What promises to make their lives richer than their environment would portend is the love and friendship they offer each other.

"Kiswana Browne"

In the third story, we move from August to autumn, from middle-aged
women whose choices in life have led to the dead-end street to a young
woman who has forsaken her middle-class home in Linden Hills to be
with "the people," whose lives she hopes to improve. Unlike Mattie's
second-floor apartment, the windows of which are blocked from the
light by Brewster's wall some six feet away, Kiswana Browne lives in a
sixth-floor apartment, from which she can easily see over the wall.
Kiswana's story, a deft sketch of a young black "revolutionary" of the
late sixties, is one of the lightest and most humorous in the novel. In the
course of Kiswana's encounter with her mother, the narrative gently
mocks some of the codes of behavior that became de rigueur for young
blacks caught up in the spirit of the "Black Revolution." We learn, for
example, that Kiswana is light-skinned and has hair "so thin and fine-
textured" that it refuses to "look African," no matter how hard she tries
(*BP*, 81). This fact is particularly infuriating to her because her brother,
who is "dark-skinned and had the type of hair that was thick and kinky
enough for a good 'Fro,'" refuses to wear one, just as he has refused to
participate in campus protests (*BP*, 80). Kiswana herself dropped out of
school because "those bourgie schools were counterrevolutionary. My
place was in the streets with my people, fighting for equality and a better community" (*BP*, 83). In the course of the novel, Kiswana learns
how little she knows about her "people," since her own class and the
experiences it has provided separate her profoundly from the other
women on Brewster Place. To her credit, Kiswana learns to listen and,
eventually recognizing the need for education, enrolls in a community
college. Her first step to understanding the other women on Brewster
Place, however, is understanding something about herself and her own
origins, which provide the focus of her story.

The conflict never far from the surface in Kiswana's relationship with
her mother is in many ways a typical generational conflict. The readiest
symbol over which Mrs. Browne and her daughter habitually argue is
Kiswana's name, which she has taken to emphasize her African roots.
Her mother quite naturally refuses to use the new name, calling her
daughter instead by the name she herself bestowed, Melanie.

At the beginning of the story, Kiswana is certain that she and her
mother are as different and far apart as possible in their values and
beliefs. Unfortunately, her mother cannot seem to recognize that
Kiswana is an adult or to realize that her own middle-class values are

corrupt. Constantly fantasizing and daydreaming, even in the opening paragraphs of the story, Kiswana angrily claims that she has not "'done that [daydreamed] in years—it's for kids. When are you going to realize that I'm a woman now?' She sought desperately for some womanly thing to do" (*BP*, 79). Soon, Kiswana and her mother are launched into a familiar argument: her mother dismisses the dreams and ideals of "the Movement" and claims, "There was no revolution, Melanie, and there will be no revolution" (*BP*, 84). Mrs. Browne urges her daughter to take advantage of the privileges of her class, gain an education, and work from within institutions to change them.

Kiswana, of course, believes that her parents are suffering from "a terminal case of middle-class amnesia" and that their involvement in groups like the NAACP is useless because the NAACP is a "middle-of-the-road, Uncle Tom dumping ground for black Republicans!" (*BP*, 85). The argument climaxes when Kiswana, after shouting that her mother is "a white man's nigger who's ashamed of being black," is utterly shocked that her mother's response is to grab her by the shoulders and spin her around (*BP*, 85–86).

Watching her own reflection mirrored in her mother's tear-filled eyes, Kiswana listens "to a story she had heard from a child," the proud story of her great-grandmother, for whom she was named (*BP*, 86). The point of the story, of course, is that Kiswana has roots, a history, a name with a proud lineage, and therefore she need not seek to prove she has roots by taking a new, African name. Mrs. Browne insists, in language reminiscent of Langston Hughes's in "The Negro Artist and the Racial Mountain," that "black isn't beautiful and it isn't ugly—black is. It's not kinky hair and it's not straight hair—it just is" (*BP*, 86). In words echoing Naylor's when she has described her own parents' efforts, Mrs. Browne states that "when I brought my babies home from the hospital, my ebony son and my golden daughter, I swore before whatever gods would listen . . . that I would use everything I had and could ever get to see that my children were prepared to meet this world on its own terms, so that no one could sell them short and make them ashamed of what they were or how they looked" (*BP*, 86).

Mrs. Browne's lecture to Kiswana, while it expresses important truths, does not signal a desire to change her daughter; indeed, she is clearly proud of her daughter's idealism and activism: "'And the one lesson I wanted you to learn is not to be afraid to face anyone, not even a crafty old lady like me who can outtalk you.' And she smiled and winked" (*BP*, 87). Mrs. Browne applauds her daughter's desire to help change the world. Though she herself is horrified by her daughter's new neighborhood, she at least seems to recognize the deficiencies of her own vision,[13] which, Kiswana reflects, does not recognize "that practically every apartment contained a family, a Bible, and a dream that one day enough could be scraped from those meager Friday night paychecks to make Brewster Place a distant memory" (*BP*, 77).

The earlier humor of the story returns at the end, when Kiswana recognizes just how similar she and her mother are: both paint their toenails because both are involved with men who are "into feet!" (*BP*, 87). Kiswana's discovery of this trivial commonality prompts her serious realization that "her mother had trod through the same universe that she herself was now traveling. Kiswana was breaking no new trails and would eventually end up just two feet away on that couch. She stared at the woman she had been and was to become" (*BP*, 87). Ebele Eko rightly observes that Kiswana "comes to understand and appreciate the source of her own dynamism, idealism, and dedication: her mother" (145).

Kiswana (like Lorraine and Theresa in "The Two") has *chosen* to live on Brewster Place, and she plays an important role in leading the other residents to organize a neighborhood group to protest the living conditions in the apartments. Her encounter with her mother makes her better able to help the other residents of Brewster Place. At the beginning of the story, for example, Kiswana "place[d] her dreams on the back of" a pigeon "and fantasized that it would glide forever in transparent silver circles until it ascended to the center of the universe and was swallowed up. But the wind died down, and she watched with a sigh as the bird beat its wings in awkward, frantic movements to land on the corroded top of a fire escape" (*BP*, 75). Unable to sustain her vision of transcendent flight through the vehicle of a pigeon, Kiswana shifts to thinking that the pigeon is "crapping on those folks' fire escape," a thought that leads her to fantasize about organizing the neighbors "to march on the mayor's office about the pigeons. She materialized placards and banners for them" (*BP*, 76).

Clearly, Kiswana has a keen desire for protest as an end in itself. She also has a genuine interest in helping the people of Brewster Place, but as her fantasy shows, she has at the outset little sense of the realities of their lives and therefore no sense of how best to help them. After her encounter with her mother, however, the reader next sees Kiswana organizing a tenants' association with realistic goals and sensible methods. She also allows herself to listen to what the women, especially Cora Lee, have to say about their lives. The sequencing of these events in the narrative suggests that Kiswana's encounter with her mother helps her exchange the fanciful daydreams with which she begins the story for more meaningful goals and dreams.

"Lucielia Louise Turner"

This story, the structural and thematic center of the novel, was the first portion of it to be written. The only story that presents an approximation of the conventional nuclear family, "Lucielia Louise Turner" offers an incisive indictment of such a family. The central character, Ciel, is the now-mature granddaughter of Miss Eva Turner; Mattie had been a kind of second mother to Ciel until Miss Eva died and Ciel returned to Tennessee with her parents. Ciel's life, like Mattie's and Etta's, is centered on a man whom she wants desperately to keep, even though he is verbally abusive and physically threatening.

Eugene resembles Basil in his refusal to accept adult responsibilities, his selfishness, and his obliviousness to the needs of those around him. As Naylor acknowledges, Eugene is a two-dimensional, undeveloped character (see appendix). Significantly, he experiences Ciel's friendship with Mattie as a threat to his dominance and control, and "he constantly felt the need to prove himself in front of her" (*BP*, 97). A liar and a bully, Eugene blames Ciel for becoming pregnant, seeing the responsibility of children as an obstacle to his own advancement in life: "'With two kids and you on my back, I ain't never gonna have nothin'.' He came and grabbed her by the shoulders and was shouting into her face. 'Nothin', do you hear me, nothin'!'" (*BP*, 95).

Despite Eugene's treatment of her and his yearlong abandonment of her, Ciel continues to take him back and to try to please him. Interestingly, though Ciel tries to convince Mattie that she takes Eugene back because their daughter, Serena, needs a father, she realizes that the

> truth went beyond her scope of understanding. When she laid her head in the hollow of his neck there was a deep musky scent to his body that brought back the ghosts of the Tennessee soil of her childhood. It reached up and lined the inside of her nostrils so that she inhaled his presence almost every minute of her life. The feel of his sooty flesh penetrated the skin of her fingers and coursed through her blood and became one, somewhere, wherever it was, with her actual being. But how do you tell yourself, let alone this practical old woman who loves you, that he was back because of that. (*BP*, 92)

Like the sugar cane and basil with which Mattie's son becomes associated in her mind, Ciel clings to the "deep musky scent" of Eugene's body, which reminds her of "the Tennessee soil of her childhood," because it is ultimately connected to "her actual being." Although the text does not clarify whether Eugene in fact shared any part of her southern past, Ciel experiences him on a sensual level that allows that past, and its associations with a natural world, to survive in the urban world of her present. Only after she has the abortion Eugene wanted and he announces his intention of leaving her does Ciel finally recognize that she has projected these values and meanings onto him: "She looked at Eugene, and the poison of reality began to spread through her body like gangrene. It drew his scent out of her nostrils and scraped the veil from her eyes, and he stood before her just as he really was—a tall, skinny black man with arrogance and selfishness twisting his mouth into a strange shape" (*BP*, 100). Although Eugene hardly resembles Joe Starks, Ciel does resemble Janie in her projection of her own desires and dreams onto him, as Michael Awkward has argued (114).

Other parallels between Ciel and Mattie become evident as the narrative continues. When her relationship with Eugene deteriorates, Ciel begins to focus her emotional life on her child, because she realizes that her child "is the only thing I have ever loved without pain" (*BP*, 93). Eventually, she loses both her child and the fetus that Eugene bullies her into aborting; these losses establish an even stronger link between Ciel and Mattie.

Awkward (114–16) offers a rich reading of the scene in which Ciel finally decides to placate Eugene by having an abortion. He usefully points to the juxtaposition of this scene, in which Ciel attempts to clean the rice for their dinner (*BP*, 94–95), to the scene in which Mattie exorcises the pain from Ciel's spirit through the washing of her body (*BP*, 102–5). The rice-washing scene receives further illumination from comparison with an earlier scene in "Mattie Michael": Mattie is trying to understand how her little boy has developed into the man he is; Basil has become "a stranger who had done away with her little boy and left her with no one and so alone" (*BP*, 42). Mattie's reflections come in the midst of a domestic chore, the sort of activity that fills women's lives:

> Mattie pondered this as her hands plunged into the soapy dishwater and she mechanically washed bowls and silverware. She tried to recapture the years and hold them up for inspection, so she could pinpoint the transformation, but they slipped through her fingers and slid down the dishes,

hidden under the iridescent bubbles that broke with the slightest movement of her hand. She quickly saw that it was an impossible task and
abandoned the effort. He had grown up, that was all. She looked up from
the sink and gasped as she caught her reflection in the windowpane—but
when had she grown old? Any possible answer had disappeared down the
drain with the used dishwater. (*BP,* 42)

Equating the past to the soap bubbles, which burst so easily and go
down the drain, Mattie soon abandons any attempt to understand how
past events—that is, her rearing of Basil—have led to the existence of
"this stranger," of whom, significantly, she does not wish to claim any
part. She is defeated in her efforts to understand the past largely because
she wishes to avoid such knowledge. Instead, soon after this scene
occurs, she places her home in jeopardy to raise Basil's bail—so that she
can keep him with her still—and this effort too is doomed to defeat.

The dish-washing scene parallels the scene in which Ciel tries unsuccessfully to clean all of the starch from the rice:

The water was turning cloudy in the rice pot, and the force of the stream
from the faucet caused scummy bubbles to rise to the surface. These
broke and sprayed tiny starchy particles onto the dirty surface. Each bub-
ble that broke seemed to increase the volume of the dogged whispers she
had been ignoring for the last few months. She poured the dirty water off
the rice to destroy and silence them, then watched with a malicious joy as
they disappeared down the drain.

"So now, how in the hell I'm gonna make it with no money, huh?
And another brat comin' here, huh?"

The second change of the water was slightly clearer, but the starch-
speckled bubbles were still there, and this time there was no way to pre-
tend deafness to their message. She had stood at that sink countless times
before, washing rice, and she knew the water was never going to be totally clear. She couldn't stand there forever—her fingers were getting cold,
and the rest of the dinner had to be fixed, and Serena would be waking
up soon and wanting attention. Feverishly she poured the water off and
tried again.

"I'm fuckin' sick of never getting ahead. Babies and bills, that's all
you good for."

The bubbles were almost transparent now, but when they broke
they left light trails of starch on top of the water that curled around her
fingers. She knew it would be useless to try again. Defeated, Ciel placed
the wet pot on the burner, and the flames leaped up bright red and
orange, turning the water droplets clinging on the outside to steam.

Turning to him, she silently acquiesced. "All right, Eugene, what do you want me to do?" (*BP*, 94–95)

Awkward argues that the "dogged whispers" with which Ciel identifies the "scummy bubbles" are the whispers "of discord that were again entering the relationship. By sadistically drowning the whisper-containing bubbles, by silencing, in other words, the voice of reality, she displays a preference for illusion, silence, and dream and an unwillingness to confront directly the implications of the voice's message. . . . Confronted by the ultimate failure of her purification rite, Ciel realizes that some sacrifice on her part is required in order to satiate Eugene" (115).

I read this scene differently. The "dogged whispers" that the "scummy bubbles" evoke seem to be the all-but-spoken words she has been hearing from Eugene for several months, words indicative of his desire that she abort the baby. The "nagging whispers of trouble" began during the months after Eugene returned home, and Ciel has "examined each one to pinpoint when" they began (*BP*, 92)—just as Mattie tries to "pinpoint" the transformation in Basil. Ciel considers for an agitated moment that the whispers started "the month that she had gotten pregnant again," but she quickly dismisses this possible origin, rationalizing that she is not sick, as she had been during her pregnancy with Serena: "No it wasn't the baby. It's not the baby, it's not the baby" (*BP*, 93).

Thus, when Ciel attempts "to destroy and silence" the whispers, she is doomed to defeat, just as she is doomed to defeat in washing all of the starch off the rice, though presumably the persistent "scummy bubbles" have not been such a problem to her in the past. Since the "dogged whispers" of Eugene's desire for an abortion cannot be silenced, Ciel tries to force their clear articulation, asking Eugene, "What do you want me to do?" Eugene's response is characteristically coercive: he forces her to make the decision to have the abortion by letting her know that, if she does not, he will leave her: "He wasn't going to let her off so easily. 'Hey, baby, look, I don't care what you do. I just can't have all these hassles on me right now, ya know?'" (*BP*, 94). Eugene's threats produce the desired response from Ciel, who has the abortion because she believes doing so will make him stay with her—just as Mattie risks all she has in the vain hope of keeping Basil.

The abortion Ciel goes through is bearable, however, only through her defensive splitting of herself, keeping "herself completely isolated" from what happens (*BP*, 95). Just as Mattie attributes the disappearance of her "little boy" to "this stranger," so Ciel attributes the abortion to someone else, some "other woman who had wanted an abortion" (*BP*, 100).[14] Her realization of what she has done occurs when, shortly after the abortion, Eugene announces his intention of leaving her. Ciel's initial response to his news is to plead with him: "'Eugene, please.' She listened with growing horror to herself quietly begging" (*BP*, 99). Ciel's language takes on added significance when it is considered in relation to later events: resonating in the novel's climax, *please* is the word Lorraine repeats over and over again both before and after she has been brutally beaten and raped. Ciel's use of the word here and her recognition of its self-demeaning implications horrify her even as she speaks.

Eventually, however, Eugene pushes Ciel too far: when he demands an explanation for why he cannot leave, she recognizes that the answer lies in the week when "she had done all those terrible things for that other woman who had wanted an abortion. She and she alone would have to take responsibility for them now. He must understand what those actions had meant to her, but somehow, he had meant even more" (*BP*, 100). But, of course, Eugene does not "understand," and when he tells her that her loving him "ain't good enough" as a reason for him to stay, "the poison of reality . . . scrapes the veil from her eyes," allowing her to see Eugene as he is. Her new accurate vision of Eugene enables her to accept responsibility for what she has done: "I'll never forgive myself for not having done it [hating Eugene] sooner—soon enough to have saved my baby" (*BP*, 100). In one of several instances of dramatic irony in the novel, Ciel's realization occurs just moments before she loses Serena, of whom she has become, since the abortion, "terribly possessive" (*BP*, 100). Just as Ciel decides that she will "get Serena and we'll go visit Mattie now," she and Eugene hear "the scream from the kitchen" that signals Serena's electrocution (*BP*, 100–101). Naylor forces the reader to recognize that Ciel's insistence on trying to placate and keep Eugene removes her attention from her child, as a result of which the child dies.

The final sections of the story, in which Mattie snatches Ciel from the despair into which she sinks after Serena's death, have rightly received a good deal of critical acclaim and attention.[15] Mattie's rocking and cleansing of Ciel constitute not only the emotional origin of the novel but its emotional center as well. "Tired of hurting," Ciel has decided to "give up the life that God had refused to take from her" (*BP*, 101), but her death is an event Mattie will not allow: "'No! No! No!' Like a black Brahman cow, desperate to protect her young, she surged into the room, pushing the neighbor woman and the others out of her way" (*BP*, 103). Taking Ciel into "her huge ebony arms," Mattie rocks Ciel until Ciel finally emits "from the bowels of her being . . . a moan . . . so high at first it couldn't be heard by anyone there, but the yard dogs began an unholy howling" (*BP*, 103).

The comfort and the ritual cleansing that Mattie gives Ciel in this scene symbolize what all the women in the novel—and by extension, the women who read the novel—need. The text makes it clear that the "murdered dreams" of Ciel's childhood and the death of her child connect her to women throughout time, from the ancient Greek women whose babies were sacrificed to appease Neptune to the Jewish mothers who watched their children die in the death camps, to the African women who "dashed" their children "on the wooden sides of slave ships" (*BP*, 103). This suffering is explicitly the suffering of women as mothers, for Mattie must rock Ciel "back into the womb, to the nadir of her hurt," to find the "slight silver splinter" rooted deeply in her. The balm that can soothe Ciel's pain and bring her back from the despair into which she has sunk is to be found in the "huge ebony arms" in which Mattie enfolds her, arms symbolizing the nurturance and love that women can give each other—the same love that Mattie offers Etta, the same love that Mrs. Browne offers Kiswana. Mattie's subsequent ritual bathing of Ciel similarly represents not simply a purification, as Awkward suggests, but a celebration of the female body.

This story thus presents the pain of grief and betrayal, including self-betrayal, as inescapable but bearable when women bond together. Like the two previous stories, "Lucielia Louise Turner" ends on a note of hope, for Ciel's tears, which were so long in coming, "would end. And she would sleep. And morning would come" (*BP*, 105).

"Cora Lee"

The story of Cora Lee, who has an apparently insatiable desire for new-born babies, is perhaps the single story in the novel in which Naylor's artifice is most evident. The central character is, of all the characters in the novel, the one who remains most distanced from the reader's emotional engagement, though the story itself has elicited a great deal of intellectual engagement from critics. In a novel treating the theme of motherhood in all its permutations, this story points most explicitly to the selfish motivations that often lie behind motherhood.

The story's title character is introduced as an "easy child to please," so long as her parents gave her a new baby doll each Christmas (*BP*, 107). A good student in school, and her parents' "most obedient child" (*BP*,

108), Cora Lee rebels only when her parents attempt to give her "a teenaged Barbie doll" or "foreign figurines" (*BP*, 107). When her father finally refuses to give the 13-year-old girl any more dolls, Cora Lee turns to sex, which for her is simply enjoying "the thing that felt good in the dark" (*BP*, 109). After her mother belatedly warns her that she must not engage in sex "because her body can now make babies and she wasn't old enough to be a mother" (*BP*, 109), Cora Lee begins systematically to use her newfound pleasure as a means of restoring her enjoyment of baby dolls—only now, of course, they are real babies.

Celeste Fraser persuasively argues that this story attacks the myth of the welfare mother, which posits that poor women have babies for profit; Cora Lee, by contrast, "has babies for the sole pleasure of having babies."[16] Fraser sees Naylor's presentation of this myth in the story as a deliberate and elaborate fantasy; hence, the epigraph to the story, taken from Mercutio's Queen Mab speech in *Romeo and Juliet*, "instructs the readers to approach 'Cora Lee' as 'nothing but vain fantasy'" (96). A compatible reading of the story is offered by Peter Erickson, who argues that Naylor "builds up the Shakespearean motif of the dream by linking Bottom's and Puck's references to dreaming with allusions to Mercutio's set piece on Queen Mab and Prospero's 'We are such stuff as dreams are made on.' Using this Shakespearean background, Naylor plays off two meanings of dream—genuine hope and futile fantasy—against each other in the immediate context of black urban poverty."[17]

Certainly it is difficult to believe that the performance of *A Midsummer Night's Dream* to which Kiswana invites Cora Lee and her children has any lasting impact on Cora Lee. Despite her resolutions to take a more active role in her children's lives and educations, the juxtaposition of those resolutions to Bottom's "I have had a most rare vision" undermines the reader's confidence that they will be lasting.

"Cora Lee" is consistent with the other stories in the novel in dramatizing the realities of women's lives without necessarily suggesting that those lives can be transformed. We have seen that what makes the lives of most of the women of Brewster Place bearable and livable is the support and nurturance they receive from each other. Like the other characters we have met, Cora Lee achieves momentary insight into her life and acknowledges responsibility for it; her ability to change that life is another question altogether.

In remarking on the changes in the urban landscape of her childhood, Naylor has stated that "younger and younger women are having children, and those children are having other children and they stay in a vicious circle. They see no way out" (Carabi, 41). Cora Lee represents one example of the phenomenon Naylor describes—she has her first baby when she is a sophomore in high school. Naylor explores but does not fully explain the possible causes for the direction Cora Lee's life takes.

The opening paragraph of the story establishes that Cora Lee's obsession with dolls was initiated by her parents' Christmas gifts to her. Awkward rightly points to the doll trope as "the clearest example of Naylor's reuse and refiguration of the deconstructed parts of *The Bluest Eye*" (105). He also points to the fact that, whereas Morrison uses the doll trope to criticize the white standards of beauty that distort the self-images of African Americans, Naylor uses it to explore "the self-destruction of the black underclass" (109). I would suggest that Naylor is also using the doll trope to further her exploration of motherhood as the primary means of female self-definition. For Morrison, the doll trope is racialized, whereas for Naylor it is genderized.

When Cora Lee is given her first baby doll, "she circled her arms around the motionless body and squeezed, while with tightly closed eyes she waited breathlessly for the first trembling vibrations of its low, gravelly 'Mama' to radiate through her breast. Her parents surrounded this annual ritual with full heavy laughter, patted the girl on the head, and returned to the other business of Christmas" (*BP*, 107). The story suggests that the earliest and clearest message Cora Lee receives about how best to please her parents is to assume the role of mother. The baby doll is presented as a "perfect" object, one that will welcome all the love Cora Lee can lavish and that will, in return, call her "Mama."

Once the dolls are replaced by real babies, Cora Lee is an excellent mother to her children as long they remain infants. Their clothes and crib are kept in spotless condition, and Cora Lee makes sure that "there was no place for" germs (*BP*, 112). What she prizes about her babies is their complete dependence on her, especially because her babies' needs are ones she can fulfill. Like Mattie, Cora Lee "wondered at the change" that occurs in babies as they develop into toddlers (*BP*, 112). Once they grow "beyond the world of her lap" (*BP*, 112), "she just didn't understand them" (*BP*, 113) and is, in fact, at a loss to know how to deal with them. Jill Matus suggests that Cora Lee's "inability to absorb the baby as developing, needy child is part of her blocking of realities that are impinging and uncomfortable. As caretaker of a small baby, she regresses into a world that reflects a comforted, comforting sense of self. The image of herself as mother—the power, the sensuous pleasure, and the closely circumscribed world of the mother-child dyad—marks the end of her desire. Cora's dream projects a static world in which the mother-infant relationship must never be ruptured—hence the necessity for infinite replacement of the newborn baby."[18]

Unlike Etta Mae Johnson or Lucielia Louise Turner, Cora Lee does not fashion her sense of self from her relationships with men. Although she "had really liked" Sammy and Maybelline's father, his violence toward her finally made her get rid of him (*BP*, 113). Eventually, her only use of men is for sex; they become "the shadows—who came in the night and showed her the thing that felt good in the dark, and often left before the children awakened, which was so much better" (*BP*, 113). Cora Lee in effect usurps the stereotypical role of men who, like Reverend Moreland T. Woods, use women for sexual pleasure and then abandon them. In an ironic reversal of this pattern, Cora Lee stops caring about even the names of the "shadows"; she is content to receive from them "the thing that felt good in the dark" and, sometimes, "the new babies" (*BP*, 114). Men are best experienced as "shadows" because "shadows didn't give you fractured jaws or bruised eyes" (*BP*, 114).

Cora Lee's life is spent watching soap operas, providing excellent care for the infant of the moment, and being constantly frustrated by her other children, whose behavior she cannot control, largely because she has little interest in them. What disrupts her life within the confines of the story is a visit from Kiswana Browne, who seeks Cora Lee's participation in the tenants' association she is organizing. Kiswana, who seems to be about the same age as Cora Lee, disturbs her, causes her to become defensive about her children. When Cora Lee suggests that Kiswana should have babies, and Kiswana points out that "babies grow up," Cora Lee is haunted by these words, as she is by Kiswana's perfume, which "left her unsettled and she couldn't pinpoint exactly why" (*BP*, 120). After Kiswana leaves, Cora Lee suddenly seems to see for the first time the chaos and disrepair of her home and her children's clothes, and she energetically cleans house, cooks dinner, and, the following day, produces her children scrubbed and neatly dressed to go with Kiswana for the performance in the park of *A Midsummer Night's Dream*.

Although initially fearful that her children will embarrass her at the play because they will not understand its language, she and the children are soon caught up in Shakespeare's magic. In the course of the play, Cora Lee spins her own fantasy of how she will become more actively involved with her children, who will, as a result, grow up to get "good jobs in insurance companies and the post office, even doctors or lawyers" (*BP*, 126). But these resolutions are as fanciful as the fairies in the play.

Significantly, Cora Lee's reaction when the play is over echoes her desire for babies: she "applauded until her hands tingled, and felt a strange sense of emptiness now that it was over. Oh, if they would only do it again" (*BP*, 126).

Nonetheless, Naylor suspends through the end of the story the question of whether Cora Lee will change her life. On the one hand, she uncharacteristically washes the children "and put them each into bed with a kiss—this had been a night of wonders" (*BP*, 127). On the other hand, when she goes to her own bedroom, "the shadow, who had let himself in with his key, moved in the bed," and Cora Lee "turned and folded her evening like gold and lavender gauze deep within the creases of her dreams, and let her clothes drop to the floor" (*BP*, 127). It is difficult to believe, as Charles Johnson does, that any real or lasting impact has been made on Cora Lee's life through her encounter with Kiswana or her experience of Shakespeare.[19]

Of all the stories in *The Women of Brewster Place*, "Cora Lee" remains the most unsettling. Erickson rightly points to the "irony in Kiswana's being the intermediary who arouses in Cora Lee a Shakespearean dream of upward educational mobility when Kiswana herself has already deliberately rejected it, having dropped out of college" (234). And while it is true, as Matus and Fraser argue, that the story explodes the myths of the welfare mother and the exalted value of the two-parent, nuclear family, the hopelessness of Cora Lee's situation seems most attributable to her own refusal or "inability to mature" (Awkward, 108). The reader's desire for Cora Lee to change is perhaps one source of the story's disturbing effects. Significantly, the other women of Brewster Place freely criticize Cora Lee but nonetheless accept her as a part of the community. And since the final glimpses we have of Cora Lee in the novel, even though they occur in Mattie's dream, show her as a leader in the destruction of the wall, Naylor seems to insist that there is hope for her as well, however tenuous. In the damage she inflicts, through neglect, on her children, Cora Lee is certainly the character most walled in by the sexist notion that motherhood should be the primary basis for female identity.

"The Two"

The lesbian couple to whom this story's title refers are denied female friendship with the other women in Brewster Place. The last two characters in the novel to be introduced, Lorraine and Theresa are distanced from the community of the street, a fact signaled by their identity as "the two"; unlike the other characters, they do not exist as "Lorraine" and "Theresa" but only as a pair whose relationship is condemned. Naylor has stated in an interview that the community of Brewster Place "could not reach over" the difference constituted by Lorraine and Theresa's sexuality; "just like the world had put a wall in Brewster Place, they had put a wall between themselves and Lorraine and Theresa" (Carabi, 41). Both the story's title and its narrative structure reflect Naylor's principal interest in what "the two" represent to the community of Brewster Place: we are four pages into the story before Lorraine and Theresa are presented directly to the reader. Although Naylor eventually allows the reader access to the interior lives of her characters, her narrative arrangement asserts their alienation from the community and the community's power to transform them into "other."

Neither Etta Mae's hustling of men nor Cora Lee's failings as a mother to her ever-increasing number of children elicit from the community the kind of self-righteous condemnation implied by the opening sentence of "The Two": "At first they seemed like such nice girls" (*BP*, 129).[20] That their appearance belies their reality quickly becomes evident when "the rumor started" and "spread through the block like a sour odor that's only faintly perceptible and easily ignored until it starts growing in strength from the dozen mouths it had been lying in, among clammy gums and scum-coated teeth. And then it was everywhere—lining the mouths and whitening the lips of everyone as they wrinkled up their noses at its pervading smell" (*BP*, 130). Although the sour smell of the rumor originates in the "dozen mouths" who speak it, that origin is forgotten when the smell becomes "a yellow mist that began to cling to the bricks on Brewster" (*BP*, 131). Quickly, then, the rumor "got around that the two in 312 were *that* way. And they had seemed like such nice girls" (*BP*, 131).

Although "the official watchman for the block" is Sophie, because she has a good view of Lorraine and Theresa's apartment, the venom that develops against the two women belongs to everyone in the community. The opening four pages of "The Two" come close to destroying any idealized vision of community that the novel may have previously created. By the end of the opening section, the narrative has established that Lorraine and Theresa will function as scapegoats for the community: "Confronted by the difference that had been thrust into their predictable world, they reached into their imaginations and, using an ancient pattern, weaved themselves a reason for its existence. Out of necessity they stitched all of their secret fears and lingering childhood nightmares into this existence, because even though it was deceptive enough to try and look as they looked, talk as they talked, and do as they did, it had to have some hidden stain to invalidate it—it was impossible for them both to be right" (*BP*, 132).

The story that follows brings together all the characters in the novel. Naylor uses the story to develop further the themes she has addressed throughout: the efficacy of female bonding as a counterforce in the lives of the women trapped on the dead-end street; relationships between men and women; and issues surrounding female sexuality. The story also considers again the relationship between fathers and daughters, an important theme in "Mattie Michael." Through the violent rape of Lorraine and her subsequent brutal murder of Ben, the emotional tensions underlying many of the earlier stories finally explode.

Although Naylor's decision to include a lesbian couple in a novel intended to represent the diversity of black women's lives and experiences was a courageous one, her handling of the relationship has been criticized for running "counter to the positive framework of women bonding she has previously established."[21] Our glimpses into the relationship reveal that Lorraine and Theresa offer less love and support to each other than do, for example, Mattie and Etta. I would not suggest, as Barbara Smith does ("Truth," 231), that Naylor is under any obligation to present this lesbian relationship as wholly positive and without problems; to have done so, in fact, would have been inconsistent with her largely realistic depictions of other relationships in the novel.

What does seem odd, however, is that the conflict between Lorraine and Theresa on their divergent views of their sexuality becomes a conflict about their relationship to the community. The discord within their relationship, in other words, mirrors the discord generated in the community by their presence. In none of the other stories is the question of how the protagonist relates to the larger community central; the one story in which it is of any importance is, significantly, "Etta Mae Johnson," whose title character, like Lorraine and Theresa, claims the right to her own sexuality. But the relationship of the individual to the community assumes enormous importance in "The Two." In each of the other stories, the supportive bonds of sisterhood are important, but they are bonds forged between two women, not between one woman and the community at large.

Lorraine and Theresa hold completely opposing views of their relation to the community. Lorraine wants desperately to be accepted into the community, as Theresa recognizes: "No, it wasn't her job she feared losing this time, but their approval. She wanted to stand out there and chat and trade makeup secrets and cake recipes. She wanted to be secretary of their block association and be asked to mind their kids while they ran to the store" (*BP*, 136). Theresa sees Lorraine's desire for acceptance as a function of her "softness" (*BP*, 135) and wishes that Lorraine would "harden" and become a valuable "sparring partner" in their relationship (*BP*, 136). Theresa, by contrast, has no interest in the community and prefers to socialize at gay clubs. Whereas Lorraine insists that being a lesbian "doesn't make me any *different* from anyone else in the world," Theresa insists that "it makes you damned different!" (*BP*, 165). Ironically, although Theresa insists that she is indifferent to the attitudes of the women in the community, it is she who is made so angry by Sophie's snooping that she throws all the makings of her meatloaf at Sophie's windows. Theresa's vaunted indifference would thus seem actually to be defensive self-protection against the community's disapproval and rejection.

The real focus of the story is not, however, on Lorraine and Theresa but on what they—as "The Two"—represent to the other women on Brewster Place. It is thus not surprising that the most significant expression of female bonding in the story is found not in the interaction between Theresa and Lorraine but in that between Mattie and Etta, who recognize in the lesbian couple a mirror of their own relationship. Their exchange occurs during the tenants' association meeting at Kiswana's apartment, after Sophie has uttered one of her many self-righteous platitudes about the "sin" of which Lorraine and Theresa are guilty. Mattie asks her more experienced friend, "How do you get that way? Is it from birth?" (*BP*, 141). Etta, who has encountered lesbianism many times, responds:

> "They say they just love each other—who knows?"
> Mattie was thinking deeply. "Well, I've loved women, too. There was Miss Eva and Ciel, and even as ornery as you can get, I've loved you practically all my life."
> "Yeah, but it's different with them."
> "Different how?"
> "Well . . ." Etta was beginning to feel uncomfortable. "They love each other like you'd love a man or a man would love you—I guess."
> "But I've loved some women deeper than I ever loved any man," Mattie was pondering. "And there been some women who loved me more and did more for me than any man ever did."

"Yeah." Etta thought for a minute. "I can second that, but it's still different, Mattie. I can't exactly put my finger on it, but . . ."

"Maybe it's not so different," Mattie said, almost to herself. "Maybe that's why some women get so riled up about it, 'cause they know deep down it's not so different after all." She looked at Etta. "It kinda gives you a funny feeling when you think about it that way, though."

"Yeah, it does," Etta said, unable to meet Mattie's eyes. (BP, 141)

This conversation, which is the most explicit articulation of female bonding in the novel, suggests that the love between Mattie and Etta—and presumably, between any two women—even though it has not been sexually expressed, is of a kind with the love between Lorraine and Theresa. As the moral center of the novel, Mattie's judgment here carries a good deal of weight. It is nonetheless significant that her insight is expressed to Etta, not to Lorraine or Theresa, and that it has no impact on the action of the story.

The only person to befriend either Lorraine or Theresa is Ben, the old janitor. Because Lorraine reminds Ben of his daughter, he initiates a friendship with her, the only positive male-female relationship we see in the novel. Both Lorraine and Ben are destined to become representative selves, she for the other women in the street, who would deny their sisterhood with her, and he for the men in those women's lives.

The first African American to move to Brewster Place, Ben leads as shattered a life as any of the women. Like Mattie, Etta, and Ciel, he is from the South, where he worked as a sharecropper. The memories he seeks to repress through alcohol are of his daughter, who was crippled. Because she was unable to work in the fields, she was forced to have sexual relations with the white landowner—an arrangement encouraged by Ben's wife, Elvira, and tolerated by Ben. When Ben tried to protest this abuse, however, Elvira retaliated by questioning Ben's manhood: "If you was half a man, you coulda given me more babies and we woulda had some help workin' this land instead of a half-grown woman we gotta carry the load for. And if you was even quarter a man, we wouldn't be a bunch of miserable sharecroppers on someone else's land—but we is, Ben" (*BP*, 153). Although Ben fantasized about killing Elvira, he eventually turned instead to alcohol as a way of tolerating the sexual abuse of his daughter—until she finally left home for Memphis, and Elvira left him for another man.

Ben's apparent impotence in producing children to work the land is matched by his actual impotence in putting a stop to his daughter's abuse, by which he and his wife profit. He is the counterpart of Mattie's father, who loved her but could brook no disobedience, and of Lorraine's father, who kicked her out of their home when she was 17 after he discovered she was a lesbian. The bond between Ben and Lorraine is forged by their mutual needs. Ironically, their friendship enables Lorraine to become stronger and more independent, changes that, in turn, place her alone in the alley on the fatal Saturday night when she is raped by C. C. Baker and his friends.

The last of the handful of male characters presented in the novel, C. C. Baker is presented as representative of the many young men roaming streets like Brewster Place: "These young men always moved in a pack, or never without two or three. They needed the others continually near to verify their existence. When they stood with their black skin, ninth grade diplomas, and fifty-word vocabularies in front of the mirror that the world had erected and saw nothing, those other pairs of tight jeans, suede sneakers, and tinted sunglasses imaged nearby proved that they were alive. And if there was life, there could be dreams of that miracle that would one day propel them into the heaven populated by their gods—Shaft and Superfly" (*BP*, 161). Both in this passage and in the rape scene itself, Naylor takes pains to establish the societal forces that have shaped a C. C. Baker. Living in a racist world that says they have no value, C. C. and his friends also have dreams—of the sort that world has provided them, dreams of being a supermasculine, violent hero. In the rape scene, Naylor halts the action to underscore the fact that C. C. and his friends are simply trying to define themselves as men according to the terms their culture itself uses. Because they will never "be called upon to thrust a bayonet into an Asian farmer, target a torpedo, scatter their iron seed from a B-52 into the wound of the earth, point a finger to move a nation, or stick a pole into the moon," they are obliged to "validate" their manhood in the only way left to them—through the sexual assault of a black woman (*BP*, 169–70). As Helen Fiddyment Levy observes, "Through the brutal gang rape of Lorraine, Naylor connects violence against women directly to the cultural ideal that privileges male aggression, acquisitiveness, and dominance."[22]

Lorraine, in turn, attempts to stop them in the only way she knows: she speaks first with her mouth and then with her eyes "the only word she was fated to utter again and again for the rest of her life. Please" (*BP*, 171). The total ineffectualness of this typically female way of confronting the world—begging for mercy from a powerful male—is made devastatingly clear in the violent, brutal gang rape to which Lorraine is subjected. As I noted earlier, Lorraine's use of the word *please* connects her to Ciel; the two women will be more explicitly connected in Mattie's dream in "The Block Party." Lorraine's rape itself may also be seen as counterpoint to Mattie's ritualistic cleansing and exorcism of pain from Ciel. Just as Mattie's love brings Ciel back from the death to which her pain is taking her, so the absence of that kind of caring and protective bond is, by implication, responsible for Lorraine's vulnerability to C. C. Baker and his gang. Barbara Christian underscores this responsibility: "Naylor implies that Lorraine's story ends as it does because the women of Brewster Place, who should have been her mothers or sisters, failed to support her, worse, castigated her" (*Feminist*, 201). It is doubly signifi- cant, then, that Mattie, who has been a life-saving agent for Ciel, sees Lorraine crawling down the alley toward Ben but is unable to arrive in time to stop the murder.

The structure of the story establishes beyond doubt that the women of the street, in their refusal to embrace Lorraine, are complicitous in the assault on her by C. C. Baker and his friends. And Mattie's recognition of the commonality of all the women underscores Naylor's argument that what happens to Lorraine could happen to all of them and has indeed happened to many of them, albeit in milder forms. Similarly, Lorraine's unwitting murder of Ben, who to her bloodied sight is only "motion on top of the garbage can" (*BP*, 172), provides a kind of poetic justice for all the women who have been assaulted by men in the course of the novel. "The manner of Ben's death can," Awkward argues, "be viewed as a form of (authorial) retribution" (124).

"The Block Party"

The final story of the novel, as its title promises, presents a celebration of sorts in which the various women of Brewster Place are united. The end- ing of "The Two" suggests, however, that at this point no kind of cele- bration is conceivable. And in point of fact, most of the narrative of the final story consists of Mattie's cataclysmic dream of the women joining together to destroy the wall against which Lorraine has been raped and Ben murdered, the wall that throughout the novel has symbolized the barriers of racism and sexism that circumscribe the women's lives.

So sustained and powerful is Mattie's dream that many readers fail, in their first reading of the novel, to recognize it as a dream—a tribute to Naylor's skill in creating narrative ambiguity. Both before the dream and within it, however, the women of Brewster Place have been united in a new way by Lorraine's rape and subsequent insanity and by her murder of Ben.

The prologue of the story suggests that these events have had cosmic effects. Incessant, biblical rains transform the street into a kind of hell: "Water snaked down the gray bricks and flowed into the clogged gutters under sulfurous street lights like a thick dark liquid" (*BP*, 175). The rain is so heavy and the weather so cold that the residents are isolated from each other, "confined to their homes and their own thoughts" (*BP*, 175). All of the women, and little girls as well, dream of Lorraine, "the tall yellow woman in the bloody green and black dress" (*BP*, 175). Some of the women even begin "to look upon the rains as some sort of sign" (*BP*, 176). Against this ominous backdrop, Mattie's dream is introduced.

Mattie dreams of the block party, a festive affair with music, dancing, and good food. Suddenly, Ciel, who has been away from Brewster Place for a long time, appears, apologizing for not having written. In a reenactment of their experience earlier in the novel, Mattie "pressed Ciel into her full bosom and rocked her slowly" (*BP*, 177). Mattie serves Ciel a piece of angel food cake, made according to Miss Eva's recipe—the first thing Miss Eva served Mattie the night she welcomed Basil and his mother into her home. Mattie's recollection of that evening prompts Ciel to inquire about Basil, the first mention of his name since early in the novel. Mattie says that she has not heard from Basil: "Guess he ain't been as lucky as you yet. Ain't run out of highway to stop and make him think" (*BP*, 178).

As Mattie and Ciel talk, Ciel explains that she is living in San Francisco and thinking of marrying and starting another family; significantly, the fact that the man is "not black" (*BP*, 178), implies, as Matus argues, "the difficulty of envisioning alternatives to Brewster's black world of poverty, insecurity, and male inadequacy" (53). What has brought Ciel to Brewster Place is a dream she has had, "one of those crazy things that get all mixed up in your head. Something about that wall and Ben. And there was a woman who was supposed to be me, I guess. She didn't look exactly like me, but inside I felt it was me. You know how silly dreams are" (*BP*, 179). In this dream within Mattie's dream, Ciel describes the woman as wearing "a green dress with like black trimming, and there were red designs or red flowers or something on the front. . . . And something bad had happened to me by the wall—

I mean to her—something bad had happened to her. And Ben was in it somehow" (*BP*, 179).

Ciel's identification with Lorraine is one of the most explicit statements the novel makes about the very real sisterhood that binds black women together. Her dream, like the dreams all the women have of Lorraine, expresses the truth that Sophie and some of the others have tried to deny. Ironically, of course, only through Lorraine's brutal rape and insanity have the women of the street come to recognize their connection to her. Perhaps out of a desire to protect the still-fragile Ciel, neither Mattie nor Etta explains the meaning of her dream to her; they also fail to tell her how Ben died.

As Mattie's dream continues, the women begin to worry that it is going to rain, and although people are eating and drinking, dancing and talking, Mattie suddenly sees their "dark faces distorted into masks of pleasure, surprise, purpose, and satisfaction—thin masks that were glued on by the warm air of the October sun" (*BP*, 180). Behind the festivities, Mattie realizes, are the pain and despair of everyday life. Both Mattie and Etta pray, however, that the sun will remain, that it will not begin to rain again.

Also present in the dream are Kiswana and Cora Lee, who have continued, it seems, their tentative friendship. Cora Lee is pregnant once more, and Kiswana is still awkwardly trying to fit in with the other women. Slowly, the clouds begin to cover the sky, and Kiswana urges the people to put the food away and unhook the stereo. To her amazement, they refuse. Even when "the dark clouds had knotted themselves into a thick smoky fist," Kiswana's pleas are ignored, until Mattie finally explains that "clouds don't always mean rain" (*BP*, 183–84). Although Mattie and Etta are desperate to prevent the rain by denying it, the rain does indeed begin to fall. Just as the first drops fall, Cora Lee discovers that blood is still on the wall. Muttering "It just ain't right; it just ain't right. It shouldn't still be here" (*BP*, 185), she begins to tear out the bricks. Soon she is joined by the other women—the men and children do not participate—who discover that the blood is all over the wall: "It's spreading all over," Mattie shouts (*BP*, 186).

A resident of Brewster Place by choice, not necessity, Kiswana insists to Ciel, "You know there's no blood—it's raining. It's just raining!" (*BP*, 187). Nevertheless, Ciel, who recognizes both what the wall represents and therefore what the women's destruction of it means, "pressed the brick into Kiswana's hand and forced her fingers to curl around it. 'Does it matter? Does it really matter?'" (*BP*, 187).

The bonds of sisterhood uniting the women as they destroy the wall together are eventually extended to Theresa, who throughout the party has been moving out of the apartment she shared with Lorraine:

> Cora Lee came panting up with a handful of bricks, her stomach heaving and almost visible under her soaked dress.
> "Here, please, take these. I'm so tired."
> Theresa turned her back on her.
> "Please. Please." Cora held out the stained bricks.
> "Don't say that!" Theresa screamed. "Don't ever say that!" She grabbed the bricks from Cora and threw one into the avenue, and it burst into a cloud of green smoke.
> "Now, you go back up there and bring me some more, but don't ever say that again—to anyone!" (*BP*, 187–88)

Cora's use of the word *please* unites her with Lorraine and Ciel, and it is appropriately Theresa who recognizes the devastating consequences of the posture in life the word implies. Supplication for what amounts to one's right to live, to be, makes women vulnerable to victimization. As Mattie knows—and we must remember that this dream is her vision of what ought to happen—the forces with which women must contend cannot be countered through supplication. To claim life requires the sort of assertion that Mattie herself made when she snatched Ciel back from the threshold of death. The "cloud of green smoke" into which the brick bursts reminds us that a beseeching posture could not save Lorraine, "the tall yellow woman in the bloody green and black dress" whose brutalization has prompted Mattie's dream. Just as the word *please* unites Cora Lee with Ciel and Theresa, the "green smoke" unites Lorraine with Etta, the only other character who wears green in the novel.

The sheer length of Mattie's dream—nearly 12 pages of the 13-page story—prevents the reader from relinquishing its vision after Mattie awakens. The united effort of the women to destroy the wall is so consistent with readers' desires that we may give our intellectual assent to its status as a dream, but not our emotional assent. The dream is one of Naylor's most successful strategies in the novel, allowing her to provide a vision of what needs to happen while at the same time withholding it.

When Mattie awakens from her dream, the day of the block party has arrived along with "a deluge of sunlight" (*BP*, 188)—an oxymoron made significant by Mattie's dream. Mattie interprets the sunshine as "just like a miracle," even though the sun is shining "on the stormy clouds that had formed on the horizon and were silently moving toward

Brewster Place" (*BP*, 188). Naylor has stated that she wanted to allow each reader to decide whether the women would, in fact, tear down the wall. The conditions resemble those in the dream—the sun is shining, with storm clouds on the horizon—but whether the women will act as they do in Mattie's dream remains, Naylor says, deliberately unanswered (Carabi, 41).

"Dusk"

The closing frame of the novel reiterates and underscores the open-endedness of "The Block Party." Whereas the opening frame describes the birth of Brewster Place, "Dusk" describes not its death but its process of dying. Although we learn that the street has been condemned and its residents evicted, Brewster Place is "dying but not dead" (*BP*, 191). It will not die until "the expiration of its spirit in the minds of its children" (*BP*, 191), and that spirit, the final paragraph of the novel suggests, continues to live in its "'Afric' children" (*BP*, 192). No matter that their dreams are shattered or endlessly "deferred"; what is important is that the "colored daughters of Brewster, spread over the canvas of time, still wake with their dreams misted on the edge of a yawn. They get up and pin those dreams to wet laundry hung out to dry, they're mixed with a pinch of salt and thrown into pots of soup, and they're diapered around babies. They ebb and flow, ebb and flow, but never disappear. So Brewster Place still waits to die" (*BP*, 192).

Although the lives of black women may be circumscribed, the text celebrates their ability to continue to dream of a better life for their children. And because they continue to dream, the many Brewster Places they inhabit will not die. Similarly, as Matus shows, Naylor's novel itself refuses closure, for the outcome of the block party remains unknown and "Brewster Place still waits to die." The novel thus offers an alternative answer to the question posed by Langston Hughes's poem, suggesting that the deferral of dreams is corollary to life itself. Brewster Place, like the settings of Naylor's subsequent novels, exists less as a place than as a "spirit in the minds of its children." That spirit, the novel suggests, is defined by its power to dream.

Chapter Three

Selling the "Mirror in Your Soul": *Linden Hills*

While Naylor was writing *The Women of Brewster Place*, she dreamed, she has said, "of having a quartet of interconnected novels that would serve as the foundation for a career I wanted to build in writing" (*Dreaming*, 170). Her most evident strategy in establishing these interconnections is referring to characters or places in one text that become significant in the next. Thus, we learn in *The Women of Brewster Place* that Kiswana Browne has fled the middle-class home of her parents in Linden Hills, the trees of which she can see from her apartment on Brewster Place. Naylor dreamed of doing "a whole treatment of her neighborhood" ("Conversation," 582), and that dream became a reality with the publication in 1985 of *Linden Hills*.[1]

Writing a novel about Kiswana Browne's neighborhood meant shifting her focus from the working-class black women who inhabit Brewster Place to the middle- and upper-middle-class blacks—chiefly men—who measure their success by their ability to live in a Linden Hills. This shift in focus in some ways reflects the shift Naylor herself experienced, both in moving from Harlem to Queens when she was still a child and in finding herself in new worlds as a result of her education and her writing. *Linden Hills* allowed her, she has stated, "to come to terms with what it meant to change class, which is actually what I did and what my parents had been working so hard for. But when a child from a poor class enters another class, there is tension" (Carabi, 42). Naylor's concerns about the moral and spiritual risks associated with a move to a higher socioeconomic class are evident in the model she decided to use in structuring *Linden Hills*, Dante Alighieri's *Inferno*, which she read in a "Great Works of Literature" course at Brooklyn College.

Naylor says that her interest in the novel was in

> what happens to black Americans when they move up in America's society. They first lose family ties, because if you work for a big corporation, you may have grown up in Detroit but may end up living in Houston. Then there are the community ties. You can create a whole different type

of community around you—mostly of a mixture of other professional, middle-class people—but you lose the ties with your spiritual or religious values. And ultimately, the strongest and most difficult ties to let go of are your ties with your ethnocentric sense of self. You forget what it means to be an African American. (Carabi, 41–42)

In the neighborhood of Linden Hills that Naylor creates, those who have broken all of these ties are considered the most "successful," the sign of their success being the location of their houses near the bottom of the slope on which the neighborhood is built; those who have kept some of these ties intact, among them Kiswana Browne's parents, live nearer the top of the slope.[2] Like Morrison's neighborhood of "the Bottom" in *Sula*, Linden Hills reverses ordinary values, but as Christian points out, the Bottom "is a distinctly African-American community with a distinct African-American culture," whereas "Linden Hills residents reject their black culture" ("Geography," 370). The reversal of values in Linden Hills also reflects the influence of Dante's *Inferno*, which "was the perfect work for symbolizing when up is down. Dante presents an image of Florentine society and then slowly moves from the lesser sins to the greater sins. So that's what I did in *Linden Hills*" (Carabi, 42).

Naylor denies that her novel inscribes the idea that "the only real black is a poor black" (Bonetti), but the novel itself fails to offer any positive, morally sound character who is not poor or dangerously close to it. Naylor's suspicion of the corrupting influence of "worldly" concerns— the residue perhaps of her years as a Jehovah's Witness—is nowhere more apparent than in this second novel, which she considers her "masterwork" (see appendix). Nor is it surprising that most of the characters whose ambitions Naylor charts in the novel are male, since, as Christian points out, black women have the least "access to power in the larger society" ("Geography," 353). Ironically, the male characters in *Linden Hills* are more numerous, and many are far more insidious and destructive, than those in *The Women of Brewster Place*, though Naylor's depiction of men in *Brewster Place* has been more frequently found objectionable by male critics.

Linden Hills represents, in fact, Naylor's most incisive critique of male patriarchy, which provides the necessary underpinnings of economic aggression and success. The novel's moral attention to both class and gender systems seems to reflect Naylor's own experiences at the time she wrote the novel. As we have seen, she began to identify herself as a feminist during her years at Brooklyn College. In the summer of 1981, following her graduation, Naylor traveled to Spain and Tangiers, where she began "the first first draft" of *Linden Hills*.³ On this her first big trip abroad, financed with the advance she received on *The Women of Brewster Place*, Naylor took a copy of James Baldwin's *Nobody Knows My Name* (1961), expecting to experience Europe in much the same way as Baldwin and Ernest Hemingway had described. Her status as a woman, however, made her experience very different: "I was harassed a lot on the streets because I was a woman traveling alone. In southern Spain the women don't walk alone. So the men assumed I was a prostitute or that I wanted them to approach me, and it was really difficult. And the freedom that Hemingway and Baldwin experienced I didn't have. . . . And I'm going to be honest—I resented that; I was bitter that I couldn't have the world like they had the world" ("Conversation," 570).

If her travel in Europe gave new dimensions to Naylor's developing feminism, her experience the following year at Yale University must equally have reinforced her suspicions of upward mobility. Naylor entered Yale in the fall of 1981, intending eventually to obtain a doctorate and "get one of those high-class union cards, which is tenure," so she would have financial security (Pearlman and Henderson, 31). She discovered, however, that she was unable to write and pursue academic studies at the same time. It seems reasonable to speculate that the incompatibility of academic and creative endeavors that Naylor experienced became associated in her mind with the class differences between urban Brooklyn College for commuter students and Ivy League Yale. Certainly her devastating portrait of an academic in the novel—the historian Daniel Braithwaite—suggests a correlation between intellectual and moral bankruptcy and material success.

Drawing on the traditions of allegory, satire, and Gothic fiction, *Linden Hills* portrays a nightmarish world in which black Americans, lured by promises and dreams of success, have achieved status and some measure of power; in the process, however, they have forfeited their hearts and their souls, though they remain, like Dante's sinners, unrepentant and therefore irredeemable.

The Model of the *Inferno* and the Meaning of Class

Naylor draws on the *Inferno*, the first and best-known *cantica* of Dante's *Divina Commedia*, as the model for *Linden Hills* in at least three significant areas. She employs what we might call Dante's moral geography in the overall conception and particular details of the middle-class neighborhood known as Linden Hills. She adapts Dante's narrative strategy of the journey into and through hell as her main organizing principle. And she offers, like Dante, an allegory intended to warn and instruct her intended audience—black Americans.

Moral Geography

Dante envisioned hell as a tripartite region consisting of nine concentric, descending circles, each the eternal home of a particular kind of unrepentant sinner. Hell is entered by passing through the gates whose famous inscription announces the end of all hope, into the Vestibule of the Indifferent, people "Whose mortal life earned neither praise nor blame," and angels who did not join in the rebellion against God but did not keep "faith with Him" either.[4] Beyond this vestibule is the river Acheron, across which Charon ferries waiting souls into the first circle, Limbo, where reside Homer, Horace, Virgil, and others who were "sinless" but never benefited from Christian baptism, having lived and died before Christ.

True hell begins beyond Limbo, though Limbo is included as one of the nine circles. The first five circles of hell comprise the section of Dante's hell designated for those guilty of incontinence, less onerous to Dante than violence and fraud, the general categories defining the two remaining sections. The sixth circle, which lies below the river Styx and behind the walls of the City of Dis, is inhabited by Heretics and represents a transition between upper and lower hell. The seventh circle, consisting of three rings, is the place of torment for those guilty of violence—against neighbor, against self, and against God.

The final section of hell—circles eight and nine—is reserved for the fraudulent and is separated from the previous section by an abyss. Shaped like a funnel, this section is reached by Dante through the help of the monster Geryon. Circle eight, the funnel's lip, is "corrugated by ten dismal troughs" (18.7) that form a series of ditches called *malebolge*. Across these ditches are bridges "like spokes, / Reaching from outer edge to inner pit" (18.11–12), and from atop these bridges Dante and Virgil view the sinners below, ranging from Panderers and Seducers at the top to Counterfeiters and Falsifiers at the bottom. At the bottom of circle eight is the Giant's Well, beyond which lies the ninth circle and the frozen floor of hell. At the very bottom Dante places Satan, whom he depicts as a horrible monster with three mouths; in these mouths are the most fraudulent of any who have lived, at least according to the fourteenth-century Italian poet: Judas, Brutus, and Cassius. Beyond hell's frozen floor is the center of the earth and the Southern Hemisphere.

Although Naylor's modern inferno does not match Dante's point by point, there are numerous similarities between the two terrains. Linden Hills is built on "a V-shaped section of land with the boundaries running south for one and a half miles from the stream that bordered Putney Wayne's high grazing fields down a steep, rocky incline of brier bush and linden trees before curving through the town's burial ground and ending in a sharp point at the road in front of Patterson's apple orchard."[5] Putney Wayne's grazing fields eventually become city blocks bounded by Wayne Avenue, on the north side of which is the business district; across from the straggling businesses are apartments, the back windows of which look down into Linden Hills. In these apartments live Ruth and Norman Anderson, who overlook but are clearly not a part of Linden Hills. A stream, equivalent to Dante's Acheron, separates this area from Linden Hills proper. Although the area corresponds topographically to Dante's Vestibule of the Indifferent, its residents, or at least the two we encounter, do not; indeed, Ruth and Norman Anderson are to some extent moral touchstones in the novel. Along Wayne Avenue is Wayne Junior High School, from which Willie Mason and Lester Tilson graduated, and the bronze plaques over its front doors inscribe a parody of Dante's "Abandon all hope."[6] Naylor thus indicts educational systems for their inculcation of the values underlying Linden Hills.

Like the concentric circles comprising Dante's hell, "eight circular drives," which ultimately lead to the cemetery and the home of Luther Nedeed, make up Linden Hills. The upper five roads, known as First, Second, Third, Fourth, and Fifth Crescent Drives, correspond to Dante's first five circles. On these streets live the Tilsons, Kiswana Browne's parents, Winston Alcott, Xavier Donnell, Chester Parker, and Michael Hollis, all of whom correspond in general ways to the Incontinents of Dante's first five circles, as Ward points out (69). Through his betrayal of his own integrity as well as of his long-standing relationship with his male lover, Winston Alcott learns that he will be moving from Second Crescent Drive to Tupelo Drive in the lower part of Linden Hills. The residents of the upper five streets have all forsaken personal and family ties, which, as noted earlier, Naylor believes are the first ties relinquished by black Americans moving "up in American society." But by the time we get to Fourth Crescent Drive, we encounter characters, like the dead Lycentia Parker, who have also lost their "ethnocentric sense of self." Michael T. Hollis, on Fifth Crescent Drive, though he retains some sense of his ethnocentric identity, has sacrificed both family ties and spiritual values. Naylor's description of what happens to upwardly mobile black Americans is thus flexibly delineated through her topography.

The counterpart to Dante's lower hell is known simply as Tupelo Drive, named as the result of protests by residents eager to have a Tupelo Drive address: they successfully blocked efforts by a city commissioner to name their streets Sixth, Seventh, and Eighth Crescent Drives. At the very end of Tupelo Drive is the house of Luther Nedeed, Naylor's Satan figure in the novel. Nedeed's street address is 999 Tupelo Drive—the number, as Naylor explains, being the biblical sign of the beast, appropriately inverted in this upside-down world (Ward, 69n). Although Tupelo Drive was named after the home of the first Luther Nedeed, Tupelo, Mississippi, Naylor has indicated that she also intended a pun on the "two pillars" in front of Dante's City of Dis (Bonetti). Accordingly, the residents of this lower—and from their perspective, most desirable—part of Linden Hills "built a private road with a flower-trimmed meridian headed by two twelve-foot brick pillars" (*LH*, 14–15).

Unlike its model, the lower part of Linden Hills does not include multiple subtypes of sinners, though it does have an abyss. Naylor presents only two residents of Tupelo Drive besides Nedeed: Laurel Dumont, who corresponds to the suicides in Dante's seventh circle (violence); and Daniel Braithwaite, who would easily fit in any number of the lower subdivisions of Dante's eighth circle (fraud). Laurel's name also seems to align her with Dante's suicides, who take the form of trees. Just as hell is ultimately the domain of Satan, so Linden Hills is controlled by a series of Luther Nedeeds. *Nedeed*, Naylor has stated, is an inversion of *de eden*, which she found "appropriate because the Nedeeds are the Satanic rulers of this false paradise" (Ward, 70n). The Nedeeds are both the realtors who lease the houses in Linden Hills for one thousand years and a day (eternity) and the undertakers who provide the final resting place for the residents.[7] The Nedeed home, like Satan's, is at the very bottom of Linden Hills, surrounded by the town cemetery and isolated by an artificial lake. Behind the Nedeed house is a chain-link fence, beyond which are Patterson Road and Patterson's apple orchard.

Naylor provides enough correspondences between the topography of her modern middle-class suburb and that of Dante's hell to make her general import quite clear. The key differences lie in the kinds of offenses she and Dante weight most seriously and in the awareness of their respective inhabitants. A central irony informing Naylor's work is found in her characters' lack of consciousness about the damnation of their souls. By contrast, Dante's sinners, though unrepentant, understand that they are being punished. Naylor's characters eagerly seek addresses farther down in Linden Hills, closer to Tupelo Drive, closer to the source of power, Luther Nedeed. By defining success in terms of their location lower down in Linden Hills, they betray their unawareness of their destructive course. Thus, for example, "there had been a dispute for years over the exact location of Linden Hills," and "its boundaries contracted and expanded over the years to include no one, and then practically everyone in Wayne County"—for everyone wants a Linden Hills address (*LH*, 1).

Narrative Strategy

Dante's *Commedia* is structured as a journey taken by the poet to the three realms of the afterlife. The poem begins on the evening of Maundy Thursday in 1300, a point of crisis for the poet, as we learn from the opening lines:

> Midway along the journey of our life
> I strayed, abandoning the rightful path,
> And found myself within a gloomy wood.
> So hard it is its aspect to describe,
> This savage, harsh and fearsome wilderness,
> That fear rekindles with the memory. (1.1–6)

After wandering all night, he sees in the morning a wonderful mountain, but he cannot climb it because it is guarded by a series of beasts. In the midst of his anguish, the soul of Virgil suddenly appears. Virgil tells Dante that, to reach the top of the mountain, he must travel indirectly, with Virgil serving as his guide, through hell and then purgatory; eventually Beatrice, symbol of divine love, will lead him through paradise. Virgil further explains that he has come to aid Dante at the behest of the Virgin Mary, Santa Lucia, and Beatrice.

Dante's journey through hell (and purgatory and paradise) is thus occasioned by a crisis in his life, a turning point that happens to correspond with the most significant days in the Christian calendar as well as with the first year of a new century. His guide is appropriately the great classical poet of Italy, Virgil, whose intervention has been brought about by three female figures. The journey they undertake will enable and empower Dante to find his way back to "the rightful path" from which he has strayed. Dante's descent into hell (the part of the *Commedia* Naylor uses) is completed on Easter Sunday, when he and Virgil surface in purgatory.

Naylor's Dante is 20-year-old Willie "White" Mason, a poor young man who left school "after the ninth grade" because "there was really nothing more they could teach him" (*LH*, 28).[8] An aspiring poet, Willie memorizes his poems rather than writing them down, in emulation of "the great slave poet, Jupiter Hammon, who memorized thousands of verses because he couldn't read" (*LH*, 29). Willie is an oral poet because he identifies written poetry with white people: "The written word dulls the mind, and since most of what's written is by white men, it's positively poisonous" (*LH*, 29).

Willie, like Dante, is at something of a point of crisis in his life. The audience for his poetry has been driven inside by the winter weather, and he is thus "forced to talk to himself, and his reflections disturbed him. He was twenty years old and the last job he had worked side by side with a twelve year old who came in after school. Would that be his fate at thirty and forty? . . . With jobs like that, he saw himself frozen in time, never becoming a man, just a very gray-haired boy. He'd think about Linden Hills and all that it offered, and wonder if perhaps there might have been another way" (*LH*, 29–30). The "all" offered by Linden Hills is what Willie's journey will make him see clearly. His journey, like Dante's, will have corrective value. That journey into Linden Hills takes place during another significant time in the Christian calendar, the Christmas season: he begins his journey on 19 December and completes it on Christmas Eve.

Like Dante, Willie has a guide to help him find his way through Naylor's modern inferno. He is led by one of the residents of Linden Hills, Lester "Shit" Tilson, who continues to live at home with his mother and sister on First Crescent Drive; Lester then, like Virgil, is a resident of the place through which he will lead his friend. Lester is also a poet, but he writes and even sometimes publishes his verse. The relationship between the two young men thus resembles the relationship between Virgil and Dante: Dante was noted for his departure from Latin and his use of the vernacular in his great poem. The decision to write in the vernacular reflects, among other things, a belief that the written word should not be accessible only to an elite group. Somewhat similarly, Willie's insistence on remaining an oral poet reflects his desire to direct his verse toward African Americans; he rejects the written word because of its association with and control by white Americans, who have used it to maintain their power over African Americans, and he places himself instead within the African tradition of the griot.

Like Virgil, Lester Tilson does not himself invent the idea of giving his friend a tour of Linden Hills. He is encouraged to do so by Naylor's equivalent of Beatrice, Ruth Anderson, who suggests that the two young men may be able to make some extra money for Christmas presents by doing odd jobs in Linden Hills. While she is not, like her counterpart Beatrice, a Christ figure, Ruth Anderson does represent the purest love we encounter in the novel. She not only initiates Willie's journey but provides assistance (as does Beatrice) when she fears that Lester and Willie may encounter difficulties.

Willie's journey through Linden Hills, like Dante's journey through hell, gives him increasingly horrifying visions of the emptiness and fraudulence of the residents' lives. Before he begins his journey, he reflects that he has perhaps erred in the choices he has made, that perhaps the people who live in Linden Hills represent a better way of life. By the conclusion of his journey, his glimpses into their lives have silenced such questions. Although he must certainly enter adulthood, the course he chooses will not be the pursuit of the American dream of material success.

Dante's Allegorical Legacy

As a medieval writer, Dante almost of necessity intended his *Commedia* to operate on several different levels of meaning, including the allegorical, although his poem is not the straightforward, one-for-one allegory that we find, for example, in Spenser's *Faerie Queene*. Dorothy Sayers offers these definitions as a way of understanding Dante's art: "An allegory is a dramatised metaphor. A metaphor is a compressed simile. A simile is the perception of likeness in unlike things, presented in such a way that the understanding of the one helps to understand the other."[9] Dante's *Commedia* uses the metaphor of the worlds of the dead to dramatize allegorically both the behavior of those in the world of the living and the rewards or punishments that their behavior warrants. As Thomas Bergin suggests, "The *Commedia* portrays our world with all its morally diversified citizenry. So the 'true' meaning is essentially . . . the revelation of the human heart, the continuous struggle between good and evil" (254).

In *Linden Hills*, Naylor reverses Dante's principal metaphor: the middle- to upper-middle-class Linden Hills becomes a metaphor for hell, one of the worlds of the dead. Its inhabitants, who have destroyed or are in the process of destroying their souls through a range of behaviors, suffer many of the torments of hell and, most important, have become hollow and dead. Linden Hills is the land of the living dead.

Linden Hills was originally created by Luther Nedeed I,[10] whose evil and corruption are evident in his having "sold his octoroon wife and six children for the money to come North and obtain" the land (*LH*, 2), and in his having later bought and married another octoroon whom he never freed. Luther's dual business interests—real estate and undertaking— quickly make him a rich man. Luther Nedeed II, in turn, takes his father's wealth and multiplies it. Nedeed II, "like his father," recognizes that the future of America "was going to be white: white money backing wars for white power because the very earth was white—look at it— white gold, white silver, white coal running white railroads and steamships, white oil fueling white automotives" (*LH*, 8). Nedeed II thus determines that, because he is black and therefore cannot rule the world, "he sure as hell could ruin. He could be a fly in the ointment, a spot on the bleached sheet, and Linden Hills would prove it" (*LH*, 8). He resolves to make his land into "a beautiful, black wad of spit right in the white eye of America" (*LH*, 9).

Luther Nedeed III further refines the visions of his father and grandfather. Recognizing that "life is in the material. . . . Success is being able to stick an 'er' on it," Nedeed III wants not only for Linden Hills to be "a blister" to the white world but "to make that sore fester and pus over" (*LH*, 9). To that end, he realizes, he will have to make Linden Hills "a showcase . . . a jewel—an ebony jewel that reflected the soul of Wayne County but reflected it black"; the reflection would be "so bright that it would spawn dreams of dark kings with dark counselors leading dark armies against the white god and toward a retribution all feared would not be just, but long overdue. Yes, a brilliance that would force a waking nightmare of what the Nedeeds were capable. And the fools would never realize . . . that it was nothing but light from a hill of carbon paper dolls" (*LH*, 9–10).

Nedeed III, like his father and grandfather before him, uses Linden Hills as a way of gaining power for himself, but that power will be made possible by the many residents of Linden Hills who match white people in their drive for material wealth, status, and power. By the time the current Luther Nedeed (the fourth) takes over the family domain, however, Linden Hills is not an "ebony jewel" reflecting the Nedeeds, for it is no longer "black" but "successful" (*LH*, 17). Nedeed IV is thus obliged to recognize that "the plans and visions of his fathers might have been misdirected" (*LH*, 18), and he is forced to find his power only in defining what is desirable and in controlling the access to what he has defined. In true Satanic fashion, he finds his pleasure in watching the inhabitants strive "to reach the bottom," to finally gain an address on Tupelo Drive, after which "they eventually disappeared. Finally, devoured by their own drives, there just wasn't enough humanity left to fill the rooms of a real home, and the property went up for sale" (*LH*, 17–18).

In Naylor's allegory, material success is identified with white culture, and its single-minded pursuit leads to the destruction of the human soul. A part of that destruction for the African American people who pursue this white dream is the loss of their ethnicity. As Nedeed IV realizes, material success does not reflect the color of those who achieve it; such success simply reflects itself. There are numerous specific allegorical meanings in Naylor's tale, but its underlying concept is the death of the (black) human soul occasioned by pursuit of the (white) American dream of material prosperity.

The Novel's Structure

Scraping off the Pinks

Although Naylor uses Dante's scheme of the journey into hell as the principal narrative device in *Linden Hills*, the novel departs from its Dantean model in presenting two journeys, which are mirror images of each other. Simultaneous with Willie Mason's journey down into Linden Hills is Willa Nedeed's journey up from the basement/morgue of her husband's house, where Luther has imprisoned her and their son. Willie Mason and Willa Nedeed, as their names and their parallel journeys suggest, are mirror images of each other. Moreover, although Ruth Anderson sends Willie with Lester down into Linden Hills for the apparent purpose of earning money, Willie's journey from the outset is a quest for knowledge of Willa. At first he is curious about the source of the unearthly howls he hears coming from the depths of Linden Hills, but as he and Lester advance on their journey, his object is to discover the name of Luther Nedeed's nameless wife.

The opening section of the novel, which serves as a kind of prologue, not only sketches the history of Linden Hills and the Nedeed men but also explains the plight of the current Mrs. Nedeed. Because the Nedeed men have, as Luke Bouvier states, "conceived of Linden Hills as a timeless space outside of history," they have attempted to create a family that suggests timelessness and permanence.[11] Thus, the successive generations of Nedeed men follow the model established by the first Luther Nedeed: each marries an octoroon woman; each woman births one child, a son; and each of these sons "grew up to carry his father's first name, broad chest, and bowlegs. Big frog and little frog, the town whispered behind their backs" (*LH*, 4). The women who marry the Nedeed men function simply as a means of reproduction, a role whose importance disappears as soon as the male heir is born. Four generations of identical Nedeed men have been reproduced, but as the novel opens, the fifth generation, a five-year-old son, threatens to destroy the Nedeed empire: although this son has "the same squat bowlegs, the same protruding eyes and puffed lips," he is white, not black, and his "ghostly presence . . . mocked everything his fathers had built" (*LH*, 18).

Although the current Luther Nedeed has broken with tradition by marrying a brown-skinned woman rather than an octoroon, he has scrupulously followed every other rule passed on to him. The Nedeed men have, they believe, perfected the art of reproduction: their "seed was only released at the vernal equinox so the child would come during the Sign of the Goat when the winter's light was the weakest" (*LH*, 19). Naylor emphasizes the Nedeed dedication to evil through their calculations for copulation, since many of the devil's physical traits are traditionally taken from Capricorn, "the Sign of the Goat"; the associations with this astrological sign include deception, greed, and wealth, as well as dryness and coldness, all qualities exhibited by each generation of Nedeed men.[12]

Despite having faithfully followed "the journals and charts" by which the Nedeeds have ensured their immortality, the current Luther has been presented, some five years before the novel's opening, with a white son. Since the journals and charts "had been infallible for generations," only one conclusion is possible: "There was no way that this child could be his son" (*LH*, 19). The current Mrs. Nedeed, unlike her predecessors, who "had been brought to Tupelo Drive to fade against the whitewashed boards of the Nedeed home after conceiving and giving over a son to the stamp and will of the father" (*LH*, 18), must harbor within herself "a deep flaw or she wouldn't have been capable of such treachery" (*LH*, 19). The son she has produced, Teresa Goddu points out, "represents the rupture that begins the process of revisioning Luther's patriarchal myth."[13] Despite generations of light-skinned wives, Luther repudiates any connection with his white son; since the Nedeed men have always denied the importance of their wives, the idea that their genes might be manifest in this son is beyond Luther's conceptual powers. Ironically, of course, his white son not only asserts, through his skin color, the undeniable significance of the Nedeed wives but also symbolizes the total rejection of their ethnicity that has come with the Nedeeds' quest for power.

Unwilling to acknowledge these consequences of the Nedeeds' patriarchal empire building, Luther locates the cause of this threat to his domain in his wife: "Obviously, he had allowed a whore into his home but he would turn her into a wife" (*LH*, 19). It is to effect this transformation that Luther has locked Willa and their son into the old morgue in the basement of their house.[14] In the course of the novel, we follow her growing recognition of her own power, a power that Luther clearly understands from the outset but intends to control, for "it took over a hundred and fifty years to build what he now had and it would be a cold day in hell before he saw some woman tear it down" (*LH*, 20). Ironically, of course, it is indeed a very cold day in what is hell when Willa succeeds in this destruction.

The connection between Willie and Willa is emphasized by the sentences, following this passage, with which the prologue concludes: "It was cold. In fact it was the coldest week of the year when White Willie and Shit slapped five on Wayne Avenue and began their journey down into Linden Hills" (*LH*, 20). Like Willa, whose gender and status as wife both marginalize and imprison her, Willie is at best a marginalized citizen of the streets; his working-class status keeps him economically powerless, and as Gates notes, his "penchant for writing poetry" threatens to make him "seem 'feminine' to others."[15]

The chapter in which Willie is introduced, titled "December 19th," juxtaposes a family from the "dilapidated garden-apartment buildings" on Wayne Avenue (*LH*, 33) with a family from First Crescent Drive. This chapter not only provides the exposition that sets up the journey Willie will undertake with Lester but also dramatizes the differences between the impoverished world in which Willie lives and the materially comfortable one of his friend. The scene in which Willie and Lester join Ruth and Norman Anderson brilliantly illustrates Naylor's use of symbolic imagery as a primary method of establishing meaning in her novel.

Willie and Lester have encountered each other on Wayne Avenue, and their primary topic of conversation before Ruth and Norman Anderson join them has been the cold weather. Willie, who "stamped his feet to keep the ice from seeping into the soles of his shoes" and has no gloves at all to protect his hands (*LH*, 30), admires "Lester's thick suede gloves

and Western boots" (*LH*, 30). His friend, however, is contemptuous of
these garments because they have been given him by his mother and sister. Willie, whose suffering from the cold is a constant motif in the
novel, suggests that "least you got someone to care about whether you
freeze or not. It must be nice to have a family in Linden Hills who can
afford that kind of stuff" (*LH*, 30). Comfortably warm in his winter
apparel, Lester complains that wearing these clothes is "torment"
because they remind him that he has no money with which to recipro-
cate, and the end result will be that "I'm nothing and they've made their
point *again* for another year. Merry Christmas, baby" (*LH*, 31). As Willie
points out later in the chapter, Lester wants to enjoy the comforts that
his family's money provides him while reserving the right to feel morally
superior to his family.

Like Willie, Ruth Anderson lacks adequate winter clothing, her "thin
beige coat" providing her with very little warmth; this fact does not prevent her from being a "golden goddess" about whom Willie frequently
dreams, though even in his dreams he never does more than "look" (*LH*,
32). Formerly married to a resident of Fifth Crescent Drive in Linden
Hills, Ruth had wanted from her marriage to Norman "that anchor of
security which comes with the weight of accumulated things" (*LH*, 35).
As the wife of Norman Anderson, she not only lacks these things but
experiences an even greater poverty than do the other residents of
Wayne Avenue: "The Andersons' poverty was a standing joke on Wayne
Avenue. People said that if Norman brought home air, Ruth would
make gravy, pour it over it, and tell him not to bring so much the next
time" (*LH*, 32).

Despite their poverty, the Andersons invite Willie and Lester to come
home with them and have some coffee, which they serve in the only
three cups—made of Styrofoam—they possess. Their apartment is likewise sparsely furnished, containing only absolute essentials for living:
"one sofa in the living room, one kitchenette set with plastic-bottomed
chairs on uncertain chrome legs, one bed" (*LH*, 33). Despite the absence
of furnishings, "it *was* a home," one into which visitors felt honored to be
invited (*LH*, 33). Similarly, though Ruth serves the coffee in Styrofoam
cups, she handles these "as carefully as she would china. And she gave
them each a plastic spoon with a paper napkin folded underneath.
Norman poured the coffee and made such a ceremony of unwrapping
Willie's cheap blackberry brandy and adding it to their cups, you might
have thought it a rare cognac. And when the two boys raised the steam-
ing coffee to their lips, that's exactly what it tasted like" (*LH*, 33). Later

in the scene, when Ruth asks Norman, "What rules in this house?" he responds, "Love rules in this house, Ruth" (*LH*, 38).

The spiritual and emotional richness found in the Anderson home is heightened by its juxtaposition to Lester's house, to which the young men go after they leave the Andersons. The Tilson house is elaborately, ornately, and rather hideously decorated—completely in green, the color of the wealth that Lester's mother and sister so desperately seek. Mrs. Tilson, a "delicate, yellow woman," makes Willie feel "big and awkward and black" (*LH*, 48). Though clearly displeased that, in her eyes, a disreputable young man is visiting in her house, Mrs. Tilson does invite him to share their dinner, though she apologetically refers to it as "peasant food" (*LH*, 48), "common food, but filling" (*LH*, 49). Compared throughout the scene to a bird, Mrs. Tilson objects to Willie's name (Willie K. Mason), especially after she realizes that his first name is not a diminutive for William and his middle initial stands for nothing: "It just never occurred to me that people lacked such imagination they had to resort to giving a child a letter for a name" (*LH*, 50). Pretentious and greedy, she and her daughter want to move further down in Linden Hills.

Although Mrs. Tilson clearly disapproves of Willie as a friend for her son, she nevertheless "set the dining room table with china, silverware, and linen napkins" in his honor, but "the starched linen kept slipping off his lap, and he spent the evening cringing every time his heavy knife hit the thin plate or his teeth clinked against the fragile Norwegian crystal" (*LH*, 54). The three Tilsons spend the evening bickering with each other, their material comfort incapable of providing emotional or spiritual harmony.

The contrast with Willie's experience in the Anderson home is striking. Naylor makes clear the spiritual and emotional richness that transforms the Andersons' dilapidated apartment into a warm, welcoming, loving home. But the process by which this transformation is made both possible and necessary represents one of the more puzzling elements of the Andersons' story. The bare furnishings of their apartment have been necessitated by Norman's periodic attacks of the mysterious "pinks": every two years, he destroys everything in their apartment because "the pinks" attack his body—his face, his hair, his skin—and he uses every object in sight to try "to scrape" them off (*LH*, 34). Eventually, after destroying everything he can find, he is taken away for a three-month sojourn in the hospital. Between these attacks, he is a gentle man, a hard worker, and a good husband.

Although little critical attention has been given to this mysterious illness, its symbolic meanings seem to be clearly suggested by the effects it
has. Ruth finally realizes "after their fourth summer" that because of the
predictable, cyclic occurrence of the pinks, she will never have "good
brocade chairs, linens, a set of company silverplate," all the sorts of
material things that the residents of Linden Hills accumulate and prize.
Given, however, that the novel dramatizes the destruction of the soul
through the pursuit of such things, Norman's periodic illness serves to
prevent Ruth from engaging in that pursuit. The "weight of accumulated things" that Ruth has wanted is conveniently rendered unachievable
because of Norman's regular attacks of the pinks. If Ruth is to stay with
Norman, her reasons will of necessity be based on the love they share,
not on the material possessions they acquire.

The episode in which Ruth decided to leave Norman reinforces these
symbolic meanings of his disease. Her decision to leave, some six years
before the present time of the narrative, came after she lost her job as a
result of a serious infection of her ovaries. Before she could call a cab to
come pick her up, Norman arrived home and "told her he felt the pinks
were coming, and he was lucky this time, he'd been able to leave the
plant before the guys saw them clinging to his flesh" (LH, 35). Out of
her own pain and despair, Ruth "lashed out at what was driving her from
everything she loved. She was through, did he hear her, through.
Because he was a maniac—a fucking, crazy maniac. And she hoped to
God that this time he would drive a piece of broken glass through his
heart. Then a sharp pain bent her over at the waist" (LH, 35).

What changes her mind about leaving him is his own act of love and
sacrifice. Although he is being attacked by "a wad of pink slime,"
although he smells "his flesh dissolving under the pinkish slime,"
although "the jellied mucus was now biting into his chest and gnawing
at his thighs and groin," he refuses to try to scrape the pink slime off
(LH, 36). He recognizes that if he begins scraping, he will not be able to
stop. And Ruth is in pain. So, "screaming . . . from his very being," he
goes to the medicine cabinet for aspirin to bring Ruth, and with utmost
difficulty manages to bring the medicine and a glass of water, which he
inadvertently tumbles onto her bed: "Norman rocked by the edge of the
bed with his arms clasped around his middle, trying to hold the pieces of
his body together" (LH, 36). Finally recognizing the enormous, self-sac-
rificing gesture of love he is making, Ruth herself begins screaming:
"'Norman!' It was the wail of a woman embracing a nightmare. 'Scrape.
Them. Off'" (LH, 36). Ruth rightly embraces this "nightmare," for it

constitutes a love that no material possessions could ever replace. She stays with Norman, accommodating their life and their home to the periodic onslaught of the pinks.

The illness from which Norman suffers is in fact the illness afflicting the residents of Linden Hills. They, however, unlike Norman, fail to recognize the necessity of fighting it, of destroying whatever possessions they have in order to scrape the pinks off; instead, "they're scraping and clawing to move closer to that weirdo, Nedeed" (*LH*, 39). Naylor reinforces the meanings of Norman's illness through her infrequent use of the color pink in the novel. For example, Xavier Donnell, whose ambitions make him fearful of loving a black woman, wears "pink silk ties" (*LH*, 55). And pink and white crepe paper decorate the limousine that takes Winston Alcott to his wedding—a ritual symbolic of his betrayal of his lover David and of his accession to the demands of being a "family man" in order to move farther down in Linden Hills (*LH*, 80). Lycentia Parker, who fought hard to prevent construction of a housing project to benefit poor blacks, is buried in a pink dress. Most important of all perhaps is the reference to the blond white woman whom Xavier Donnell takes to Winston Alcott's wedding: using a common slang expression, Lester refers to her as "that pink job" (*LH*, 84).[16]

The association of the color pink with white people, and of white people with obsessive materialism, provides us with an understanding of Norman Anderson's illness. Something within Norman causes him to develop the pinks just about the time he and Ruth have managed to accumulate a few furnishings for their home. The pinks thus express the materialism entering the Andersons' lives, which Norman rightly experiences as a threat to his very being and to his marriage, both of which he preserves by destroying the material possessions he and Ruth have acquired. The pinks thus constitute a powerful trope for the sickness underlying African Americans' embrace of white values. Although Ruth does not understand the reason for the pinks, she comes to accept them as a permanent, recurring feature of life with Norman; the love and concern he displays for her finally enable her to reject the desire to accumulate possessions.

The love ruling the Anderson home is glaringly absent from the houses in Linden Hills. And it is a love that extends beyond the Andersons themselves to embrace all who enter their home, a fact that Willie learns firsthand. In a moment of jealousy over not being able to have Ruth himself, Willie deliberately strikes out at Norman, hurtfully suggesting that Norman paint their home pink. Immediately Willie is covered with

shame and guilt, as well he should be. Instead of taking offense, however, Ruth, who interprets Willie's ensuing sadness as the result of not having money for Christmas presents, suggests that Lester and Willie do
odd jobs in Linden Hills. Willie is elated to be forgiven, thinking, "Ruth
wanted him to go into Linden Hills and he would go. He was just sorry
that she hadn't asked him to go to hell for her so he could really prove
himself" (*LH*, 41). His attempt to wound Norman—behavior uncharac-
teristic of the Willie we come to know in the novel—is perhaps comparable to Dante's straying from the right path; as a consequence, Willie,
like Dante, does indeed "go to hell . . . so he could really prove himself."

Significantly, it is at the end of the visit with Ruth and Norman that
the sound of Willa Nedeed's howling is first heard—and it is Ruth who
hears it, then opens the window so they all can hear (*LH*, 42). Later,
when Willie and Lester are walking to Lester's home on First Crescent
Drive, Willie hears the sound again, though Lester cannot. Only late
that evening, when Willie and Lester turn out the lights and open a window to smoke a joint, do they both hear the sound of "a long, thin wail
as it trailed along the floor" (*LH*, 60). Willa's howl, the emotion behind
which Lester and Willie are too young to identify, frightens them and
makes Willie want to assure himself that "the world he understood was
still intact" (*LH*, 61). Clearly, his journey into Linden Hills will be a journey toward the woman who voices that howl, and at journey's end "the
world he understood" will no longer be intact. From this point forward,
Willie's journey is counterpointed by Willa's, a fact of which Willie has
some awareness and Willa has none. Naylor's juxtaposing of their apparently unrelated narratives continues to develop the call-response pattern
(a defining feature of African American music) that she initially establishes here.[17]

"The Mirror in Your Soul"

In the remaining chapters of the novel ("December 20th," "December
21st," "December 22nd," "December 23rd," and "December 24th"),
Naylor presents a complex narrative that interweaves Willie and Lester's
journey down through Linden Hills, Willie's thoughts and dreams about
that journey, Willa's journey of self-discovery, Luther's thoughts and
plans, and the stories of the individual residents of Linden Hills whom
the two young men encounter. The narrative fragmentation underscores
the fact that Linden Hills is a neighborhood but not a community, as
Christian points out ("Geography," 354).

In some instances, the reader is given access to the residents' thoughts and feelings through Naylor's third-person limited narration, although the narrative is often decidedly satiric; such narrative is provided for Xavier Donnell and Maxwell Smyth, Reverend Michael T. Hollis, and Laurel Dumont. We are given access to the pre-wedding conversations of the gay lovers, Winston Alcott and David, whose relationship is being disrupted by Winston's marriage. In the cases of Chester Parker and Daniel Braithwaite, the reader's access is limited to what Lester and Willie see and hear. Naylor thus controls and varies her readers' engagement with her characters; some of the residents of Linden Hills enter into our sympathies, while others remain distanced from us and removed from our sympathies.

These characters have all, however, sold "that silver mirror God propped up in your soul" to which Grandma Tilson refers in the novel's epigraph. In the modern inferno Naylor depicts in *Linden Hills*, this "silver mirror" is not sold to the devil, but "just to the highest bidder." Grandma Tilson's grandson, Lester, explains to Willie what the old woman meant. Selling the mirror in your soul, he says, means "giving up that part of you that lets you know who you are. She would often say, 'Child, there's gonna come a time when you'll look at the world and not know what the blazes is going on. Somebody'll be calling you their father, their husband, their boss—whatever. And it can get confusing, trying to sort all that out, and you can lose yourself in other people's minds. You can forget what you really want and believe. So you keep that mirror and when it's crazy *outside*, you look inside and you'll always know exactly where you are and what you are. And you call that peace'" (*LH*, 59).

Mirrors have been given symbolic value throughout antiquity and in all cultures. The mirror seems to derive its significance from the notion of a magical connection between an object and its reflection (Biedermann, 222). Naylor uses Grandma Tilson's metaphor of the mirror as a unifying thematic device: the residents of Linden Hills have all sold their sense of who they are—that which gives them integrity—to achieve material success. References to mirrors recur frequently in *Linden Hills* as a way of suggesting loss of integrity. We have already seen that the Nedeed conception of Linden Hills as an "ebony jewel" eventually reflects not blackness but simply success. Other examples reinforce this point.

Luther Nedeed IV, for instance, experiences "the shining surface" of the residents' "careers, brass railings, and cars" as painful, because "it only reflected the bright nothing that was inside of them" (*LH*, 17). At the wake for Lycentia Parker, which, as Ward points out, is a grotesque parody of the Last Supper (75), Lester and Willie watch the gluttonous guests from the second floor of the Parker home, where "the brass chandelier reflected the changing faces bent over the tabletop as clearly as a mirror" (*LH*, 130). Not only the brass chandelier but the plates and tabletop reflect the souls as well as the faces of the guests up to Willie, who "hadn't really been listening so much as looking down into the faces that were looking up through the clear dinner plates from the glass-topped table. And something was haunting him about the rhythm of the knives and forks that cut into the slices of roast beef. . . . The plates never seemed empty of the brown and bloody meat. The utensils worked their way from center to edge, exposing an ear here, a chin there. Parts of a mouth, a set of almond-shaped eyes" (*LH*, 133). Naylor emphasizes the gluttony of the guests through the mirroring effects of the plates and table, by which the guests are reductively fragmented into their individual body parts.

One of the most elaborate examples of Naylor's use of the mirror occurs in the section describing Reverend Michael T. Hollis's preparations for preaching at Lycentia Parker's funeral. Significantly, when he looks at the mirror as he is dressing, he does not look at his face: "Turning toward the mirror over his dresser, he surveyed himself intently from the neck down and reached for his Aramis body lotion. *Put on the whole armour of God that ye may be able to stand against the wiles of the devil.* His bronze skin was almost as even and firm as the day he entered college, with just a few gray hairs mixed in with the auburn on his chest. His hands smoothed the lotion over the lean muscled arms and torso" (*LH*, 158). As this extended passage continues, Naylor juxtaposes the process of Hollis clothing himself with passages from Paul's Epistle to the Ephesians, in order, as John N. Moore demonstrates, "to underline his spiritual vacuity."[18] Dressed not in "the whole armour of God" but in the finest and most expensive designer clothes, Hollis is finally forced to look at his face when he brushes his hair: "He told himself the usual lie, it was a face that looked like death. Harsh as it was, it was better than the truth: it was a face that looked like it had no reason to live" (*LH*, 164).

Significantly, after Hollis's conversation on the way to the church with Willie, who fondly remembers the Christmas parties Reverend Hollis gave for the poor when Willie was young, Hollis takes another look in the mirror, but this time he begins with his face: "He forced himself to look at the mirror on the inside of his closet door, starting with his face and moving all the way down. Is this what that young man saw? A six foot, aging disappointment who had to put on a clown's outfit once a year to feel that he really counted at the pulpit" (*LH*, 177).

Just as looking in the mirror obliges Hollis to see the emptiness of his soul, so Laurel Dumont, in the depths of her despair, visits her grandmother and hopes that the rooms will be dark and that there will be "no mirrors" so that she can believe that she is still a vibrant little girl, not a hollow woman (*LH*, 230).

Willa Prescott Nedeed's Journey

Alice Walker has stated that her novel *The Third Life of Grange Copeland* (1970) "is ostensibly about a man and his son [but] it is the women and how they are treated that colors everything."[19] Very much the same thing is true of Naylor's novel, which seems to be primarily about men but at the heart of it is a woman—as Willie's lines, composed the night before he goes to Luther Nedeed's house, reveal: "There is a man in a house at the bottom of a hill. And his wife has no name" (*LH*, 277). Willie's journey in the novel, like Willa's, is in part a quest for her name—or more accurately, for her right to a name, to a presence. Locked with her son in the old basement morgue by her husband, whose denial of food and water results in the child's death, Willa is forced to make some sort of sense of her marriage.

Willa's process of discovery entails regaining exactly what the residents of Linden Hills have relinquished: history. From the outset, the Nedeed men have realized that those people "who had hopes of building on, not over, their past" were "fools who could do the most damage if he let them stay" (*LH*, 11). The Nedeeds have instead sought out people willing to "forget what it meant to be black" in order to stay in Linden Hills; "you step outside Linden Hills and you've stepped into history" (*LH*, 16). In the same way, not only do the Nedeed men use and then politely ignore their wives, but they virtually expunge them from memory; for instance, Luther's ignorance about his maternal ancestors makes him unable to acknowledge the white son his wife bears as his. He must even "pause a moment in order to remember his mother's first name, because everyone—including his father—had called her nothing but Mrs. Nedeed" (*LH*, 18). When Luther decides to "turn" Willa from a "whore" into a "wife" by locking her in the basement, "her absence was much more intrusive than her presence had ever been" (*LH*, 66), underscoring just how slight her presence had been.

Although Willa eventually determines, in another ironic twist, to reclaim her role as wife, her conception of that role is decidedly different from Luther's. Her process of self-discovery originates in her discovery of the sundry remnants of the lives of the previous Nedeed wives: Luwana Packerville Nedeed, Evelyn Creton Nedeed, and Priscilla McGuire Nedeed, the very women whose presence has been manifest in the white skin of Willa's now dead son. Buried away in the trunks of the old morgue where Willa has been imprisoned are the documents by which she can reclaim a lost history: Luwana's Bible, on the blank pages of which she has written; Evelyn's cookbooks, recipes, and shopping lists; and Priscilla's photograph albums. Significantly, these women, through their documents, are the only characters in the novel who are privileged to have their stories told in the first person. The historical records they left behind stand in contrast to, and represent a sharp correction of, the formal (male) history of Linden Hills that Daniel Braithwaite has dedicated his life to writing. Only someone who has had a similar experience, the experience of being Mrs. Luther Nedeed, could understand the history revealed by the documents these women left. And Willa's comprehension of the meaning these documents hold can be accomplished only through her willingness to recognize her own life in theirs.

Each previous wife's documents describe or reveal both the condition of being Mrs. Nedeed and the emotional and spiritual impact of that condition on her. Thus, Luwana Packerville Nedeed used her Bible to record her gradual discovery of her relationship to her husband. Between the Books of Jeremiah and Lamentations, for example, she wrote of learning that Luther owned her, that as a slave she had "only exchanged one master for another," and that even her son belonged to her husband (*LH*, 117). Before Leviticus, she recorded Luther's instructions about housekeeping and diet. On the page before the New Testament, she wrote that Luther, having read of a slave woman in the South who poisoned her master's soup, decided that Luwana would no longer be allowed to cook for either him or their son. By the time Luwana had been married for 15 years, she had become so isolated that in desperation she "split" herself, so that she could write letters to herself. The part of herself that recognized the brutality of Luther's treatment inscribed her outrage in letters to the part of herself who had been well schooled in the proper behavior of a woman and a Christian; this part of her self attempted to dismiss the other part's complaint because of its universality: "This senseless prattle about evil is unhealthy for your soul. There is nothing—do you hear me—nothing that is going on in your home that is not repeated in countless other homes around you" (*LH*, 123).

This rebuff led Luwana to discontinue the letters for a year, during which time she resorted instead to inscribing on her body (with a silver hat pin) the number of times she had been called upon to speak: "To the day it is exactly 665 times that I needed to open my mouth to speak— 332 times to answer their good morning's and 333 times to do the same in the evening. It would have been 720 times but this was not a leap year and they were both traveling for a little over a month—32 days in exact reckoning—viewing different schools for the boy. When they returned on the evening of the 33rd day, that gave me the additional good evening" (*LH*, 124). As she explained in this final letter to her other self, the 666th time would be when she said good-bye to her son, but as Willa realizes, "there was no record of what happened to Luwana Packerville on the morning she made the six hundred and sixty-sixth utterance" (*LH*, 125). The only record, in fact, is what Willa read first, on the front page of the Bible, the words Luwana wrote last: "There can be no God" (*LH*, 125).[20]

Reading Luwana's inscription of the nightmare of her life finally releases "the flood" in Willa herself, "for all those silent mornings" she has spent with Luther and for her realization that, "if her life depended on it, the man she had lived with for the last six years wouldn't be able to tell the executioner" anything of her life—not even the unimportant details known by her beautician, grocer, and mailman (*LH*, 125). Although Willa is not, like the nineteenth-century Luwana, literally a slave, she recognizes that she too had unsuccessfully sought a kind of freedom through her marriage to Luther. The freedom Willa wanted was freedom from being an unmarried woman of 30 and from the social stigmatism associated with that status. Taught to believe that something must be "wrong with you if no one's wanted you by now," Willa was "free to marry a man that she didn't love because there was no question of asking for love in return. It had been enough that he needed her" (*LH*, 117). Because she has wanted to be "needed," she has become Mrs. Nedeed without realizing that her marriage constitutes a legal bond only; in no other way do she and Luther share a marital relationship: "Then what had happened six years ago? Was she so busy being needed that it never dawned on her she wasn't being married?" (*LH*, 118). Like Winston Alcott, whose success can be ensured only by replacing his relationship with another man with marriage to a woman he does not love, Willa marries Luther to escape the social ostracism attached to single women. As Luther himself rightly understands, Willa "would never have looked at him if it weren't for the feel of the name *Mrs. Luther Nedeed* as she slipped on that white satin and brocade, the cold smooth rings" (*LH*, 69). Luwana's records of her status as the first Mrs. Nedeed enable Willa to begin to recognize the realities of her own marriage and to accept responsibility for her participation in the lovelessness of that marriage. Luther may have married her only to produce an heir, but she married him only to gain the social status marriage can provide.

Searching for more information about Luwana Packerville, Willa discovers a whole other set of records: the recipes and cookbooks left by Evelyn Creton Nedeed. At first, she thinks she has found a wad of papers written by Luwana, but she quickly discovers they are Evelyn's canning records; she throws "them down in disgust. She was wasting her time. Forty years were gone. These recipes were from another lifetime. Evelyn Creton probably never knew Luwana Packerville. As she roasted her meats and canned her apple butter year after year, she didn't know that a woman had gone insane because she was barred from the very kitchen that Evelyn Creton later filled with her damned cookbooks. . . . Evelyn Creton had obviously found joy in that kitchen as she filled her shelves with these recipes" (*LH*, 140). Blinded by her own male-inspired assumptions about what constitutes history, Willa is unable at first to discover any meaning in Evelyn's recipes, canning lists, and shopping notations. Then she begins to notice that the quantities of food Evelyn prepared were vastly disproportionate to the needs of the three people who would have eaten it; Willa rightly concludes that "the woman cooked as if she were possessed" (*LH*, 141).

Willa eventually discovers that not only was Evelyn an obsessive cook but her ingredients were rather unusual. Recognizing one of these—shameroot—Willa suddenly realizes that Evelyn used aphrodisiacs in her recipes in an effort to attract her husband back to her bed. Willa again identifies her own experiences with those to which Evelyn Creton Nedeed's recipes are a witness, for every Luther has followed the same pattern of ignoring his wife once she has borne him a son. Like Evelyn, Willa has thought the problem "must lie in something that she just wasn't doing right. If she hung in there long enough, he would change" (*LH*, 148). As Willa further realizes, however, the problem manifested itself "long before she walked into Tupelo Drive" (*LH*, 148): even on their honeymoon they had had separate bedrooms, but she had not wanted to acknowledge, until now, that Luther's behavior was "*unnatural*" (*LH*, 149). Like Evelyn, Willa has tried all the modern aphrodisiacs—perfumes and cosmetics—"confident that Lancome had told her to 'believe in magic,' so that change was definitely on the way" (*LH*, 149).

But Willa's efforts to change herself, based on her assumption that there must be something wrong with her, have been as unavailing as Evelyn's. Only by connecting herself and her experiences with those of the previous Mrs. Nedeeds is Willa able to consider that Luther's treatment of her is based on his hatred of women, not on some failing in her. In her isolation from women's history, she has repressed the knowledge she furtively sought by following Luther out one evening: she found him working in the mortuary, carefully preparing a female corpse, and as she watched, he "lift[ed] a fish head out of a plastic bag and turn[ed] it gently in his hands before inserting it in the spread body before him" (*LH*, 175). Of necessity, Willa believes, she had convinced herself that this vision "had to be a dream," one of the many "insane nightmares that threatened to break through on reality" (*LH*, 174), for if it were not, how could she continue to live with him?[21] Willa begins to accept her own complicity in concealing from herself the "unnaturalness" of Luther's morbid preference for dead women, a preference that is clarified and emphasized in the primary narrative immediately following Willa's memory. Here, at Lycentia Parker's funeral, we are made privy to Luther's recollections of the lessons about being a mortician that he learned from his father: "Female bodies were different. With the proper touch, you could work miracles. . . . Just the right pressure and resistant muscles in the face, neck, arms, and legs gave themselves up completely to your handling. . . . But it was a power not to be abused; it took gentleness and care to turn what was under your hands into a woman" (*LH*, 185). This is the loving care that Willa watched Luther lavish on the female corpse the night she followed him, but it brought a knowledge that she has, until now, denied and repressed.

As Willa continues to read the meanings behind Evelyn's shopping lists and recipes, she recognizes how horrifying Evelyn must have found her own "raw and personal needs," for Evelyn "had been such a proper woman" (*LH*, 187), and though she had lived in the twentieth century, it brought her no new words "to validate these types of desires in a Mrs. Evelyn Creton Nedeed" (*LH*, 188). Carefully reading and rereading Evelyn's notes, Willa finally discovers that Evelyn, like many contemporary women, embarked on a cycle of binging and purging as a way of defending herself against her husband's rejection. Eventually, she ingested more purgatives than nutrition, grew thinner and thinner, and finally poisoned herself with prussic acid in vanilla ice cream.

Willa's role in the reclamation of this lost history is crucial. The documents left behind are successively less explicit, their interpretation requiring fuller and deeper participation from her. Thus, while Luwana actually recorded her thoughts and feelings in the pages of her Bible, Evelyn's shopping lists and recipes are far more cryptic, and Priscilla, Willa discovers, left only photographs. Willa must bring Evelyn's life into clear focus by learning to read her notes with intelligence and empathy. Based on Evelyn's "careful and meticulous handwriting," for example, Willa constructs a "vision of quiet dignity and immaculate grooming" (*LH*, 187). By the time Willa reaches Evelyn's final notation, made on 24 December, she is able to construct in her mind the whole scene of the delivery boy's journey to the Nedeed house, with his package containing the ice cream and poison. Unlike Braithwaite, who prides himself on being an "objective" recorder of history, Willa can reclaim the very different historical documents left by the Nedeed women only by entering subjectively and imaginatively into their reality.

More than intelligence, however, is required for such a re-visioning of these women's lives: Willa must risk the pain that ensues from her identification with these women if she is to read their documents accurately. And it is precisely this pain that Willa rejects after she finishes her survey of Evelyn Creton Nedeed's recipes and lists. Telling herself that "she wasn't crazy like these other women; she had coped and they were crazy" (*LH*, 204), Willa desperately attempts to break her connection with the previous Mrs. Nedeeds. She wants to "strike out at what had happened, to destroy those beginnings" (*LH*, 204), and so she begins tearing the pages out of the books, shredding letters and diaries, determined to "read nothing else. Nothing. She just didn't care anymore about their sad, twisted lives" (*LH*, 205). But in the process of destroying the documents left by women whose lives were indeed so much like her own, Willa is suddenly stopped "by a pair of soft, compassionate eyes" (*LH*, 205) in a photograph from an album she is trying to tear up: "almost against her will, she turned the page" (*LH*, 206). The final Mrs. Nedeed before Willa, Priscilla, used her photograph albums to record the nothingness that her marriage made of her. Willa realizes that the annual family portraits of Priscilla McGuire Nedeed, her husband, and their son were not, as the captions suggest, "recording the growth of a child; the only thing growing in these pictures was her absence" (*LH*, 209).

Willa's process of self-discovery is not a continuous narrative, as my summary may suggest, but is actually presented in the novel piecemeal, interspersed with the stories of the Linden Hills residents and of Willie and Lester's journey. One of the ways Naylor connects Willa's discoveries to the activities in Linden Hills is through a variation on the metaphor of the mirror. Juxtaposed to Willa's inadvertent discovery of Priscilla McGuire Nedeed's photograph albums is the story of Laurel Dumont, the only woman besides the Nedeed wives whose story is fully told in the novel. Immediately preceding Laurel's story, and immediately after Willa's discovery of Priscilla's photograph albums, the narrative recounts one of the nightmares Willie has as a result of his journey. He dreams of going into a store to buy a camera, where he is told by the saleswoman, "You can't use my camera because you have no face" (*LH*, 211). This dream (like the others Willie has) connects Willie to Willa and Priscilla as well as to Laurel Dumont.

Already "a crippled bird" sunk in a "void" from which even her grandmother cannot rescue her (*LH*, 242), Laurel has resigned herself to the fact that "despite all of her efforts and on top of everything else—it was going to be a White Christmas" (*LH*, 239). The image takes on ominous overtones. The final blow to her tenuous existence is delivered by Luther Nedeed, who informs her that she must vacate her residence on Tupelo Drive because it is leased to her husband, who has filed for divorce. Since her husband does not plan to live in the house, it reverts to Luther's Tupelo Realty Corporation; Laurel herself, being merely a wife, has no claim to it. Following this news, Laurel dives into her empty swimming pool. When Willie finds her body, face down, "without thinking, he turned her over" (*LH*, 249). Naylor thus establishes, through almost dizzying mirror reflections, links between the now faceless Laurel, Willie's symbolic dream, and Priscilla McGuire Nedeed's growing absence from the family photographs. Willie also discovers that Nedeed not only precipitated but watched this suicide and did nothing to prevent it, a fact that further locates the oppression of all these women in male control and power.

Immediately after Willie turns Laurel's body over, the narrative shifts back to Willa: "Her face was gone. The photo album trembled in her cold hands as she realized there was no mistaking what she now saw: Priscilla McGuire ended at the neck—and without her features, she was only a flattened outline pressed beneath cellophane" (*LH*, 249). As Willa realizes, Priscilla deliberately demonstrated her absence and insignificance by removing her face from photograph after photograph with "cleaning fluid. Bleach. A drop of hot grease" (*LH*, 249). On the last photograph, "scrawled across the empty hole in lilac-colored ink was the word *me*" (*LH*, 249).

Willa's unearthing of her history—the history of those women
whose lives have been defined, as hers is, by their marriages to the
Nedeed men—culminates in this realization of female erasure, female
absence. Importantly, that erasure is expressed through the source of
identity, the face. It is thus significant that Willie's discovery of Laurel
Dumont's now-faceless body and Willa's concomitant discovery of
Priscilla McGuire Nedeed's faceless photographs are followed in the
narrative by Willie's visit with Daniel Braithwaite, the resident who
lives nearest Luther Nedeed on Tupelo Drive; Braithwaite's house, in
fact, allows him to see "what Luther Nedeed has seen" (*LH*, 258). Like
Nedeed, Braithwaite has watched the self-destruction of the residents
of Linden Hills and done nothing but record it, from Nedeed's perspective. As insidious as Nedeed in many respects, Braithwaite, according
to Naylor in an interview, is "a dried-up voyeur, the worst kind of academic you can have" (Bonetti). In his conversation with Willie and
Lester, Braithwaite brings together the key metaphors of the mirror
and the camera. He remembers, he says, Grandma Tilson's words
about "that silver mirror God propped up in your soul," but he avows
that "she was wrong about that" (*LH*, 260). While she thought the residents of Linden Hills "were selling little bits of themselves" in order to
live in Linden Hills, he is confident that "they've sold nothing; pieces of
themselves were *taken* away" by the white world they had to work in so
that they could live in Linden Hills (*LH*, 260). Braithwaite thus
removes responsibility and power—*will*—from the residents of Linden
Hills. He acknowledges that Linden Hills is "as broken and disjoint-
ed—as faceless—as Laurel Dumont's body," but as a historian, he
assigns neither praise nor blame to Nedeed (*LH*, 261). Braithwaite
espouses a theory that history must be written with complete neutrali-
ty; moral judgments cannot be made even about slavery, since the
question of its wrongness depends "upon who you were talking to and
when—black or white" (*LH*, 261). To Braithwaite, "done properly, history becomes a written photograph" (*LH*, 261). What he forgets, or
conveniently ignores, as Goddu points out, "is the perspective of the
viewer; subjectivity enters this experiment as soon as the scientist picks
up the camera and looks through its lens" (218). Willie, however,
whose unconscious identification with Laurel and Willa gives him a different sensibility, recognizes that "Braithwaite would have gotten a
much different picture all these years" by looking down the hill at
Luther Nedeed's own house rather than up the hill at the rest of Linden
Hills (*LH*, 266).

Naylor suggests not only that Braithwaite ignores parts of history—the parts Willa has been discovering in the course of the novel—but that he is as misogynistic as Nedeed. Braithwaite's house is surrounded by dead willow trees: "My trees are dead," he explains to Willie and Lester. "I killed them when I realized that they might interfere with my work. I didn't cut them down because I was so terribly fond of them. Willows are the most elegant of all trees. And, you see, in the fall and winter I can still imagine that they will bud again in the spring, and my sense of loss isn't so great" (*LH*, 264). Just as Luther Nedeed prefers dead women to living ones, so Braithwaite prefers his willows dead—and the echo of Willie's and Willa's names in the trees he kills has unmistakable implications.

Despite the efforts of her husband and his historian to expunge her from life and from history, Willa Prescott Nedeed will not be erased; she will claim for herself an identity and a will. The narrative section in which she takes the first step toward self-determination immediately follows the Braithwaite section. Naylor uses the mirror image once more as a way of insisting on the mirror's accurate reflection of self. Willa, after "staring at the gaping hole that was once Priscilla McGuire," begins "to touch her own face" (*LH*, 267) in an effort to assure herself of her own substantiality. But the image her fingers attempt to create dissolves quickly, until she "closed her eyes and used both hands, trying to form a mirror between her fingers, the darkness, and memory. What formed in her mind might be it, but she needed to be sure" (*LH*, 267). To guarantee that her mental image is indeed accurate, Willa takes the small pot in which she has collected water when Luther opens the pipes, and she manages to use the water as a mirror. Though she cannot make out the "shape of her eyes," she is able to see enough of her other facial features to be certain: "No doubt remained—she was there" (*LH*, 268).[22]

Seeing her face in the mirror she has created allows Willa finally to cry, but this time it is not for the ghosts she has resurrected in this basement morgue: "The tears belonged to none of them. The gentle drops were falling from her bowed head into the pot because this was the first time she had known peace" (*LH*, 268). The benefits Willa receives from seeing her reflection in the water recall the benefits Grandma Tilson attributed to "the mirror in your soul": "So you keep that mirror and when it's crazy *outside*, you look inside and you'll always know exactly where you are and what you are. And you call that peace" (*LH*, 59). Having found such peace, Willa takes nourishment from herself: she drinks "the cold, rusty water" in the pot that now has her own tears intermingled with it. The end of the section underscores the nature of the process Willa has undergone: "Now . . . she had actually seen and accepted reality, and reality brought such a healing calm. For whatever it was worth, she could rebuild" (*LH*, 268).

The Apocalyptic Ending

The concluding chapter of *Linden Hills* ("December 24th"), in which an increasingly feminized Willie finally meets Willa just seconds before the Nedeed house goes up in flames, has been variously interpreted. Larry Andrews, for example, argues that Willa "has achieved selfhood and poetic justice" (16), a reading consistent with Bouvier's claim that "Willa reasserts her identity and image" (150). Margaret Homans acknowledges that "Willa literally brings down the house of patriarchy," but she sees this as "an act of negation . . . since it destroys her even as she destroys it."[23] Concurring with Homans, Goddu sharply criticizes the novel's ending, claiming that because she "unknowingly catches her bridal veil on an ember and starts a fire, Willa neither acts willfully in burning down the house of patriarchy nor lives to tell her story. Willa's self-determination, like all female history in this book, ends in self-destruction and disappearance" (225). Goddu further argues that Willa "might escape the basement but she never leaves the house" because Naylor "can finally only imagine a black male poet" (226).

Goddu raises serious questions about Naylor's ultimate analysis of the system of gender oppression her novel presents. The novel, however, presents not simply gender oppression but class oppression as well, and its depiction of middle-class black suburbia as a kind of hell seems to preclude the possibility of a solution beyond destruction. Although Naylor suggests that any alternatives to the soul-destroying values of patriarchy must reside in a feminized, working-class, male artist—Willie K. Mason—the novel's ending does not suggest any real solutions or the building of any kind of new society, despite the rich suggestiveness of Willie's name.[24] Naylor's long affiliation with the Jehovah's Witnesses seems to be expressed in the novel's conclusion, for indeed the evil of the world she creates in the novel is so absolute that it can only be destroyed; it can never be redeemed.

The novel nevertheless creates in the reader a sense of triumph and victory in Willa's final moments of life and a sense of hope, however small, in Willie and Lester's final conversation. For Willa claims responsibility for her marriage, and in doing so "she gained strength and a sense of power" (*LH*, 280). She undergoes a rebirth described as "an unconscious journey in toward the power of will" (*LH*, 288), and with that will she reasserts her right to her life: "Yes, she was Willa Nedeed and so this was the end of the month. It wasn't the most perfect exis- tence to begin with, or even the best time of the year. But it was all she had" (*LH*, 289).[25] And so, with determination and resolve, she cleans the basement and begins her way up the 12 steps to the kitchen door. After she cleans the kitchen and heads toward the den, she and Willie simul- taneously see her image in the mirror: "There in the mirror next to the open kitchen door was a woman, her hair tangled and matted, her sunken cheeks streaked with dirt. Her breasts and stomach were hidden behind a small body wrapped in sheer white lace. The wrinkled dress was caked under the arms with dried perspiration, the sagging panty- hose torn at the knees and spotted with urine" (*LH*, 298–99). No longer an attractive woman, certainly far removed from the perfection Luther has sought in his female corpses, Willa at this moment is nevertheless a formidable human being. That she is prepared to match her will to Luther's is evident when she speaks: " 'Luther,'—her voice was cracked and husky as Willie's hand went toward his tightening throat—'your son is dead'" (*LH*, 299). Her insistence on confronting Luther with the corpse of the child whose paternity he has tried to deny is the first step toward her defeat of him.

Her victory is ensured when Luther, thinking that "Willa was leaving the house" and reading "the determination in her eyes as madness" (*LH*, 299–300), tries to block her passage. When he attempts to push her into a chair that is positioned in the direction of the kitchen, and there- fore of the basement door, "every cell in her body strained against his hands" (*LH*, 300). Finally, when he reaches for the child, she locks them in an embrace "and the three were welded together"; when they stagger against the fireplace, the bridal veil in which she has wrapped the child "brushed an ember, the material curling and shrinking as orange sparks raced up its fine weave. There was no place in her universe to make sense out of the words, 'My God, we're on fire.' No meaning to his struggle except that it was pushing her back into the kitchen. And now no path to the clutter by the door except through the lighted tree. They went hurling against it, the top smashed a side window, and the December wind howled in" (*LH*, 300).

As a close reading of this passage reveals, Willa may not intentionally have set fire to the bridal veil, but contrary to Goddu's reading, the con- flagration of the whole house occurs because Willa refuses to be moved back in the direction of the basement. Although Luther's intention at this point may not be to imprison Willa again, any hint of such an outcome is what she will, and does, resist, even if the alternative is death. And this resistance unquestionably constitutes a victory of sorts.

Similarly, the conversation between Willie and Lester on the novel's closing page suggests some sense of hope. Willie, having unsuccessfully tried to find help from some of the residents on Tupelo Drive, is stunned by the realization that they have allowed Luther's house to burn; to him, such a gesture suggests complete inhumanity. After the excitement is over, as Willie and Lester walk toward Patterson Road, their conversation suggests their different interpretations of the event:

> There was silence until Willie told the biting wind, "They let it burn, Shit."
> "Yeah."
> Silence again. Suddenly Lester stopped walking. "But they let it burn, White."
> "Yeah."
> "No, don't you see—they let it burn."
> A deep sob caught in Willie's throat as he told the wind once again, "They let it burn, Shit."
> "Yeah."
> *They let it burn.*
> Each with his own thoughts, they approached the chain fence, illuminated by a full moon just slipping toward the point over the horizon that signalled midnight. Hand anchored to hand, one helped the other to scale the open links. Then, they walked out of Tupelo Drive into the last days of the year. (*LH*, 304)

While Willie seems to indict the residents of Linden Hills for their apparent indifference to the fire in the Nedeed house, Lester uses the same words to suggest that their indifference constitutes a recognition of the need for the destructive fire. And since the fire destroys only the Nedeed house, the heart and center of Linden Hills, there is perhaps some hope that the neighborhood, free of its Satanic ruler, may change.

Naylor perhaps intends to suggest some sense of hopefulness through the novel's final image of the joined hands of the two young friends. Certainly the ending does not project the kind of affirmation we find at the conclusion of *The Women of Brewster Place*—there are no female ebony phoenixes here. Nonetheless, the human bond between Lester and Willie and their departure from Linden Hills do temper, ever so slightly, the otherwise horrifying vision of the novel.

Chapter Four

Belief and the Recovery of Peace: *Mama Day*

Reflecting on her identification as a writer, Gloria Naylor commented in an interview that "after *Linden Hills* I became a writer in my own mind" (Bonetti). Her third novel, published in 1988, not only validated that claim but can legitimately be regarded as a tour de force. Although Naylor regards her first four novels as a quartet of sorts, *Mama Day* marks a signal change in the novelist's development; it is the work of a fully confident and accomplished storyteller and a brilliant prose stylist.

Mama Day departs significantly from *The Women of Brewster Place* and *Linden Hills* in numerous ways; in the writing itself, the most important of these is point of view. Naylor has said that, because she had successfully mastered third-person point of view, she decided to use it once again in *Mama Day* but her story simply would not allow itself to be written from that point of view. Suffering from a serious writer's block, Naylor came upon William Faulkner's *As I Lay Dying* (1930), which she had never read, and his strategy in that novel of using a shifting, first-person narration provided the key she needed (*Dreaming*, 174–75). One of the most remarkable accomplishments of *Mama Day* is its alternating narrators: George, Cocoa, the first-person plural voice of the Willow Springs community, and the consciousness of Mama Day. This formal device both reflects and reinforces the novel's thematic concerns with reality and truth. As Cocoa asks near the end of the novel, "What really happened to us, George? You see, that's what I mean—there are just too many sides to the whole story."[1]

Mama Day also differs from the first two novels in its smaller cast of major characters and in its alternation between an urban, northern setting and a rural, southern one. Naylor's creation of the all-black, matriarchal island of Willow Springs, which cannot be found on any map, marks her departure from the modes of naturalism and realism used in the first two novels. Naylor deliberately wrote *Mama Day* in a mode closely resembling magical realism because, she has said, she "needed to find a way structurally to have you walk a thin line between that which is real and that which is not real" (Bonetti).[2] Through various uses of "magic," Naylor found ways to explore her central concern with "the intangible" and with "belief" (Bonetti). In an interview, she contrasted her need to "exorcise demons" in her first two novels with her desire in *Mama Day* "to rest and write about what I believed. And I believe in the power of love and the power of magic—sometimes I think that they are one and the same. *Mama* is about the fact that the real basic magic is the unfolding of the human potential and that if we reach inside ourselves we can create miracles" (Carabi, 42). This celebration of love and magic makes *Mama Day* Naylor's most positive and life-affirming fiction to date.

The Novel's Structure

The Magical Willow Springs

The alternating voices that narrate *Mama Day* and the alternating settings of New York and Willow Springs together provide the keys to our understanding of the novel's most important themes and meanings. Although the principal story line concerns the two lovers George and Cocoa, the fact that their respective narrative sections constitute a conversation without words conducted in Willow Springs some 14 years after George's death suggests that a good deal more is at stake in the novel than the love between these two individual characters. The larger concerns of the novel are made manifest by the emphatic placement of the narrative section belonging to the communal voice of Willow Springs: it opens the novel. The communal voice also introduces us to George and Cocoa and instructs us about how we, as readers, can hear and understand their conversation "without a single living soul really saying a word" (*MD*, 10). The island setting of Willow Springs—its history, its values, and most important, its matriarchal structure—embodies the novel's most important meanings.

Located in the Sea Islands, Willow Springs is not only an all-black but a black-owned island off the coasts of Georgia and South Carolina; the island "ain't in no state" (*MD*, 4) and is connected to the mainland by a "wood and pitch" bridge that must be rebuilt every 69 years (*MD*, 5). Geographically, socially, and culturally, Willow Springs is closer than any other location in the United States to Africa, and it thus allows Naylor both to celebrate the African heritage of black Americans and to contrast the values of that heritage with those of the white world, dismissively referred to as "the mainland." Lindsey Tucker has recently pointed out that historically "the dominant ethnic groups that have comprised what is known as the Gullah language and culture of the Sea Island region have been from the Kongo-Angolan area" of Africa, and that these groups "were considered the most rebellious."[3] Naylor draws on such historical realities to create in Willow Springs an island whose inhabitants are guided by the spirit of one rebellious slave, Sapphira, whose name has been lost to them but who has acquired the status of a goddess. Her spirit and her power live on in her descendant Miranda "Mama" Day.

Although Naylor has said that she did not consciously use Shakespeare's *The Tempest* in the novel, there are evident parallels between the two works. Through her creation of the magical Willow Springs and its "ruler" Mama Day, Naylor joins other twentieth-century African American writers for whom Shakespeare's play has assumed special significance. Elaine Showalter discusses the importance of *The Tempest* to American literature, pointing out that it has long been believed to have "some historical relation to the establishment of the Jamestown colony in 1607."[4] Whereas most African American writers have been interested in the Caliban-Prospero relationship, Naylor not only has no Caliban figure but usurps the white male power of Prospero through her creation of Mama Day. Although Mama Day carries the same name as Prospero's innocent and subservient daughter, Miranda, the fact that she is more commonly referred to as "Mama" suggests "the possibility of escape from Shakespearean entrapment in the subservient daughter role" (Erickson, 243). Naylor's text thus stands as a revision of both Shakespeare's play and of African American male appropriations of Caliban as a figure of black male power. As Valerie Traub argues, "In Naylor's work, the tension between feminist and anticolonialist politics inhering in Caliban's figure is elided in favor of a matriarchal, female-centered, post-colonial scene."[5]

The Prefatory Documents

The novel's prefatory documents emphasize the centrality of Willow Springs and of Sapphira Wade, its "great, great, grand, Mother" (*MD*, 218), whom Traub sees as a newly configured Sycorax, Caliban's mother in Shakespeare's play (155).[6] There are three prefatory documents: a "map" of Willow Springs; a family tree of the Day family; and a bill of sale for Sapphira. Given that George is frustrated by his inability to locate Willow Springs on any of his maps and therefore does not know how to pack for his first trip to the island, the playful map in the front of the novel functions on one level certainly as a kind of joke.

The second prefatory document, the Day family tree, stands in sharp contrast to the obliteration of such history in the lives of most African Americans. It also celebrates the extraordinary woman who was able to defy that kind of obliteration and who therefore could never be explained or controlled by the bill of sale that follows the family tree. It serves, Traub observes, "as an antidote to and exorcism of that initial sale of human flesh as property" (155). The asterisked note explaining the last name of the Day family explicitly imbues Sapphira with the divine power of creation: " 'God rested on the seventh day and so would she.' Hence, the family's last name." The family tree visually links the living members of the Day family—Miranda, Abigail, and Cocoa—to the dead members, a connection that is central in the novel itself, for both Miranda and Cocoa hear the voices of their ancestors when they visit their graves, and Miranda actually communes with her ancestors. This connection between the living and the dead, which is also represented in the silent conversation between the dead George and the living Cocoa that comprises much of the narrative, points to the African belief system operating in Willow Springs.[7]

The final prefatory document, the bill of sale for Sapphira Wade, similarly accumulates multiple meanings. Significantly, only the reader of the novel has access to the bill of sale in its entirety. Late in the novel, Miranda finds this document hidden at "the other place" (the Day family's home), but most of its text has been obliterated, including all but the first two letters of Sapphira's name. The incompleteness of the bill of sale within the novel proper reflects the islanders' subversive refusal to be defined by the "discourses of the oppressor" (Tucker, 183). Although Miranda, "in her dreams . . . finally meets Sapphira" (*MD*, 280), she "can't tell you her name, 'cause it was never opened to" her (*MD*, 308). The discovery of the name, Miranda says, will be left to Cocoa (*MD*, 308). Even though "the *name* Sapphira Wade is never breathed out of a single mouth in Willow Springs" (*MD*, 4), all of the inhabitants know of and believe in her power, which receives verbal and symbolic expression for them in the date they were deeded the land, 1823. Only the rational, logical George, who requires empirical evidence for everything, remains skeptical about Sapphira's existence: "I wondered if that woman had lived at all. Places like this island were ripe for myths, but if she had really existed, there must be some record. Maybe in Bascombe Wade's papers: deeds of sale for his slaves" (*MD*, 218). George's desire for white-inscribed documentary evidence of Sapphira's existence is a measure of his denial of his own history as a black American. It reflects as well his willingness to accept white definitions of black identity. Were George to be given the same access to the complete deed of sale that is accorded the reader, he would be incapable of reading it correctly.

The bill of sale documenting Bascombe Wade's purchase of Sapphira withholds from the purchaser "all warranty against the vices and maladies prescribed by law," for Sapphira has proven unwilling to become or be defined as a slave; she is "inflicted with sullenness and entertains a bilious nature, having resisted under reasonable chastisement the performance of field or domestic labour." The language used in this document that George finds so necessary for "proof" is chilling. The "reasonable chastisement" directed at Sapphira, for example, typifies a white discourse that cloaks even while it assumes the violence and brutality by which Africans were made into slaves. Still worse than the euphemistic "chastisement" is the inhumanity that could so confidently see degrees of "reasonableness" in such violence and brutality. An archetypal subverter of such oppression, Sapphira demonstrated a self-possession that no amount of brutality could shake and that no bill of sale could revoke, as Bascombe Wade eventually learned. The white assessment of Sapphira's healing and creative powers as indicative of her "delving in witchcraft" will also, in the opening pages of the novel, be contrasted with the black assessment of those same powers. She was, the narrative voice of Willow Springs assures us, "a true conjure woman" who used her powers to heal and to free her people (*MD*, 3).

The Prologue

The opening narrative section of the novel instructs readers in how to read the prefatory documents—and the story about to unfold—correctly. To achieve a correct understanding, readers are cautioned, we must open ourselves to a distinctively African, distinctively female, angle of vision; in a sense, we must develop, like Mama Day, an "ability to read signs . . . which is . . . an important component of African belief systems" (Tucker, 181). We must shed the assumptions that guided those who sold Sapphira and countless other Africans into slavery and that continue to control the "mainland" United States today, assumptions that the novel identifies as both white and male. To comprehend what

Sapphira and Willow Springs are "about," we must be receptive to the
world of Willow Springs itself: "It's about a slave woman who brought a
whole new meaning to both them words, soon as you cross over here
from beyond the bridge" (MD, 3). To understand the world of Willow
Springs, in other words, we must shed our mainland understandings of
"woman" and of "slave"; this world will open for us new meanings of
femaleness and of blackness. The legends about Sapphira differ, even
those about the color of her skin: "satin black, biscuit cream, red as
Georgia clay: depending upon which of us takes a mind to her" (MD, 3).
Like any goddess, Sapphira takes her attributes in part from those who
recognize and honor her. But also like any goddess, Sapphira has
achieved her status as a result of her irrefutable actions. Although the
details of what transpired between her and her putative owner Bascombe
Wade are wildly contradictory, the end results are not: "Mixing it all
together and keeping everything that done shifted down through the
holes of time, you end up with the death of Bascombe Wade (there's his
tombstone right out by Chevy's Pass), the deeds to our land (all marked
back to the very year), and seven sons (ain't Miss Abigail and Mama Day
the granddaughters of that seventh boy?)" (MD, 3).

The communal narrative voice of the opening section represents one
of Naylor's most significant accomplishments in the novel. We as readers are drawn into the world of Willow Springs by this seductive voice
that invites us to shed our assumptions about time, about reality, about
truth. We are told, for example, that Sapphira's name has been lost to
her descendants in Willow Spring, and yet we are given this information
through the narrative's *use* of that same name. Such an apparent contra-
diction, however, matters as little as the contradictory descriptions of
Sapphira herself. Levy rightly points to Naylor's success through this
narrative voice in bringing the reader "immediately and intuitively into
Willow Springs as she insists on direct personal communication" (214).

The introductory narrative urges us to understand Willow Springs by
learning to listen to its voices as well as to the voices within ourselves.
We are cautioned, through the example of Reema's boy—"the one with
the pear-shaped head" (MD, 7)—not to bring the perspective of the
world "beyond the bridge." Although born in Willow Springs, Reema's
boy was corrupted by the college education he received on the mainland.[8] Using the methodologies for discovering "truth" that he learned
on the mainland, Reema's boy wrote a book about Willow Springs that
purported to explain the mystery of "18 & 23" as "really 81 & 32, which
just so happened to be the lines of longitude and latitude marking off

where Willow Springs sits on the map" (*MD*, 8). Registering disgust and contempt, the narrative voice tells us that the book explains the inversion of the numbers as "'asserting our cultural identity'" and "'inverting hostile social and political parameters'" (*MD*, 8). Levy points out that the book "allows Naylor to juxtapose Mama Day's maternal language with the impersonal associational language represented by the writing of Reema's boy—he is known in Willow Springs by his mother's name— and the language and calculation of the mainland investors who seek to persuade Miranda to sell the island for 'development'" (215). After Mama Day sets the price at $1 million an acre, "you shoulda seen them coattails flapping back across The Sound with all their lies about 'community uplift' and 'better jobs.' 'Cause it weren't about no them now and us later—was them now and us never" (*MD*, 6). The narrator right- ly recognizes that Reema's boy has been transformed by such people beyond the bridge: "The people who ran the type of schools that could turn our children into raving lunatics—and then put his picture on the back of the book so we couldn't even deny it was him—didn't mean us a speck of good" (*MD*, 8). Instead of interviewing the Willow Springs islanders with a tape recorder, he should have just asked. Then he would have been sent to Abigail and, eventually, to Mama Day: "Everything he needed to know coulda been heard from that yellow house to that silver trailer to that graveyard" (*MD*, 10).

Reema's boy, however, "didn't really want to know what 18 & 23 meant, or he woulda asked" (*MD*, 8). "But on second thought," the nar- rator concludes, "someone who didn't know how to ask wouldn't know how to listen. And he coulda listened to them the way you been listen- ing to us right now" (*MD*, 10). We as readers are invited to reject the "objective" scientific methods of understanding represented here by Reema's boy—and later in the story, by George—and to identify our- selves instead with the ways of understanding used by the inhabitants of Willow Springs. We must learn to "really listen," not only by paying attention to the small details and nuances of meaning but also by sub- mitting ourselves willingly to the rituals and traditions that constitute the world of Willow Springs. Only by entering Willow Springs' ways of knowing can we as readers understand the narratives of Cocoa and George that follow. The communal voice offers us the opportunity to identify ourselves with Willow Springs; it assures us, Suzanne Juhasz comments, that if we "can read outside of the dominant culture—which is white and male, the world beyond the bridge—[we] too can partici- pate in the heritage of Sapphira Wade."[9]

Narrative Strategy

The prefatory documents and the opening narrative section set the stage
for the love story of Cocoa and George. The remainder of the novel is
pieced together like the quilt Mama Day and Abigail make for Cocoa
and George's marriage. The first-person narratives of Cocoa and George
alternate with each other and with narratives using either the Willow
Springs voice of the opening section or a third-person point of view limited to the consciousness of Mama Day. Although there are no chapter
divisions, the novel is divided into two parts, and the narrative sections
belonging to George and Cocoa are separated from those belonging to
Willow Springs or Mama Day by three symbols, squares within diamonds. The first-person narratives of George and Cocoa are separated
simply by blank space. These patterns are altered only once, in the climactic scenes toward the end of the novel (*MD*, 283–93). If we use the
diamond symbols as markers in the text, then part 1 contains a total of
13 sections: 6 belong to Willow Springs and/or Mama Day, and 7 are
the alternating narratives by Cocoa and George. The sections belonging
to Willow Springs/Mama Day are roughly equal in length to the sections
given to Cocoa and George. The length of individual sections changes in
part 2, where there are 45 sections plus an epilogue: 23 belong to
Willow Springs/Mama Day, and 22 belong to Cocoa and George. In
terms of length, however, George receives more pages than Cocoa in
part 2, a disparity explainable by the fact that Cocoa is ill. Since parts 1
and 2 are of comparable length (143 and 151 pages, respectively), and
yet part 2 has more than three times as many identifiable sections, it is
evident that the pace of the novel speeds up in part 2, where each narrative piece is considerably shorter than those in part 1.

This brief description makes clear the appropriateness of the quilt as
a metaphor for the novel's structure. In *Linden Hills* we see Naylor's
interest in presenting simultaneous action from varying points of view;
in *Mama Day* she literally constructs the narrative by stitching together
numerous individual "pieces" to create a unified whole. These pieces,
moreover, range over past, present, and future time, thus disrupting our
normal expectations of linear, chronological narrative movement.
Margot Anne Kelley, in a recent article on African American women
writers' use of "quilting aesthetics" in their fiction, suggests that such
disruptions are similar to the quilt maker's practice of piecing together
old and new fabrics; the novelist's use of such a strategy thus obliges us
to "rethink" our "understanding of space and time—both their signifi-

cance and their relation to what we name 'real.'" Kelley also points to the characteristic habit of "Afro-traditional" quilters of relying "on strong, highly contrasting colors," a habit yielding "a concurrent awareness of parts and wholes."[10] This technique finds its counterpart in the novel's juxtaposition of George, Cocoa, and Mama Day.

Naylor herself provides in her description of the quilt that Mama Day and Abigail make for Cocoa and George an apt analogy for how the novel is pieced together. Sitting up alone after Abigail has gone to bed, Mama Day finds herself "almost knee deep in bags of colored rags, sorted together by shades" (*MD*, 137). The double-wedding-ring quilt the sisters are making for the young couple will be of brilliant hues: "The overlapping circles start out as golds on the edge and melt into oranges, reds, blues, greens, and then back to golds for the middle of the quilt" (*MD*, 137). Organized by colors rather than materials, the pieces of cloth Mama Day selects tell the history of the Day family: "A bit of her daddy's Sunday shirt is matched with Abigail's lace slip, the collar from Hope's graduation dress, the palm of Grace's baptismal gloves. Trunks and boxes from the other place gave up enough for twenty quilts: corduroy from her uncles, broadcloth from her great-uncles. Her needle fastens the satin trim of Peace's receiving blanket to Cocoa's baby jumper to a pocket from her own gardening apron" (*MD*, 137). Even though Mama Day knows that her sister will "have a fit," she nonetheless includes a snippet from their mother's "gingham shirtwaist" (*MD*, 137). Eventually, the bags of scraps produce "a piece of faded homespun" that Mama Day realizes had to have belonged to Sapphira herself (*MD*, 137). When the pieces have been stitched together properly, Mama Day reflects, "you can't tell where one ring ends and the other begins. It's like they ain't been sewn at all, they grew up out of nowhere" (*MD*, 138). Houston and Charlotte Baker, in their study of the cultural meanings of African American quilting, suggest that the "patchwork quilt, laboriously and affectionately crafted from bits of worn overalls, shredded uniforms, tattered petticoats, and outgrown dresses stands as a signal instance of a patterned wholeness in the African diaspora."[11] Certainly the quilt made by Abigail and Mama Day functions similarly to create from fragments a whole and "patterned" history of the Day family.

Like the quilt, Naylor's narrative is stitched together of many fragments, but the stitching is so perfect that they do not appear to have "been sewn at all." The absence of chapter titles or even divisions and the unobtrusiveness of the few markers provided in the text contribute to the "patterned wholeness" of the novel. The unity achieved through the stitching together of narrative fragments tends also to make us less aware of the individual fragments and more aware of larger patterns and themes.

Major Narrative Lines

The principal narrative line or pattern in the novel is the story of the "star-crossed" (*MD*, 129) lovers, George and Cocoa, the reference linking them, of course, to Romeo and Juliet. The conversation without words that we "overhear" between Cocoa and her dead husband represents their attempt to understand how and why their love and marriage came to such a tragic conclusion. Part 1 of the novel traces their courtship and first four years of marriage in New York City, during which time Cocoa makes her yearly visits to Willow Springs alone because George always saves his vacation time to attend the professional football playoff games. At the end of part 1, Cocoa has graduated from college, and she and George are ready to try to have children. This decision is apparently what prompts George to announce that this August he will go to Willow Springs with Cocoa. Part 2 charts George's first and last visit to Willow Springs, which results in his death.

Three other narrative lines develop in the novel. The first, introduced early, concerns Bernice Duvall's experiences with motherhood. Frustrated by her inability to become pregnant, Bernice eventually goes with Mama Day to the other place, where the miracle of conception is made possible through the ritual Mama Day performs. This narrative line follows the birth of Bernice's son, her attempts to shelter him from the forces of life, and eventually his death during the big storm that hits the island.

The second minor narrative line concerns the marital adventures of Ruby, who uses her knowledge of voodoo to destroy those who spark her possessive jealousy: she has killed her first husband for being unfaithful, worked roots on Junior Lee to seduce him away from Frances (*MD*, 112), and driven Frances crazy. In part 2, we watch as her jealousy of Cocoa, to whom Junior Lee seems attracted, prompts her to place Cocoa in the life-threatening illness from which George tries to save her. Ruby's house is destroyed and she herself is seriously injured by lightning during the big storm—lightning induced by Mama Day.

The final narrative line concerns Mama Day's attempts to recover and understand the history of the Day family, particularly the relationship between Sapphira and Bascombe Wade and that between her own mother and father, Ophelia and John-Paul. Mama Day's journey to this knowledge (which requires a sojourn at the other place) is necessitated by Cocoa's marriage to George—by the introduction, in other words, of a new person, an outsider, into the Day family. Although her journey to this knowledge becomes most pressing after Ruby harms Cocoa, the journey itself begins as early as the quilt-making scene, when she first begins to intuit that George may be the third in a line of men whose hearts are broken by women they love but try to possess. Mama Day's journey to knowledge is completed when the spirit of Sapphira comes to her in her dreams and instructs her about the measures she must take to save Cocoa.

Reduced to their most elemental features, the various narrative lines in the novel reveal an important common pattern: the destructive power of possessive love. George loses his life because he will not accept Cocoa's ties to Willow Springs but insists instead on acknowledging only her ties to him. Bernice Duvall loses her son because she believes he belongs to her, rather than to life and to himself. Ruby mistakenly believes that she can own her husbands. And as Mama Day discovers, her own father helped destroy the peace in his family by refusing to let his wife go, just as his wife lost her sanity because she could not accept the loss of her child. Reaching back to the beginnings of the Day family, and trying to understand the male roles in its history, Mama Day further realizes the enormity of the loss experienced by both John-Paul and Bascombe Wade, the latter of whom never accepted the fact that he could not own the woman who refused to be a slave. Both men "*believed*—in the power of themselves, in what they were feeling" (*MD*, 285), but their refusal to recognize anything beyond their love led them to try to possess, thereby losing, the women they loved.

Although the narrative lines concerning Bernice and Ruby indicate that possessive love is not the exclusive province of men (as does the insanity of Mama Day's mother), the greater weight given in the novel to George and the connections drawn between him and John-Paul and Bascombe Wade suggest that men have a greater proclivity for it. The novel insinuates a connection between the oppressive institution of slavery and the oppressive institution of marriage. The insidious idea underlying slavery, that human beings can be owned, finds parallel if less horrifying expression in male attempts to possess and control the women they love. Bascombe Wade's relationship with Sapphira, the mother and creator of Willow Springs, represents the nexus of gender and racial oppression in the novel. Although the novel acknowledges the love these men feel, it also insists that such love threatens the very life of the women toward whom it is directed. George succeeds in reversing the pattern established by Bascombe Wade and John-Paul by dying himself so that Cocoa may live; however we interpret George's death, the fact remains that he dies while Cocoa lives. And Cocoa's living is crucial to the continuing recovery of the history of Sapphira, "the great, great, grand, Mother," as Mama Day reflects toward the end of the novel.

Setting, Character, and Conflict

Naylor's Rewriting of *Tar Baby*

Toward the end of Toni Morrison's *Tar Baby* (1981), a novel that also revises Shakespeare's *The Tempest*, the narrator comments on the conflict between the lovers, Jadine and Son. The passage has special relevance to Naylor's novel, which can in many ways be seen as a rewriting of Morrison's text, and it therefore bears quoting in full:

> This rescue was not going well. She thought she was rescuing him from the night women who wanted him for themselves, wanted him feeling superior in a cradle, deferring to him; wanted her to settle for wifely competence when she could be almighty, to settle for fertility rather than originality, nurturing instead of building. He thought he was rescuing her from Valerian, meaning *them*, the aliens, the people who in a mere three hundred years had killed a world millions of years old. From Micronesia to Liverpool, from Kentucky to Dresden, they killed everything they touched including their own coastlines, their own hills and forests. And even when some of them built something nice and human, they grew vicious protecting it from their own predatory children, let alone an outsider. Each was pulling the other away from the maw of hell—its very ridge top. Each knew the world as it was meant or ought to be. One had a past, the other a future and each one bore the culture to save the race in his hands. Mama-spoiled black man, will you mature with me? Culture-bearing black woman, whose culture are you bearing?[12]

In Morrison's novel, Son and Jadine are representative characters whose conflict about appropriate gender roles is grounded in part in their differing notions about the past and about racial identity. Son identifies Jadine's desire to transcend the role of nurturer as an abnegation of her blackness, a result of her contamination by the white world and white values. Jadine, on the other hand, sees Son's attachment to the past, to black traditions, to a form of cultural nationalism, as an attachment to primitivism that would confine her to a subservient and unfulfilling role. Although Jadine is initially disturbed by her alienation from her "true and ancient properties," as is evident by her response to the African woman in yellow who makes her feel inauthentic (*Tar Baby*, 48), she eventually decides that she must shape her own identity as a black woman.

The passage from *Tar Baby* quoted above, though written in a language neither Cocoa nor George would use, aptly describes at least the larger terms of the conflict between them, with, of course, one major difference: whereas Morrison uses her male character to represent an Afrocentric worldview and traditions, Naylor not only makes her female character that representative but celebrates the maternal, Afrocentric island of Willow Springs and finds little to recommend in the white world associated both with postindustrial civilization and with men. As a self-proclaimed feminist and black cultural nationalist, Naylor suggests through her depiction of Willow Springs a striking alternative to Morrison's all-black town of Eloe, which offers Son a form of male camaraderie but otherwise lacks the idealized, nurturing, life-renewing traditions and ways of living represented by Willow Springs. Unlike Eloe, where women nurture but are subordinate, Willow Springs is guided by the spirit of Sapphira as that spirit lives on in Mama Day (and will one day reside in Cocoa). *Mama Day* insists on the restorative powers for black Americans of the past and of female and African-derived traditions and ways of looking at the world. The parallels between the two novels suggest that Naylor is deliberately revising Morrison's inscription of the contemporary black woman. While the epigraph to Morrison's novel (with its reference to "contentions" in the "house of Chloe") and the novel itself suggest that the contemporary black woman is no longer willing to define herself in terms of past traditions, Naylor's novel celebrates those same traditions as restorative and healing. In Naylor's vision, it is the black male who has been corrupted by the value system of the white world, not the black female.[13]

George, or the "Man Who Looked Just Like Love"

Shortly after the publication of *Mama Day*, Naylor stated that its "major male character became a conflation of all the good I had known in men."[14] Somewhat more recently, she commented that she actually had to work at not being kind to George in the course of writing the novel: "I had to go back and do some rewriting because I was too kind to George, knowing he was going to die. I said, No, you cannot feel sorry for this man at this point. He doesn't know he's going to die. He's being a bastard. Go ahead and let him be nasty in this fight" (*Dreaming*, 173–74). At the end of the novel, after George has been dead for many years, Cocoa tells her son that "he was named after a man who looked just like love" (*MD*, 310).

Taken together, these comments point to the challenge Naylor faced in placing a hero who is basically a good character in a story that requires his death even though that death saves the life of Cocoa and restores peace to the Day family. Just as we may understand Hurston's reasons for killing Tea Cake Woods at the end of *Their Eyes Were Watching God* (a novel Naylor repeatedly read while she was working on the storm scene in *Mama Day*) but nevertheless regret his death, so George's death in *Mama Day* leaves the reader as well as Cocoa with an enormous sense of loss and regret.[15] There remains for many readers a sense that George's outbreak of violence against Mama Day's chickens—associated throughout with female powers and values—in the moments before his death is inconsistent with the character we have come to know and care about. Juhasz explains the inconsistency by arguing that George is a "maternal hero" (193), by which she means "that fantasy women create so that true love is possible for us as grown women living in a patriarchal culture"; his violence demonstrates the fact that he is a fantasy—but a fantasy we do not enjoy seeing die (202).

Having acknowledged that the character Naylor creates in George does not necessarily *deserve* to die but lives in a novel that requires his death, we might most usefully focus on those qualities that make George a representative of the white, male, mainland, postindustrial world. Although the text does not support Susan Meisenhelder's claim that the orphanage George grew up in is "run by whites," there is no question that, as she argues, he has assimilated into white culture.[16] His alienation from the past and from black cultural traditions is both explained and underscored by the fact that he is not only an orphan but illegitimate. He is keenly aware of and sensitive about both his lack of parents and his belief that his mother was a prostitute.[17] His sensitivity about being illegitimate emerges most clearly in his identification with Shakespeare's Edmund, the bastard son in *King Lear*. George's alienation from African American history is ironically reflected in his identification with Edmund, for the systematic rape of slave women by white men made illegitimacy inevitable for thousands of African American sons and daughters.[18] And it is in part because he is ignorant of his own cultural history that he so easily believes that his mother was a prostitute and focuses his anger more frequently on her than on his father. The only time we see him physically strike Cocoa is when she, suspicious and anxious about his failure ever to talk about his past, asks him, "Why do you hate being called a son-of-a-bitch? A pompous, snide, uptight son-of-a-bitch?" (*MD*, 128). After slapping "the living daylights out of" Cocoa, George explains: "My mother was a whore. And that's why I don't like being called the son of a bitch" (*MD*, 130).

George has been well schooled in the American principles of self-reliance and self-sufficiency, and he is completely committed to the idea instilled by Mrs. Jackson, who ran the orphanage, that "only the present has potential, *sir*" (*MD*, 23). Nonetheless, a sense of inner emptiness and loss haunts George, binding him to the past in ways he cannot acknowledge. Levy rightly remarks that "George's lonely life represents the emotional costs to men as well as women of the mother's loss" (218). George is accustomed, however, to denying the pain of his loss and to projecting the anger he feels about it onto the person who reminds him of it, as we see when he strikes Cocoa. His comments to Cocoa in this scene further reveal the anger he feels toward both his mother and the fact that she abandoned him by drowning herself in the river:

> "I feel that men will often grow up thinking of women in the same way they think of their mothers. You see, when I was growing up, there was no reason for me to neglect her on the days that would have been important: her birthday, anniversary, or the second Sunday in May. I didn't forget to call now and then to ask her how she was doing. I didn't find her demands annoying, or her worries unnecessary. I was the kind of son who didn't refuse to share my friends, my interests, or my hopes for the future with her. Yeah, that's pretty close to the kind of son I was." (*MD*, 131)

George's congenital heart defect works symbolically on a number of different levels, but certainly one of the most important seems to be related to his abandonment by his mother. His sarcasm notwithstanding, the words he speaks in the passage above take on importance when we consider George's ways of relating to women. He has been, he says, accustomed to "pampering" women because "a little time and silly little attentions, and they would purr. Add some sort of personal gift to that now and then, and they'd walk on water for you" (*MD*, 123). He has also discovered that women's insecurities "could be nipped in the bud by ran-

domly checking off days in your appointment calendar to have your secretary mail out a Hallmark card. That way you're 'thinking' about her—
whether you are or not" (*MD*, 123). George's cavalier attitude here seems
only apparent, not real, when we consider the actions he enumerated that
he did not need to do for his mother because she was not there. Cocoa
intuitively recognizes George's desire to please when she calls to thank
him for the roses with which he begins their courtship: "The caring in
your silence stunned me. And it wasn't directed toward me personally. It
was like when a kid labors over a package—the wrapping paper is poorly
glued, the ribbon is half tied—and all of his attention is directed toward
that space between the hands that offer and the hands poised to receive.
It's the gesture that holds the heart of a child" (*MD*, 59).[19]

In his one outbreak about his mother, George provides the key to
much of his behavior with Cocoa, especially perhaps to the tenacity with
which he holds on to his football games. Precisely because he is so keenly aware of all the things he could not do for his mother because she was
not there, George seems to have determined to protect himself from any
future emotional vulnerability as compulsively as he monitors his heart.
Thus, during his courtship with Cocoa he reflects that "the more you
were beginning to mean to me, the more close-mouthed I became, waiting" (*MD*, 125).

Any reminder of his mother, however, brings out a hostility in George
that he directs against Cocoa. During the second part of the novel,
Cocoa suggests that such incidents were frequent enough for her to have
seen the connection, although the occasion of her relating this information is actually the first time George has varied from the pattern. The
incident arose, Cocoa says, when she and George were visiting Bernice
and Ambush, and Bernice, knowing nothing of George's background,
made a casual reference to George's mother. Afterwards Cocoa dreads
going back to Abigail's because she knows that George is "going to talk
about my breasts," for "Bernice had guaranteed that" with her innocent
comment (*MD*, 201). Cocoa reflects:

> "I regretted having never told her the whole truth. But how could I reach
> cab drivers, storekeepers, news commentators, a dozen waitresses—all of
> whom were likely, through casual remarks, to freeze the muscles in the
> lower part of your jaw? Put that cold light in your eyes. When I finally
> made the connection, it was in the realm just beneath thought. To have
> thought it would be too ugly and so how to speak about the unthink-
> able? We held this secret between us that we couldn't even reveal to our-

selves. I knew after one of those incidents there was nothing to do but wait. You had to hurt me—just a little." (*MD*, 201–2)

George's disruption of this pattern of behavior on this particular occasion may be attributed to the beneficial influence of Willow Springs, for instead of talking in a hurtful way about Cocoa's breasts, he says to her, "I'd like you to nurse our children," nestles his head on her breasts, and cries (*MD*, 202). Such direct expression of the loss he feels is not, however, characteristic of George; instead, he usually lashes out at Cocoa and zeroes in on "an insecurity I had shared at some previous time" (*MD*, 202). From the information we are given here, those insecurities seem most typically to be about her body, a fact that assumes great importance later in the novel when George and Cocoa have their "worst fight ever" (*MD*, 230, 232).

George's loss of his mother, the fact that he is an orphan, is not unusual: we know that Cocoa also lost both her parents and that Mama Day and Abigail were abandoned by their mother long before her actual death. What makes George's case different is that he lacks the extended family, the surrogate parents, and the connection to a past history that would sustain him. Growing up in an institution instead of in a home has taught George to detach himself from his emotional life. It has further trained him to believe only in himself, because "I had what I could see: my head and my two hands" (*MD*, 27). He has no past and does not believe in the future. He also believes in no spiritual power greater than himself: "I never knocked on wood. No rabbit's foot, no crucifixes—not even a lottery ticket" (*MD*, 27). George's sequence here collapses gambling, superstition, and religion into equally meaningless forms of belief.

When Cocoa enters his life, she turns all of his assumptions about reality upside down, as he acknowledges when he says, "Until you walked into my office that afternoon, I would have never called myself a superstitious man. Far from it. To believe in fate or predestination means you have to believe there's a future, and I grew up without one" (*MD*, 22). Because "fate" and "superstition" are not a part of the reality in which George believes, however, he not only ignores the conviction he suddenly has that Cocoa "would be in my future" but transforms that conviction into something he can more easily accommodate: "The feeling is so strong, it almost physically stops me: *I will see that neck again.* Not her, not the woman but the skin that's tinted from amber to cream as it stretches over the lean bone underneath. That is the feeling I actually had, while the feeling I quickly exchanged it with was: *I've seen this woman before*" (*MD*, 27).

Because George cannot entertain the possibility of a reality different from and larger than the empirical world to which he anchors himself, he quickly reduces Cocoa to a "type" whom he "knew . . . well" (*MD*, 32). He insists to himself that "all I wanted was for you to be yourself," and then he quickly sketches for himself what that self would be. Given Cocoa's southern accent, he attempts, in their first meeting, to get her to speak his name, because "there isn't a southerner alive who could bring that name in under two syllables" (*MD*, 33). He even claims that "it was a fact that when you said my name, you became yourself" (*MD*, 33), a statement that reveals George's desire for Cocoa's identity to be a function of her relation to him. When she speaks his name, he is able "to imagine you as you must have been: softer, slower—open. It conjured up images of jasmine-scented nights, warm biscuits and honey being brought to me on flowered china plates as you sat at my feet and rubbed your cheek against my knee" (*MD*, 33). Significantly, George's visit to Willow Springs does nothing to make him adjust this original fantasy inspired by Cocoa's accent. As Cocoa observes when they visit the other place, where she hears whispering voices from the past, George "wanted to sit in the rocking chair and play southern gentleman with me on your lap" (*MD*, 224).

This same desire is manifest in George's adamant refusal to use the pet name "Cocoa." Early in their relationship, George reflects that "it was a pity you didn't like being called Ophelia. It was a lyrical name, pleasant to say because my tongue had to caress the roof of my mouth to get it out" (*MD*, 63). But George's persistence in calling Cocoa by her birth name—when no one else does—suggests that the pleasantness associated with saying the name goes beyond the physical sensation he describes. Cocoa's birth name of Ophelia is another of the many references to Shakespeare in the novel. The only time anyone other than George uses Cocoa's birth name comes during Cocoa's first visit to Willow Springs after she and George have married. As a married woman who will eventually give birth to a new generation of Days, Cocoa is ready, Mama Day believes, to learn about the family's tragic history. The signal that the lesson is about to be given is Mama Day's use of Cocoa's birth name:

> "Ophelia, I got me some gardening to do at the other place. Pick up them baskets."

"What did you call me?"

"Don't stand there with your mouth gaping open. I called you by your name."

"But in my entire life, you've never used that name."

"That ain't true. The day you dropped into my hands, I first used it. Your mama said, 'Call her Ophelia.' And that's what we did. Called you that for a whole week to fix it into place. So you've heard me say it before, but you don't remember."

"You mean, I can't remember."

"I mean just what I said. Pick up them baskets." (*MD*, 150)

As Mama Day's final words emphasize, our access to the past beyond our memory is a question of will and desire, not of ability. And in fact, when she dutifully follows Mama Day to the other place, Cocoa is able to hear the voice of her own dead mother and learns that her mother, Grace, named her Ophelia "out of vengeance. Let this be another one, I told God, who could break a man's heart" (*MD*, 151). Named out of vengeance for her grandmother, whose excessive grief for the loss of her baby led to her suicide by drowning, Cocoa has been as loath as her family to use her given name. Mama Day's use of it on this particular occasion signals her recognition that the family's history cannot be forgotten or denied.

George, however, who knows nothing of the Day family history but is an avowed lover of Shakespeare, perhaps prefers to call Cocoa by her birth name as a way of fixing her in the female identity suggested by Ophelia's role in *Hamlet*. As Traub has argued, Cocoa's family's habit of calling her by her pet name represents their desire to distance her from Shakespeare's Ophelia, "whose suicidal madness is born of the indifference of *Hamlet*'s plot to represent women as autonomously desiring subjects" (155). George's preference for Cocoa's given name reflects an attitude consistent with his early image of her lounging at his feet and with his later conclusion, after reading several books about women, that women's bodies keep them "on an emotional roller coaster," making them "normal only about seventy-two hours out of each month" (*MD*, 141). The appeal of Cocoa's birth name to George may also indicate his identification of Cocoa with his mother, also a suicide by drowning.

Although George's loss of his mother has made his life lonely and painful, it also has resulted, as we have seen, in his distancing and detachment from women as well as in a residual hostility toward them. George betrays both a fear of and a repulsion toward women, especially their sexuality and the creative powers it represents. Naylor emphasizes this fear and repulsion through her placement of George's attempts to educate himself about women. This narrative section directly follows the most mysterious episode in the novel, Mama Day's fertilization of Bernice at the other place: "She ain't flesh, she's a center between thighs spreading wide to take in . . . the touch of feathers. Space to space. Ancient fingers keeping each in line. The uncountable, the unthinkable, is one opening. Pulsing and alive—wet—the egg moves from one space to the other. A rhythm older than woman draws it in and holds it tight" (*MD*, 140).

The reverence for and celebration of female powers of creation that we find in this section serve to highlight George's fear of and repulsion toward those same powers, expressed in the section immediately following. George feels that he is "living with a stranger" because Cocoa is "the first female I had lived with" (*MD*, 141). In previous relationships, George gave little attention to female creative powers as they are made manifest in the menstrual cycle; a woman's period "had brought relief if a mild inconvenience when it coincided with a night I wanted to sleep with a girlfriend" (*MD*, 141). Identifying himself with all men, George acknowledges that "it made you squeamish if you dwelt on the fact that you were constantly surrounded by dripping blood, and a little frightened, too" (*MD*, 141). After reading books written by both men and women, George concludes that he is "never going to find a totally objective guide to what was going on inside of females," and he shares his surprise that Cocoa becomes furious when he attributes her moods to being "premenstrual" (*MD*, 142).

Seeking "objective," rational ways of understanding Cocoa, whom he sees as typically female, George is discomfited by her ability to "manage disruptions and absorb ambivalences" (*MD*, 142). He himself has organized his life to the minutest detail. He views relationships—and indeed, all of life—in the same way that he views engineering problems in his job. For example, when he and Cocoa marry and she moves to his house, she recalls that he used a slide rule and graph paper to measure her "closets and figure out how much of our clothing we would have to store in the basement in order to share the space in your bedroom. And then when your damn diagrams didn't work out, you carried on as if I was purposely trying to sabotage our marriage because I hung up an extra linen blazer" (*MD*, 145).

Naylor uses such details about George with great comedic effect, but while his determination to impose his objective, rational, problem-solving approach on the small details of everyday life is only humorous, it becomes much more serious and significant when he attempts to impose it on the world of Willow Springs. After he has decided to visit Willow Springs, he immediately becomes frustrated because he cannot locate it on any map. As he reflects, "I really did want to go, but I wanted to know exactly *where* I was going" (*MD*, 174). Once they arrive, he recognizes that he "was entering another world. Where even the word *paradise* failed once I crossed over The Sound" (*MD*, 175).[20]

George's recognition that he has entered another world does not, however, influence either his behavior or his ways of determining truth and reality, even when the world of Willow Springs carries him back to his childhood habit of chanting himself to sleep: "I did something I hadn't done since a child. When you can't sleep and you know there is no one to call down those long corridors, you close your eyes and tell yourself over and over again, I can't find it because it's waiting in my dreams. A slow, rhythmic chant. The 'it' could be anything, and I would drift off to sleep, more often than not, to dream of a new bicycle, a good test score—my mother's constantly changing face. But that night I dreamed of you" (*MD*, 183). Again, Cocoa becomes identified in George's mind with his mother, but even though he dreams a cautionary dream, he will fail in his waking hours to follow the dream's lesson. For in the dream he hears Cocoa calling him, and he tries unsuccessfully to swim across the Sound to reach her. Mama Day shouts that he should stand up and walk, but he, characteristically, pushes "out of the water to scream in her face, You're a crazy old woman! And I found myself standing up in the middle of The Sound" (*MD*, 184). Later in the novel, of course, George will again regard Mama Day's advice as craziness and will miss the miracle they could have achieved together if he had only been able to believe.

Even before that climactic test of his character, George reveals himself as unable or unwilling to read the reality of Willow Springs correctly. The episode in which he attends Dr. Buzzard's poker game symbolically foreshadows his behavior in the chicken house. Baffled by the willingness of the men to play with Dr. Buzzard even though they consistently lose their money because he cheats, George decides to figure out exactly how Dr. Buzzard is cheating. George's "solid grounding in analyzing problems of conflict by abstracting common strategic features from an infinite number of conflict situations" (*MD*, 210) allows him "to discover exactly how he was cheating in each hand and then weigh those variables out to my advantage. In a way, the other guys were doing that, but to minimize their losses. I was going to win" (*MD*, 211). When he succeeds, however, he is surprised to see that "a pall began to fall over our circle," and that when one of the other players wins the pot, he takes the money "as if the coins were dirty" (*MD*, 212).

George's assertion of power at the poker game betrays his need to control and to dominate. Ignoring the fact that the poker game is a long-standing tradition among the men on the island, George, like a colonialist, arrogantly disrupts the conventions of this world in which he is only a visitor, confident that the inhabitants will applaud the changes he brings and surprised when they do not. George neither recognizes the welcome he is given as a privilege nor respects it, believing instead that the game is merely a contest, which he is determined to win by revealing Dr. Buzzard as an old cheater. Thus, the hospitality Dr. Buzzard offers George in the form of "a special canvas chair" and "a six-pack"—because George is unaccustomed to sitting on the ground and to drinking moonshine—is much less important to George than his host's cheating (*MD*, 208, 209). Equally clear is the fact that something other than the chance to win brings the men to their regular poker games. Their desire for fellowship and their commitment to believing in Dr. Buzzard's power over the cards are far more important to them than the money they lose.

The conclusion of the poker game reinforces these ideas. First, Dr. Buzzard's refusal to acknowledge that George is outwitting him is evident in the way he keeps his eyes on George's—and with mesmerizing effect. For in the final hand, when only the two of them are playing, George's rational knowledge that he holds the winning cards is insufficient to inspire any emotional certainty: "I kept doubting what was in front of my face," he says, "my mind knew it, but somehow the message hadn't reached my gut" (*MD*, 213). Dr. Buzzard's self-possession convinces George, against what his mind rationally knows, that Dr. Buzzard has won, even after the hole card has been thrown out: "I sat there staring at it stupidly, wondering why he didn't pick up the pot. Then with a wave of disappointment I realized he had not won" (*MD*, 213).

George's disappointment at winning suggests that he has some insight into the human realities that have been at stake in the card game. In the emotionally overpowering clapping and singing that follow the card game, George tries "to dissolve the lump" in his throat by drinking. The "dirge" that Dr. Buzzard and the other men begin to clap with their hands is followed by their singing "Take My Hand, Precious Lord" while Dr. Buzzard stands on his hands. George does not join the singing because he does not understand the rhythm, but he at least recognizes that he "had only to listen to the pulse of . . . [his] blood" and he would have understood the rhythm. He reflects that he wanted the singing "to go on forever" (*MD*, 214).

Had George only been able to absorb the lesson he learned at the poker party, he would perhaps have been able to save both himself and Cocoa by joining his hand with Mama Day's. But the meaning of the old spiritual "Take My Hand, Precious Lord" is lost on George. Instead of building a bridge between himself and Cocoa, he focuses on building the bridge to the mainland that has been blown down by the storm. Dr. Buzzard attempts to tell George that a "grown man" would recognize that "really believing in himself means that he ain't gotta be afraid to admit there's some things he just can't do alone" (*MD*, 292). George, however, is determined to save Cocoa alone, even if he has to swim to the mainland and even if he is unsuccessful in the attempt: "Yes, I would begin to swim. And at that point in time, finishing would not be the issue" (*MD*, 283). Unable to recognize that his own attitudes may be prolonging Cocoa's illness, George believes her salvation depends upon her removal from Willow Springs, which has been transformed in his mind from the "paradise" it initially seemed to be to a "godforsaken place" (*MD*, 266).

That what is required is for George "to clasp hands with women," as Meisenhelder points out ("Picture," 412), is evident from the mission Mama Day gives him: armed with Bascombe Wade's old ledger and John-Paul's walking stick (both of which connect him to earlier men who tried to possess women), he must go to the chicken house (associated throughout the novel with female power and creativity), search in the back of the nest of the "old red hen that's setting her last batch of eggs," and bring back to Mama Day whatever he finds (*MD*, 295). He must, in other words, find a way to embrace the female world and its powers. George, however, who had whitewashed the chicken house earlier for Mama Day even though he "was a little afraid of live chickens" (*MD*, 221), is enraged when he finds nothing behind the nest "except for my gouged and bleeding hands" (*MD*, 300). He maniacally uses John-Paul's walking stick to destroy the chickens, the eggs, and the chicken house itself, for he decides that "these were *my* hands, and there was no way I was going to let you [Cocoa] go" (*MD*, 301).

Significantly, when George, whose heart is giving way, staggers from Mama Day's chicken house across the road to Abigail's home, where Cocoa is dying, "the road felt like water," and he found it "impossible to cross over, make it up those porch steps, and into our room. I did it. But I was too cramped to even unbend my body on the bed beside you"

(*MD*, 301). George's masculine inability to enter the different reality he finds in Willow Springs prevents him from being able to live once he has "crossed over" the road that feels "like water." Only as a ghost can George and the secular, scientific, white, male world he represents become a part of Naylor's spiritual, natural, female island. Perhaps Juhasz is correct in suggesting that he is better dead because, "as a ghost, George has shed the encumbrances of his masculinity. Now he can stay on in Willow Springs and in the life of its next mother" (203).

Baby Girl/Cocoa/Ophelia

George's death leads to Cocoa's abandonment of New York and her return to the South—not to Willow Springs but to nearby Charleston. By the time we overhear the conversation she is having with the ghost of George, she has remarried; her second husband is "a decent guy" but, in the words of Mama Day, "a good second-best" (*MD*, 309). Most important, she has had children, thus ensuring that the Day family will continue, that the Day property will stay in the Day family, and that Mama Day, who at the novel's close is 104 years old, can die.[21] The events in Willow Springs that resulted in George's death have lifted the curse on the Day family; as Mama Day reflects in the novel's final paragraph, Cocoa's face is "a face that's been given the meaning of peace" (*MD*, 312). Cocoa is ready, moreover, to receive the mantle of Mama Day and to "go in search of answers" about the history of the Day family, Sapphira, and Willow Springs. Since George met Cocoa in New York, where she had been living for seven years, their relationship clearly enables these changes in Cocoa to evolve. Naylor's placement of Cocoa in Charleston rather than in Willow Springs suggests that she intends her character to be understood as a realistic representative of contemporary black women. At novel's end, Cocoa lives in the white, male, postindustrial world of the mainland, but she lives close enough to Willow Springs to visit it easily and to stay connected to its values.

Ironically, the peace that neither Cocoa nor her two mothers, Abigail and Mama Day, possess at the novel's beginning is tied to their inability to come to terms with the past.[22] Although Mama Day visits and grows herbs at the other place, the locus of so much pain, Abigail has not gone there for more than 20 years—until Cocoa's life-threatening illness compels her.

Cocoa's illness symbolically figures the self-doubts and insecurities that threaten her own attainment of peace. Her habit of using food metaphors to describe other people—a habit that infuriates George—is perhaps only a projection of the anxieties she feels about her appearance. Self-confident in her abilities at work, supported and nurtured by her home in Willow Springs, Cocoa has nevertheless been uncertain all her life about the way she looks. Her image of herself is evident from her first visit to George's office, to which she has come for a job interview. Another applicant, who is the color of "licorice," looks at Cocoa, and Cocoa reflects: "The way she looked me up and down—dismissing my washed-out complexion and wilted linen suit—made me want to push out my pathetic chest, but that meant bringing in my nonexistent hips. Forget it, I thought, you're standing here with no tits, no ass, and no color" (*MD*, 20). We have seen that George is aware of Cocoa's insecurities about her breasts and uses his knowledge to hurt her, but even more significant is her insecurity about her color. Her pet name of Cocoa was in fact given to her when she was five years old to " 'put color on her somewhere,' Miranda had said" (*MD*, 40), though Abigail and Miranda continue to call her Baby Girl to themselves.

Willow Springs, where white values have not intruded, is "an island of soft brown girls, or burnished ebony girls with their flashing teeth against that deep satin skin" (*MD*, 232), and among such girls Cocoa has been at a serious disadvantage. As she reflects, "If some brave soul wanted to take me out, [the other girls] would tell him that I had some rare disease that was catching" (*MD*, 233). When she was a child, she ran "home crying and almost taking off her middle finger with a butcher knife, fearing she really had the white blood she was teased about at school—she wanted red blood like everyone else" (*MD*, 47).

Although Cocoa is insecure about her skin color when she is in Willow Springs, in New York her lightness is an advantage, just as she is "Ophelia" as George's wife in New York, not "Cocoa." Only when George finally comes to Willow Springs do these two areas of her identity collide in ways she finds overwhelming. Initially, she worries about how George will respond to seeing her in Willow Springs, because "regardless of how well you thought you knew me, it was only one part of me. The rest of me—the whole of me—was here. And I wondered how you would take the transformation, beginning with something as basic as my name. Outside of my family, no one else in Willow Springs knew who in the hell Ophelia was" (*MD*, 176). Cocoa tries to assure herself that "Ophelia and Cocoa could both live in that house with you. And we'd leave Willow Springs none the worse for wear" (*MD*, 177).

Cocoa and George's "worst fight ever" arises in part out of Cocoa's desire to make herself darker—and therefore, according to Willow

Springs standards, more attractive—for the party Abigail and Mama Day throw. Cocoa is anxious about the party because "it had taken four years to get you down here, and each time I came home alone it was the same doubt in their eyes. Who could possibly want the leper?" (*MD*, 232). Not only has Cocoa married, but she has married a successful man, so she "couldn't wait for them to meet you so I could gloat. And I was going to be dressed for the part. Eat your hearts out—and he's all mine" (*MD*, 233). When George refuses to give her the reassurance she wants—and in all likelihood he could not give it to her even if he so desired—an explosion between them is inevitable.

That Cocoa's insecurities about her physical appearance and her identity, both connected in turn to her relationship to George, are what Ruby exploits is evident. As Mama Day reflects, "Baby Girl done tied up her mind and her flesh with George, and above all, Ruby knew it" (*MD*, 265). Naylor once again uses the mirror as a motif, as she does in *Linden Hills*: Cocoa's illness is most evident to her when she looks at her reflection. Significantly, Cocoa initially believes that the crack in her bedroom mirror "had just distorted" her reflection (*MD*, 275). The crack was the result of her fight several years earlier with Mama Day, who, recognizing Ruby's treachery, had prevented Cocoa from going to a concert with Ambush, Dr. Buzzard, and Junior Lee. It is evidence of Cocoa's own willfulness as well as of her ignorance about the existence and power of evil.

Cocoa has occasion to look in the mirror when, after her initial illness seems to be passing, she tries "to fix myself up a bit; a little powder and rouge to cover the paleness" (*MD*, 275). Predictably, her efforts to improve her appearance result in a horrifying reflection: "I put a dab of powdered rouge on the brush, and when I stroked upward on my cheekbone my flesh gummed on the brush bristles and got pushed up like molten caramel. I brought the brush back down and the image frowning at me had a gouged cheek with the extra flesh pushed up and dangling under the right ear. I moved over; the image moved and remained the same. Bringing my fingers up to my cheek, I felt it intact and curved while the fingers in the mirror were probing a gross disfigurement" (*MD*, 275). As we have been reminded countless times in this novel about belief, "the mind is everything" (*MD*, 90); "folks see what they want to see . . . to see what's really happening here . . . [folks] gotta be ready to believe" (*MD*, 97). Thus it is with Cocoa's illness. As Bonnie Winsbro convincingly argues, "Although much of what Cocoa sees and experiences—such as worms cascading from the shower's nozzle—

continues to be hallucination, there comes a point when she stops recognizing that her perceptions are false (i.e., hallucinations) and begins to believe that worms have invaded her body. As soon as Cocoa begins to believe that the worms are real, they become real."[23]

The spiritual and emotional sources of Cocoa's illness, which have been maliciously set in motion by Ruby, require spiritual and emotional cures. Thus, Abigail nurses Cocoa by singing spirituals and stroking her back. But as Cocoa recognizes, Abigail has only "one hand against so many of them [the worms]. If only there was a way to bring me this kind of peace forever" (*MD*, 290). The lasting peace Cocoa requires can be provided only by George's willingness to share her with Mama Day or to relinquish her through his death, for her identity is tied up with him. Her love for him entails her willingness to be Ophelia, and her illness sets her on as sure a course toward death as that taken by both her great-grandmother and Shakespeare's Ophelia. Thus, both George's love and his death are what save Cocoa and bring her peace.

That peace will enable her to become the true inheritor of Sapphira Wade's legacy. That she *is* a modern-day Sapphira is made clear several times in the novel. Early on Mama Day contrasts Cocoa with her cousin Willa (of *Linden Hills*), who did not have "a whit of courage," whereas Cocoa "came into the world kicking and screaming—kicked her right in the eye as she brought her up to her lips to suck the blood and mucous out of her nose. A little raw demon from the start" (*MD*, 39). Though Cocoa's birth name might be Ophelia, George's death frees her from that identity and allows her to receive the mantle of Sapphira, a name Naylor deliberately invokes in order to redefine. The Sapphire figure, which derives from a character on the "Amos 'n' Andy" radio and television shows, has become a stereotype of the African American woman, depicted as "obstinate, domineering, and contemptuous of the African-American man."[24] Naylor, however, reclaims this figure in much the way described by bell hooks: grown black women, hooks says, "claimed Sapphire as their own, as the symbol of that angry part of themselves white folks and black men could not even begin to understand."[25] To become the independent black woman symbolized by Sapphira, Cocoa must free herself from George's attempts to define and control her.

That Cocoa is indeed the true descendant of Sapphira is made clear when Mama Day connects Cocoa's skin color to Sapphira's, claiming that Cocoa's golden color could only come from pure blackness: "Me and Abigail, we take after the sons, Miranda thinks. The earth men who formed the line of Days, hard and dark brown. But *the* Baby Girl brings back the great, grand Mother. We ain't seen 18 & 23 black from this time till now. The black that can soak up all the light in the universe, can even swallow the sun. Them silly children didn't know that it's the white in us that reflects all these shades of brown running around Willow Springs. But pure black woulda sucked it all in—and it's only an ancient mother of pure black that one day spits out this kinda gold" (*MD*, 48). Cocoa's insecurity about her skin color is the result of allowing herself to be defined by "them silly children," and her illness reflects the necessity of her shedding such insecurity in order to see herself accurately. Even George recognizes that Cocoa "could have easily descended from that slave woman who talked a man out of a whole island" (*MD*, 219).

The novel thus appropriately closes with an image of Cocoa that reverses the history of the island. Whereas Bascombe Wade's attempts to possess Sapphira result in her flying off the island, leaving Wade to his lonely, painful vigil, George's death leaves Cocoa free to visit the rise over the Sound, where "on the east side of the island and on the west side, the waters were still" (*MD*, 312).

Miranda "Mama" Day and the Meanings of the Novel

Although *Mama Day* is without question a novel about star-crossed lovers and the different worlds and value systems that collide through their relationship, it is ultimately and perhaps most definitively about its title character. Mama Day, the motherless woman who has brought so many children into the world and nurtured them with her wisdom and her love, exists as that true and perfect maternal figure we all yearn to have known. That she is indeed a kind of archetypal mother figure is underscored by her improbable age as well as by her creative powers. She defines the values of Willow Springs and guides its inhabitants just as surely as she exercises the powers of nature to fight the evil work of Ruby. She also embodies and articulates the philosophy and moral values that Naylor seems to recommend as an antidote to the gender and racial oppression she depicts in *The Women of Brewster Place* and *Linden Hills*, as well as to the spiritual emptiness and corruption she sees at the core of contemporary urban life.

Mama Day possesses extraordinary vision—an ability to "read" both the natural and human worlds with greater understanding than others. Commenting on her character, Naylor has remarked that she herself believes "in psychics. There are dimensions that we are not privy to, those of us who use what we're told is about 10 percent of our brain."[26] Mama Day's psychic powers are what enable her to learn things about the past as well as to perceive events in the future. Unlike her sister Abigail, Mama Day is willing to open herself to the pain of the past, thereby coming to know and understand it. As she reflects when she is working on the quilt for Cocoa and George, the quilt must include all of Cocoa's history, both the joyful parts and the painful ones: "Could she take 'em all out and start again? With what?" (*MD*, 138).

Mama Day's connection to a rich African American tradition of healing and conjuring is given symbolic expression in the novel through the emphasis on her "gifted hands" (*MD*, 88). In tracing Naylor's use of African American traditions of homeopathy and conjure, Tucker points out that central to much African American folklore "is the activity of making and the metonym of hands" (Tucker, 184). The image of hands is in fact one of the most dominant in the novel.[27] The central spiritual ritual of Willow Springs revolves around the image of hands as indicators both of creation and of spiritual guidance. This is the ritual of Candle Walk, which Willow Springs celebrates instead of Christmas and on December 22, the day of the winter solstice. The islanders "take to the road," each carrying a candle or some kind of light, and as they see each other, they exchange gifts, the only stipulation for which is that the gift come "from the earth" and be "the work of your own hands" (*MD*, 110). Originally designed to provide help to those who needed it "without feeling obliged," the ceremonial exchange of gifts is followed by "a lift of the candle and a parting whisper, 'Lead on with light'" (*MD*, 110).

Just as the gifts of Candle Walk emphasize the importance of creating from the materials the earth provides, so the intonation of "Lead on with light" is connected to the spiritual guidance provided by the ancient mother Sapphira. The Willow Springs myth about the origins of the ritual makes this clear: "The island got spit out from the mouth of God, and when it fell to the earth it brought along an army of stars. He tried to reach down and scoop them back up, and found himself shaking hands with the greatest conjure woman on earth. 'Leave 'em here, Lord,' she said. 'I ain't got nothing but these poor black hands to guide my people, but I can lead on with light'" (*MD*, 110). Mama Day's position as a spiritual leader, and the gifted hands with which she uses the materials of the earth to heal and help bring forth new life, connect her to the original mother, Sapphira.

Not only are hands the symbol of our connection to both the earth and the divine, but they are the symbol of our need for connection to each other. (Recall the significance of the image of hands at the end of *Linden Hills*.) To refuse to join hands in a recognition of our human interdependence is to invite our own destruction, as the novel makes so painfully evident through George's unwillingness to join hands with Mama Day. In terms of the novel's larger meanings, the Afrocentric, maternal world of Willow Springs, symbolized by Mama Day and her gifted hands, cannot be joined to the white, patriarchal world of the mainland because that world, represented by George, refuses to acknowledge this interdependence. As a consequence, at novel's end Naylor's ideal black community remains a closed circle of women's hands.

Chapter Five
Delta Dust Blues: *Bailey's Cafe*

Published in 1992, *Bailey's Cafe* completes the quartet that, in Naylor's mind, established the "foundation" for her career as a writer.[1] Less ambitious structurally and thematically than *Mama Day*, *Bailey's Cafe*'s subject matter is in many ways implicit in the earlier novels, especially the first two. Like *The Women of Brewster Place*, *Bailey's Cafe* presents a series of female portraits, but unlike that first novel, which celebrates black women, this novel concerns itself with female sexuality and female sexual identity. "The core of the work," Naylor has stated, "is indeed the way in which the word *whore* has been used against women or to manipulate female sexual identity" (see appendix).

One might expect that such a focus would result in a series of female characters who are the victims of an oppressive patriarchal society, and in fact *Bailey's Cafe* contains some of Naylor's most horrifying delineations of female suffering. But the novel resists the simplistic "woman as victim" paradigm that informs the polemical fiction of less accomplished writers. Although women's internalization of patriarchal values may ultimately account for much of the damage inflicted on the female characters of this novel, Naylor equally emphasizes the ways in which women themselves become "the handmaidens of the oppression" (see appendix). Furthermore, the male characters in *Bailey's Cafe* are among Naylor's most three-dimensional, and certainly the principal male characters offer the women friendship and support.

Structured around a series of monologues, the novel has an underlying linear narrative movement that begins in the summer of 1948 and moves through the autumn to the holiday season, climaxing on New Year's Eve. It then skips over the intervening months to culminate, in the summer of 1949, with the birth of George Andrews. George's birth is miraculous both because "no man has ever touched" his mother and because no child has ever been born on the street in limbo where the novel is set.[2] Perhaps, Nadine speculates, "it's meant for this baby to bring in a whole new era" (*BC*, 160). The novel's progression toward George's birth, which is the occasion of all the characters coming together for the first time, offers a final sense of hopefulness that balances, if it

121

does not outweigh, the despair that has brought the novel's characters to limbo in the first place.

The coexistence of pain and beauty represented by this narrative movement reflects and reinforces the novel's use of the blues. The monologues that make up the novel are presented as individual "songs" or solos of a blues or jazz session, over which Bailey presides as the "maestro." Beyond this structural simulation of the blues, the novel's prevailing spirit is the spirit of the blues. As Bailey remarks at the opening of "The Wrap," the novel's concluding section, "I don't believe that life is supposed to make you feel good, or to make you feel miserable either. Life is just supposed to make you feel" (*BC*, 219).

The Metaphysical Setting

We know from *Mama Day* that Bailey's Cafe is located on Riverside Drive in New York City, but to an even greater extent than Linden Hills or Willow Springs, Bailey's Cafe is a metaphysical setting, representing an emotional and spiritual condition. As Peaches comments, "You can find Bailey's Cafe in any town" (*BC*, 112). Offering no menu and no set prices, the cafe's proprietor goes by the name of Bailey because that was the name on the window when he walked into the cafe "from that wharf in San Francisco" (*BC*, 27); he does not bother to correct the customers who call him Bailey, because "these people aren't my lifelong buddies; they don't need to know my name" (*BC*, 28). Although customers are sometimes slow to realize that they do not come to the cafe for the coffee, or Nadine's peach cobbler, or the company (*BC*, 3), eventually they learn it is "a way station" (*BC*, 159), a place where time is frozen (*BC*, 219), a "limbo" (*BC*, 221); it provides a space for those who are "hanging on to the edge" of the world "to take a breather" (*BC*, 28) while they decide whether to resume their lives or end them (*BC*, 221).[3]

Physically, the cafe has a "sparseness" that can be comforting because it evokes no memories (*BC*, 163). Bailey's wife, Nadine, has helped him "make a lot of improvements" by sewing and hanging red-checkered curtains and by suggesting the addition of a "double-door Frigidaire" and a jukebox (*BC*, 28). When the novel opens in the summer of 1948, Bailey has been the proprietor for three years, having been led into the cafe by Nadine after his experiences in the Pacific during World War II left him feeling hopeless. As he says, "At the very moment of Hiroshima happening, it all stopped being worth it" (*BC*, 27). For some of his customers, Bailey's Cafe is "the last place before the end of the world" (*BC*,

68). It "sits right on the margin between the edge of the world and infinite possibility," and its "back door opens out to a void" (*BC*, 76). The
"void" at the back of the cafe seems in part to represent the past of the
person who looks out on it, since we are told that those who go out the
back door determined to commit suicide simply plan "to stay out back
until a certain memory becomes just too much to bear" (*BC*, 163).

Although the "songs" of the various characters are sung in the cafe,
Bailey's is only the middle station on this street in limbo; collectively, the
stations function as "a relay for broken dreams" (*BC*, 144). Flanking the
cafe on opposite ends of "the narrow back street" (*BC*, 212) are Gabe's
pawn shop and Eve's boardinghouse. The pawn shop's window overflows
"with the broken relics of uncountable dreams" (*BC*, 212), appropriately
represented by "rows of guitars, saxophones, and clarinets" (*BC*, 212).
Beyond these, "at the far end of the counter," is a "locked gun case" containing "neat rows" of revolvers (*BC*, 212). The pawn shop is run by
Gabriel, an ancient Russian Jew who is "old enough to have just about
seen everything" of the world and human beings (*BC*, 162). Named for
the archangel of the Annunciation, Gabe is appropriately the one who
discovers the pregnant Mariam. Just as Bailey's Cafe never closes, Gabe's
pawn shop "is never open"; one side of the sign "hanging on his front
door has a painted clock with movable hands. It reads, Back at ———,
and each hour he keeps moving the hands one hour forward. And under
the clock is a red-and-gold arrow pointing down the street to us [the
cafe]. After two or three hours, if the person keeps coming back without
getting the message, and he thinks they're still worth it, he'll flip the
sign over to where it reads, Out of Business, with that same arrow pointing down the street to us" (*BC*, 144–45).

Gabe sends "a certain kind of person" to the cafe, and Bailey sends "a
certain kind of woman" to the establishment at the other end of this
street in limbo, Eve's boardinghouse (*BC*, 145), which "has always been
right down the block from" the cafe (*BC*, 80). Eve was, in fact, Bailey's
first customer when he opened the cafe on a Tuesday in 1945. The kind
of establishment Eve runs in her four-story brownstone (*BC*, 214) is a
topic of endless debate among Bailey's customers: some claim that it is a
boardinghouse, while others argue that it is "nothing but a whorehouse"
(*BC*, 81) whose female inhabitants are "sluts and whores and tramps"
(*BC*, 80).

Those who see Eve as a female pimp and her establishment as a
whorehouse base their claims on the fact that every evening at about six
o'clock the women at Eve's begin receiving "gentlemen callers" (*BC*,

214), each of whom must bring the woman he is visiting the flower of her choice. Since Eve insists that the flowers be fresh, and since she herself grows them, the gentlemen callers "think it's cheaper to buy them from Eve than some other florist" (*BC*, 93). Bailey, however, recognizes that Eve runs her boardinghouse in much the same way that he runs his cafe—sometimes charging the women for their rooms and sometimes not. He also remains neutral about what exactly goes on at Eve's: "I figure it's none of my business since I'm not a woman and would have no reason to go there looking for a place to stay" (*BC*, 80).

Eve's life story underscores the biblical connotations of her name, for she was expelled from Pilottown by Godfather when, as an adolescent, she was discovered by him to have sexual appetites. Ageless while she lived in Pilottown, Eve had no "real mother or father" and owed her life to Godfather. She blames the women of Pilottown for her expulsion, because "their slitted eyes and evil questions" led Godfather to stop showing her any affection and to clothe her in shapeless dresses (*BC*, 83). As Eve entered puberty, she learned from pressing herself against the earth to give herself physical pleasure, which was enhanced by Billy Boy's stomping: "I sought [Billy Boy] out and sought out the earth whenever I needed release from the tight silence in my home, tightening to the point of danger the closer I grew toward womanhood" (*BC*, 87). Her "first chores" in Godfather's home were to bring the wood and make the fire in which he burned all of her clothes after he discovered her and Billy Boy. Since Godfather had found her "naked and hungry," he would send her away in the same condition.

Naylor has commented that one of the first images she had for *Bailey's Cafe* was "of Eve, of a young woman down in the dust, and she's afraid."[4] The portrait of Eve in the novel identifies her completely with the original Eve, the mother of humankind whose sin led to the Fall. Naylor's Eve has created her own garden; each of the women who want to stay in Eve's boardinghouse must find it on her own. When they ask Bailey where it is, he tells them, "Go out the door, make a right, and when you see the garden—if you see the garden—you're there" (*BC*, 81). The stone wall around Eve's garden is covered with wildflowers, and inside the wall is a border of flowers that "Eve keeps blooming in cold weather: camellias, coltsfoot, winter jasmine, pearly everlasting" (*BC*, 92). Although she grows flowers throughout the yard, all of which "are for sale," the center of the yard is dominated by "the stump of her only tree," surrounded by "circles and circles of lilies" of every kind, but "none of them have a price" (*BC*, 92).

Naylor's ironic and symbolic intentions with her portrait of Eve and Eve's garden are evident, even if they are not altogether clear. The "only tree" in her garden is, significantly, no longer a tree (presumably of knowledge), but merely a stump surrounded by lilies; like her boarders, Eve has her own special flower. The abundant lilies, associated with purity and virginal love, overshadow the phallic tree, already diminished to a stump. And Eve's willingness to sell "all of her other flowers" but not the lilies seems to point to her insistence that her sexuality belongs to her, to be defined and used as she pleases.

Eve's role with the women who live in her boardinghouse is clearer. Like the cafe, her house is "a way station" (*BC,* 159), which only women who seek some kind of healing can find. Even the calling cards she gives out in the women's house of detention have no directions since, as Bailey observes, "there's no need to waste directions on someone who's just going to spend her life staying lost" (*BC,* 133). Moreover, not every woman who finds her way to Eve's is taken in. Even when she is "tempted to let a woman stay here because of the pain in her story," she does not unless the woman knows about "delta dust" (*BC,* 81), the dust that worked its way so thoroughly into Eve's own body during her trek from Pilottown to New Orleans that "it's not a part of me—it is me" (*BC,* 82).

Once Eve takes a woman into her boardinghouse, however, "she passes no judgment on" her behavior or her visitors (*BC,* 92). Eve's sole stipulation is that the women can "only entertain men who are willing to bring them flowers. If he can't do that much for you, he doesn't need to waste your time" (*BC,* 93). The first component in her strategy for enabling the women to heal is, then, to let them begin to believe in their own inherent value.

From what we see of Eve's strategy with Peaches and Jesse Bell, her healing methods also include allowing the women to continue, with no recriminations and no difficulties, the self-destructive behavior that brought them to her in the first place—with several important differences: they will act out the behavior in a protected, structured environment, among other women, and they will act it out in style. Thus, she employs Miss Maple as both housekeeper and bouncer; gentlemen are allowed to call only between six o'clock and midnight; and the midnight curfew means "no more visitors or music, and her boarders can't have hard liquor at any time" (*BC,* 116).

Eve assures Daddy Jim, father of Peaches, that if he leaves his daughter with her, she will "return her to you whole," not by limiting the number of men Peaches entertains but by teaching her to "accept no less than what" she deserves (*BC*, 113). Thus, although Eve's parlor is filled with "eager men waiting to visit Peaches" because they know she "takes on all callers" (*BC*, 113), each week Peaches "spends much more time with each gentleman caller than she spent the week before" (*BC*, 114). Eve recognizes that "whatever she's doing up in that room, she's doing it feeling beautiful," for she is learning to demand "more perfect and more perfect daffodils. They will be gotten at no florist for any price. And it will take a special man to give Eve what she'll ask for hers. A man special enough to understand what the woman upstairs is truly worth" (*BC*, 114).

Similarly, Eve proves effective in her treatment of the heroin addict Jesse Bell. After nursing Jesse through withdrawal, Eve presents her with a gift: a velvet case "lined in sky blue silk. The eyedropper was made of crystal, the teaspoon and syringe pure silver, the book of matches embossed" (*BC*, 139). Jesse is certain this gift must be some sort of elaborate joke because she cannot believe that Eve thinks she would use dope again after the agony of having quit. Eve, however, rightly recognizes that the pain Jesse has endured does not mean she is prepared to live her life rather than destroy it. Eve thus presents the gift because she wants to ensure that "the next time you shoot up, it's going to be with style" (*BC*, 139).

Jesse's second round of withdrawal almost kills her, but Eve nevertheless gives her "yet another velvet case," this one containing a gold needle (*BC*, 142). Although Jesse tells Bailey that Eve is an "icy icy mama" (*BC*, 118), Bailey reflects that Eve "went the distance and cured her—and I mean, cured her—in less than a month" (*BC*, 136). Eve succeeds, Bailey implies, because she makes Jesse take responsibility for her own life. Jesse claims that "Eve wouldn't have cared if she had died. The funny thing is that Jesse is probably right. *But I said unto thee when thou wast in thy own blood, Live*" (*BC*, 136). As the quotation from Ezekiel (one of many biblical references in the novel) makes clear, Jesse herself has been choosing death rather than life through her heroin addiction, and she must therefore be the one to whom her life most matters.

The Women of *Bailey's Cafe*

The "relay for broken dreams" constituted by Gabe's pawn shop, Bailey's Cafe, and Eve's boardinghouse does, then, extend the possibility of hope—and therefore of a return to life—for some of those whose despair brings them to the street. Significantly, however, only the woman in this relay, Eve, seems able to offer actual healing, as opposed to a simple respite. Naylor shapes her character after the biblical Eve but inverts the meanings evoked by Eve in both biblical and Western cultural traditions. Eve's disobedience in the Garden of Eden, the original sin that led to the Fall, did not involve sexuality, although her punishment included pain in childbirth (Genesis 3:16). But because redemption was achieved through a woman as well—the Virgin Mary—Eve's sin became, in Western traditions, associated with sexuality. Mary, in fact, is often referred to as the "new Eve," and during the Middle Ages, "the first word of the angelic salutation *Ave Maria* was read symbolically backwards as *Eva* (Eve)."[5] This doctrinal opposition came to be expressed in both popular and high culture through the oppositional images of whore and virgin, and these images in turn have often controlled the ways in which women are viewed in Western societies.

Bailey's Cafe deconstructs these images that define women exclusively in terms of their sexuality. Naylor's Eve, whose thousand-year trek leaves her with "poor eyesight, no sense of humor, and a body of mud" (*BC*, 91), enters New Orleans "neither male nor female—mud," but leaves it 10 years later "with three steamer trunks of imported silk suits, not one of them brown; fifty-seven thousand, six hundred and forty-one dollars, not one of them earned on my back; and a love of well-kept gardens" (*BC*, 91). Her success in New Orleans leaves her "overqualified" for just about any political job, whether as mayor, governor, or anything else "on up the line" (*BC*, 91). Overqualified or not, Eve recognizes that "there was nowhere on earth for a woman like me" (*BC*, 91).

Naylor suggests through this portrait of Eve that the world is indeed inhospitable to a woman who, like Eve, insists on defining herself and is indifferent to what others think. This indifference allows her to extend to other women the space and the conditions they need to heal themselves of the injuries they have suffered in a world that would define them as "whore."

The female characters whose lives Naylor portrays in the novel would all be condemned, by many, as whores. With one exception—Sadie—they are all boarders at Eve's, and again with the exception of Sadie, they are all based, to varying degrees, on the biblical women whose names they share.[6] The order in which these characters appear in the novel is also significant. Sadie, the first of the women presented in the novel, never finds her way to Eve's boardinghouse (*BC*, 80), a fact that perhaps explains why she has no biblical parallel. Her story is followed by Eve's,

Esther's, Mary's, Jesse Bell's, and Mariam's. The principle underlying both the individual stories and the overall arrangement of the stories is the musical principle of counterpointing. Bailey cautions us from the outset that we need to remember that "nobody comes in here with a simple story. Every one-liner's got a life underneath it. Every point's got a counterpoint" (*BC*, 34).

Sadie's story, the first we hear, establishes the tone and mood for all the stories to follow; it is appropriately entitled "Mood: Indigo." Her story is also perhaps the most lyrically painful section of the novel and certainly among the most powerfully written. Naylor attempted with Sadie to make the word *whore* "sing for you, sing beauty for you" (see appendix), and in fact Sadie's story represents one of Naylor's most accomplished and poetic pieces of writing to date.

Denied knowledge of her name "until she was about four years old," when her mother beat it into her, Sadie before that time heard herself referred to only as "The One The Coat Hanger Missed" (*BC*, 42). Sadie's story presents the survival strategies of the prototype of the unwanted and unloved child who believes she is not loved because she herself is not good. She survives, the text says, because she loves the mother who does not love her (*BC*, 42), and she spends her childhood trying to earn that mother's love, first by being good, then by being very good, "and when very good didn't work, she tried very very good" (*BC*, 43). Sadie's story becomes almost a case study of the abused child, and it certainly stands as Naylor's most serious indictment of women who victimize their children. Sadie's mother is one of the few female characters in Naylor's fiction who remains completely outside the reader's sympathies and beyond any kind of redemption.

The prostitution into which her mother forces her drives Sadie to take refuge in dreams, which eventually crystallize into a single image of desire: "There was to be a trim white bungalow with a green picket fence, and she would keep the front yard swept clean of leaves and pick all the withered blooms from their fence full of roses" (*BC*, 44). Eventually, Sadie is willing to approximate this dream in the home she gains through her marriage to the taciturn Daniel, "a man older than enough to be her father," who turns out to be a drunkard like her mother. But Sadie is denied even the approximation of the dream after Daniel dies and his daughters force her out of her home.

Although Daniel resembles Sadie's mother, he at least allows her to have a home. Repeatedly in Sadie's story, women are made responsible for abusing Sadie, from the mother who tried unsuccessfully to abort her; to Daniel's daughters, who greedily and heartlessly take her house away; to the white prostitute for whom the young Sadie once worked and who, made wealthy through her marriage to one of her customers, refuses even to recognize Sadie when Sadie most desperately needs a job. Naylor's outrage over the inhumanity of those who victimize Sadie is given eloquent expression in a sequence that first contrasts "the laws of Nature" that made Sadie a widow with "human nature that threatened to take away her home" (*BC*, 56), and then goes on to contrast "man's law" with "God's law": "Nowhere was God's law working in all of this, or lightning would have been dancing around those railroad tracks as Sadie sold everything the two daughters couldn't claim" (*BC*, 57).

Naylor also insists on the incorruptibility of the innocent and pure, for Sadie's innate moral sensibility remains intact long after her mind has been destroyed; she is, in Bailey's terms, a "lady" who transforms Bailey's "thick mug" into "china" and his "bent tin spoon and paper napkin" into "monogrammed silver and linen" (*BC*, 40). Forced into prostitution by her mother, Sadie again resorts to it in a last attempt to save her home; when that effort fails, she sells her body only for the amount needed to buy the five-star wine that allows her to keep her dream image of a house intact: "She knew she'd been given a second chance and she'd make no more mistakes. She'd make sure that she always had enough money to keep her house" (*BC*, 66).

Sadie's story "really gets sad," Bailey says, when Iceman Jones offers Sadie the first kindness and friendship she has ever experienced. But by this point in her life, Sadie has learned to keep the real world at a great distance; she knows that her dream can stay intact only if she protects it. She refuses Iceman Jones's marriage proposal, for "she knew this dear sweet man was offering her the moon, but she could give him the stars" (*BC*, 78).[7]

Unlike Sadie, the other women portrayed in the novel have found their way to the protective and potentially healing environment of Eve's boardinghouse. "Sweet Esther," the shortest story in the novel, presents a young woman whose brother sold her, when she was only 12 years old, to a man whose sexual desires found fulfillment through bondage and brutality. Esther is one in an endless line of young female children whom this man abuses until they run away. Although the experience has instilled in Esther a hatred so profound that it turns the corner of Bailey's Cafe "into a block of ice" (*BC*, 94), the details of her story make women equally complicitous in her victimization. Esther was groomed and taught, for example, by the "hag" who worked for the man. And

Esther stayed "with this man for twelve years. . . . I stay one year for each year my older brother took care of me against the shrill protests of the fat wife" (*BC*, 98). Naylor makes it clear that the brother's wife is as guilty as the brother himself for the sexual slavery into which Esther was sold.

Esther's story seems to be Naylor's re-visioning of the biblical Esther, who is celebrated in Jewish religion for her role in saving thousands of Jews from death, the event commemorated in the Jewish feast of Purim. Reaching behind the courageous action that made Esther a heroine, Naylor amplifies the details of how Esther came to be in a position to save her people. The original wife of Esther's husband, King Ahasuerus, was Vashti; she was commanded by her husband to parade her beauty before the people of his kingdom. When she refused, King Ahasuerus's counselors advised him that her disobedience would have contagious effects on the other women of the kingdom, and they urged him to abandon Vashti, making her an example to all wives. The king accepted their advice, issuing a proclamation to all the people in his kingdom "that every man should bear rule in his own house" (Esther 1:22). The king then announced that he would choose a new wife and queen from among the many virgins who were to be brought to him. Mordecai, Esther's cousin and adoptive father, sent Esther, and she was the virgin selected. Naylor's "Sweet Esther" postulates and inscribes the actual experiences of the young child and woman as an antidote to the patriarchal text's emphasis on the woman's actions for her people.

In "Mary (Take One)," which follows the story of Esther, Naylor offers an extended critique of the biblical Mary Magdalene. Like Eve, the biblical figure of Mary Magdalene has received great amplification in Christian and Western cultural traditions. Although in the Bible she is a woman out of whom Jesus "had cast seven devils" (Mark 16:9) and who is noteworthy for having been the person to whom Jesus first appeared after the Resurrection, Christian tradition has shaped Mary Magdalene into the prototypical reformed prostitute. The figure of Mary Magdalene has been a frequent subject in Western paintings, including one that may have influenced Naylor's portrait: a painting by Georges de la Tour, in New York's Metropolitan Museum, that depicts Mary Magdalene at the turning point of her life, looking at herself in a mirror.

In Naylor's re-visioning of the Mary Magdalene figure through the character of Peaches, mirrors are central. We have seen Naylor's fascination with the mirror in both *Linden Hills* and *Mama Day*, but it receives its clearest treatment in *Bailey's Cafe*. Her Mary Magdalene is the seventh child and only daughter of a Kansas City bricklayer, who nick-named his daughter Peaches because she was "yellow and sweet" and beautiful (*BC*, 102). Daddy Jim's pride in his beautiful baby led him to show her off to everyone and then to build a wall around his house to protect his prize exhibit. He enjoyed the fact that his teenaged daughter was sought after by boys, and he took pleasure in trying to get her suit-ors to acknowledge their sexual designs and desires (*BC*, 103). Even before she reached adolescence, Peaches was fondled by adult men, including the choirmaster. She thus came to see herself mirrored in the eyes of all the men who desired her and all the women who envied her; all of those mirrors reflected her as a naked, available body that, as Bailey himself says, was "born to be fucked" (*BC*, 104, 102).

In an effort to reclaim some value and worth for herself, to be some-thing other than the object of men's sexual desires, Peaches divorced her-self from her body and pretended that her true self was different from the reflection mirrored in others' eyes. The compelling need to believe in her own worth prompted her rebellion against the many actual mirrors with which her father surrounded her; every Christmas, every Valentine's Day, every birthday, Daddy Jim had yet another expensive, elegant mir-ror placed in Peaches's bedroom, so that "everywhere I turned, I could see her. But what was she doing in my room? She was a whore and I was Daddy's baby" (*BC*, 104). So frightened was she of the self reflected in the mirrors that Peaches smashed "the swan-shaped mirror, my tenth-birthday present" (*BC*, 104). But after Daddy Jim spanked her for smashing it, she "never broke another" (*BC*, 105).

The self-division created by her father's and the world's insistence on seeing her only as a sexual object intensified as Peaches grew up; her inner self struggled to differentiate itself from her outer beauty and to establish its value through good deeds and high achievements. Finally, the only recourse her inner self has for maintaining its sense of value is to give the beautiful outer self to all who want her: "Free, at last *I* was free as I gave them her. . . . Any race, any age, any size—any son of any man—had the power to drive away that demon from the mirror. Over and over, they became my saviors from *her*" (*BC*, 105).

Such methods did not work indefinitely, however, and eventually Peaches lost the ability to maintain the self-division that allowed her to value and care about her inner self while hating her outer self. Once she began to "see her" in the mirror of her own eyes, Peaches succumbed to a hatred that unified her personality: "Before, I had only hated her. Now I wanted to hate myself" (*BC*, 107). By the time she takes up with the crippled gambler who "never called me anything but Mary," her self-hatred and her *desire* for self-hatred—her belief that her inner self deserves to be hated as well as her outer self—can be arrested only through literal self-mutilation.

"Mary (Take One)" may well be the most powerful fictional analysis ever written of the devastation caused by the patriarchal reduction of women to their physical appearance. Naylor suggests, moreover, that extraordinary beauty does not cause but simply intensifies the preexisting male tendency to see women primarily as sexual objects. The self-division to which Peaches resorts stems from the same desire voiced by Nadine when Bailey is courting her: "I'm more than my body," Nadine insists, giving Bailey "a whole different way of looking at her—and women" (*BC*, 19). Being defined by the world exclusively in terms of their bodies is the bond shared by all the women in the novel.

Although Naylor's description of Peaches's mutilation of her face with a beer-can opener is brutal and painful, the story concludes on the more hopeful note of her recovery at Eve's, and this note is continued in the next monologue, "Jesse Bell." Jesse's voice is in many ways the female counterpart of Bailey's; like the first half of Bailey's monologue, Jesse's section of the novel is humorous and witty. Naylor in fact seems to have a good deal of fun in this re-visioning of the biblical Jezebel and relies extensively on verbal punning and witty allusions to biblical details.

The story of the biblical Jezebel is found in 1 and 2 Kings. Of a different race and religion from her husband Ahab, a king of Israel, she helped lead him away from the true worship of God and eventually arranged to have Naboth killed so that Ahab could have Naboth's vineyard, which he had coveted. For this wickedness, Elijah prophesied that Jezebel would be eaten by dogs. When Jehu came to arrest Jezebel, she painted her face, looked out her window, and attempted to seduce him, but to no avail. She was thrown out of the window, Jehu's horse trampled her, and when the people went to retrieve her body to bury her, they discovered that her flesh had been eaten by dogs. Thus, Elijah's prophecy was fulfilled, "and the carcase of Jezebel shall be as dung upon the face of the field" (2 Kings 9:37).

All of these details about the biblical Jezebel find their way into Naylor's portrait of the working-class Jesse Bell, who married into the snobbish, middle-class King family. Her customs and beliefs differed from those of the King family. Presided over by the patriarchal Uncle Eli, the Kings did their best to let Jesse know she was not as good as they were. Sensual and full of life, Jesse freely acknowledges to the reader that she was not "what you might call a nice girl" when she met her husband (*BC*, 122). Unlike his family, her husband accepted and loved Jesse; he even accepted the fact that she had a "special friend," a female lover. Jesse was careful to keep knowledge of her special friend from Uncle Eli, until his success in alienating her son from her drove her to heavy drinking. Eventually, she turned to dope, the "dyke club" she patronized was raided, and the Kings, led by Uncle Eli, made sure Jesse's "name hit the papers": "So I'm out there by myself, on display like a painted dummy in a window as the name Jesse Bell came to mean that no-good slut from the docks and the nineteen years I'd put into my marriage didn't amount to dog shit; the care I'd given my son—dog shit; the clothes I wore, the music I liked, the school I went to, the family I came from, everything that made me *me*—dog shit" (*BC*, 129). Like her biblical counterpart, Jesse was condemned and humiliated publicly. Nonetheless, her resilient spirit and sense of humor are the most striking notes in her monologue. Perhaps because Jesse never defines her sexuality exclusively in terms of men, she emerges from the novel considerably less damaged than the other women.

The hopefulness of Jesse's story (Eve has, after all, cured her of her heroin addiction) is counterpointed by the horror of "Mary (Take Two)," in which Naylor's re-visioning of the Virgin Mary includes painful descriptions of female circumcision and infibulation. This section of the novel is in some ways the least successful, for Naylor is obliged to transport an Ethiopian Jew from Addis Ababa to Gabe's pawn shop, primarily it seems for the purpose of dealing with the subject of female genital mutilation. Although it is true that the setting of the novel is outside the parameters of real time and space, it is also true that in no other instance does Naylor go outside the continental United States for her characters.

That Mariam gives birth to George, thus providing the novel with a hopeful ending, is indisputable; whether it is, as Eve claims, a virgin birth depends upon each reader's willingness to suspend disbelief. Since no birth at all has ever occurred on this street, however, the mere fact of George's birth seems to be sufficiently miraculous to make Mariam's virginity, on one level of meaning at any rate, unnecessary.

Again, however, Naylor's primary goal in the story of Mariam seems to be to complete her exploration of the patriarchy's efforts to define women by their sexuality. The mutilating "purification" process that Mariam must experience highlights the idea that even virginity is not sufficiently virginal to make a girl marriageable. Central to the infibulation ritual, moreover, is the fact that it is carried out by women and that

Mariam's mother plays a crucial role. Eve explains to Nadine that Mariam's mother was prompted by love of her daughter: "Finding her a decent husband would be difficult with so many other virgins to choose from, and that is why she had the midwives close her up that tightly. It raises a woman's value" (*BC*, 152). Like Sadie and Esther, Mariam has been most victimized by women, but in her case the victimization results from her mother's protective desire to prepare her for successful negotiation of the patriarchal world in which they live. Nonetheless, Naylor seems to place heavy responsibility on Mariam's mother and the other women, for the text implies that they should have found some way of resisting the patriarchy. This implication seems evident from the repetition throughout Mariam's story of the sentence, "No man has ever touched me." Expressive on one level of Mariam's virginity, the sentence functions at another level of meaning to indict the women who have brutally and violently "touched" the young girl.

Unlike Peaches, Jesse, and Esther, Mariam cannot ultimately be healed by Eve; unlike Sadie, she does not turn to artificial and self-destructive ways of supporting the dreams necessary to life. Alone of the women in the novel, Mariam dies, although her intentionality in dying remains ambiguous: "After Eve tried to return the baby to Mariam, she was met with a wall of water. In Eve's absence Mariam had tried to create a running stream to bathe in. And the void out back produced exactly what her childlike mind called up: endless water" (*BC*, 228).

The Men of *Bailey's Cafe*

Framing the stories of the women in *Bailey's Cafe* are two central male characters, Bailey and Miss Maple, who counterpoint each other in every way and are intended, Naylor said in her interview with me, to function as "bookends."[8] Because the novel explores female sexuality and female sexual identity, Naylor added, it must also address the issue of "male sexuality and male sexual identity, because you cannot have one without the other" (see appendix).

To a certain extent, *Bailey's Cafe* does explore male sexual identity. Naylor presents Bailey as a man accustomed to looking at women primarily in terms of their bodies, and she depicts Miss Maple as a man who has learned not to define his manhood through his physical prowess or, most significantly in the text, through the clothes he chooses to wear.[9] Yet it is difficult to see just how, beyond these characteristics, the text actually explores the sexual identities of the two men. They share, in fact, a privilege denied the women in the novel, namely, the privilege of maintaining privacy about their sexuality and their sexual identity. For example, although Bailey presents himself as having been, prior to his marriage to Nadine, quite the ladies' man, we hear nothing of his behavior with women. The text is equally silent about Miss Maple's attitudes toward and behavior with women. His job at Eve's boardinghouse suggests that he is more trustworthy and more caring than other men where women are concerned, but we do not actually see those qualities that uniquely fit him for the job. His defiance of gender role expectations by wearing dresses may indicate that he does not require social approval, but it does not necessarily mean anything more. The presentations of Bailey and Miss Maple focus on their responses to and ways of handling other sorts of issues, especially public issues such as the war, the atomic bomb, racial segregation, and racial discrimination—issues that never really get raised by the women. In fact, the issue of racial identity is addressed only by Bailey and Miss Maple in the novel; the women whose stories we hear see themselves—and are seen by the reader—almost exclusively as women, not as black women.[10]

The text privileges these male characters in other ways as well. The controlling narrative voice of the novel, Bailey shapes the reader's responses and certainly serves as a moral touchstone. He also exercises a certain degree of control over the women's stories, especially Sadie's, which he himself narrates. One of the longest sections of the novel is given over to Miss Maple, whose story, though certainly not always a happy one, contrasts significantly with the horror of Mariam's, which it follows. In a review of the novel, Peter Erickson objected to the fact that the joyous, multicultural ritual of baby George's circumcision is shared only by Bailey, Gabe, and Miss Maple. Erickson comments, "Political and ceremonial discourse is made to seem a largely male affair."[11] Of equal significance, however, is the fact that even the private discourse of the male characters reveals them to be multifaceted human beings whose sexuality is just one aspect of their lives. Not only is the discourse of the female characters limited to private concerns, but even their private worlds are narrowed to an almost exclusive focus on sexuality. By contrast, the single male character in the novel's cafe frame whose discourse focuses on the topic of sexuality is Sugar Man, a pimp who plays a very minor role in the novel.

In a novel concerned with the ways women have been defined by their sexuality and with the ways in which the concept of "whore" has been used against them, we might expect the one-dimensionality we find in the portraits of the women. But this one-dimensionality becomes disturbing because it exists in juxtaposition to the three-dimensionality of the principal male characters. Furthermore, these male characters are constructed very differently from the men portrayed in the women's stories. The male characters the novel develops—Bailey and Miss Maple—leave us wondering just how the female characters came to suffer the experiences their stories describe.

Bailey's Cafe and the Blues

Both the formal divisions of the novel and its epigraph reflect Naylor's intention to employ the blues and jazz in her novel's structure and themes, an intention shared by many African American writers, including Langston Hughes, Amiri Baraka, Nikki Giovanni, Richard Wright, James Baldwin, and Toni Morrison. Ralph Ellison's now-classic description of the blues provides a useful and accurate gloss on Naylor's novel: "The blues is an impulse to keep the painful details and episodes of a brutal experience alive in one's aching consciousness, to finger its jagged grain, and to transcend it, not by the consolation of philosophy but by squeezing from it a near-tragic, near-comic lyricism. As a form, the blues is an autobiographical chronicle of personal catastrophe expressed lyrically."[12] The various monologues comprising *Bailey's Cafe*, in most of which the characters tell their own stories through the first-person point of view, conform to Ellison's description of the blues. They present "the painful details and episodes of a brutal experience" in language that is indeed often lyrical. The telling of their stories itself constitutes the characters' resistance to the almost overwhelming pain inherent in those stories.

As the "maestro," Bailey begins the novel by setting "the tempo with a few fascinating tidbits" about himself (*BC*, 4). He warns us that if we are to understand why he and his customers find themselves in his cafe, we must not expect "to get the answer in a few notes," because "there's a whole set to be played here if you want to stick around and listen to the music" (*BC*, 4). Bailey's own blues song, signaled in the text by a shift to italic type, records his nightmarish experiences in the Pacific during World War II. His opening piece is followed by a section entitled "The Vamp," the double meanings of which term point to both the form and the subject of the novel. In musical terms, a vamp is an improvised musical accompaniment; it is usually "a short passage, which is simple in rhythm and harmony, played in preparation for the entry of a soloist," and often used before and after or even during solos.[13] The vamp in

Bailey's Cafe is provided by Sugar Man and Sister Carrie, who "sound" farther "apart" than they are. To see how close Sugar Man and Sister Carrie are, Bailey cautions us, we have to "take" them down to a "lower key" (*BC*, 34). Most important, if we are to understand them—and the soloists we are about to hear in this musical set—we must "listen below the surface" (*BC*, 34).

A *vamp* is also, of course, a term for a woman who uses her charms to seduce; it is suggestive of, if not quite synonymous with, *whore*. This meaning of the word provides the subject matter of the notes played by Sugar Man and Sister Carrie, the pimp and the religious fanatic who frequent Bailey's Cafe and whose identifying notes are "Five-alive" and "Lord Jesus" (*BC*, 35). Each finds the other wholly objectionable, but in reality they share a rather similar perspective on women. Sister Carrie, who is "afraid of her own appetites" (*BC*, 33), is obsessed with what she sees as the dirtiness of female sexuality, and her obsession is projected onto her daughter Angel, whose developing adolescent body horrifies Sister Carrie. Sugar Man believes that women are weak and in need of male protection, "a little like children—but a whole lot like angels" (*BC*, 34). He sells women's bodies because he is confident that "they were gonna sell it anyway. I just knew the highest rollers" (*BC*, 34). Sister Carrie and Sugar Man also share a common perspective on Eve's boardinghouse: they both regard it as a whorehouse. Like a musical vamp, they enter the text periodically to sound these familiar notes.

The blues themselves are, as Sherley Anne Williams states, "essentially an oral form meant to be heard rather than read," the roots of which are found in the call-response pattern of slave work songs.[14] In a blues or jazz set, the vamp provides such a call-response pattern, and Naylor simulates this pattern by allowing the voices of Sister Carrie and Sugar Man to surface periodically during the novel. The importance of the pattern is its insistence on seeing individuals in relation to a community. As Williams notes, "Even the selection of songs in a blues performance underscores the relationship of singer and audience and the manner in which communal values are incorporated into the presentation of the blues performer's act" (545). Naylor's use of the cafe for the setting of the novel also reinforces the relationship of the individual and the community. Although we as readers overhear the stories narrated by the individual characters in the course of "The Jam," their primary audience consists of Bailey, Nadine, and their regular customers—Sugar Man, Sister Carrie, Eve, Miss Maple, and Gabe.

This primary audience is at its fullest and becomes something of a real community in the final section of the novel, "The Wrap" (again, a musical term), which describes the first birth ever to happen in this limbo. To ease the pain of Mariam's childbirth, Eve puts on a light show: "Sparkling. Shimmering. Waves of light. . . . Cascades of light flowing in, breaking up, and rolling like fluid diamonds over the worn tile" (*BC*, 224–25). The miracle of George's imminent birth brings all of the characters to the cafe: "Besides the few customers, everyone who lived on the street was gathered inside. And I mean everyone, even strange little Esther" (*BC*, 224–25). When the baby's first cry is heard, "the place went wild," with people hugging, cheering, and dancing; then, "wonder of wonders, Esther smiled" (*BC*, 225).

The climactic moment comes, however, when Peaches begins to sing the spiritual "Anybody Ask You Who You Are." "Soon," Bailey says, "we were all singing, a bit ragged and off-key. But all singing" (*BC*, 226). Peaches's choice of song here resonates with special poignancy for readers familiar with *Mama Day*'s George, whose parentage is of such importance to him. Within the context of *Bailey's Cafe* itself, both the particular spiritual and the fact that it is a spiritual are significant. The spirituals were created by a people who were stripped of their names and their history and whose humanity was denied by their status as slaves. The slaves' creation of the spirituals represented their *resistance* to slavery and its attempt to define them as less than human. A spiritual like "Anybody Ask You Who You Are" asserts the slaves' right to define themselves. As James H. Cone has argued, "The basic idea of the spirituals is that slavery contradicts God; it is a denial of his will. To be enslaved is to be declared *nobody*, and that form of existence contradicts God's creation of people to be his children. Because black people believed that they were God's children, they affirmed their *somebodiness*, refusing to reconcile their servitude with divine revelation."[15] When Peaches and the other characters in *Bailey's Cafe* sing "Anybody Ask You Who You Are," they may be said to be saying, collectively, to the newborn baby (and to themselves) that he must remember, whenever the world challenges or attempts to deny his humanity, that he is "somebody":

> Anybody ask you who you are?
> Who you are?
> Who you are?

> Anybody ask you who you are?
> Tell him—you're the child of God. (*BC*, 225)

The meaning of this spiritual has deep relevance to the characters who sing it. To a world anxious to define them as whores, these women must learn to say, "I am not a whore but the child of God." The flowers Eve requires her boarders' gentlemen callers to buy symbolically make the same statement.

The miracle of George's birth at the end of the novel and the community it creates together evoke an underlying optimism, a belief in the ultimate resistance of the human spirit to attempts to destroy it. Naylor's reliance on the blues for the structure and themes of the novel itself points toward this intention, for the blues, like the spirituals, "affirm the somebodiness of black people. . . . The blues are a transformation of black life through the sheer power of song" (Cone, 117). Even Mariam's subsequent death does not diminish the novel's sense of hope and affirmation. While most of the "songs" comprising the novel are painful to listen to, they stand as testimony to what Ellison called "the sheer toughness of spirit" by which "the agony of life" can be "conquered" (94). Only Sadie and Mariam remain outside the possibility for healing offered in the novel; significantly, they are the only characters whose stories are narrated by someone else. For most of the characters, telling their own stories, singing their own songs, empowers them to generate the hope necessary for living.

Chapter Six

Spiritual and Moral Sanctuary in Gloria Naylor's Fiction

At the beginning of this study, I suggested that Naylor's deep and extended involvement with the Jehovah's Witnesses has had a profound influence on her fiction. Some of the ways in which Naylor's fiction reflects her early years with the Jehovah's Witnesses are certainly apparent. Her novels draw extensively, for example, on the Bible, of which she most clearly has a detailed, even exhaustive, knowledge. In addition, Naylor has an affinity, as do the Jehovah's Witnesses, for apocalyptic images and events: in *The Women of Brewster Place*, the rape of Lorraine is followed by unrelenting rains; in *Linden Hills*, the evil Nedeed house goes up in flames; in *Mama Day*, the big storm, a metaphor for middle passage, destroys the bridge connecting Willow Springs to the mainland; and in *Bailey's Cafe*, Mariam is swallowed up by the waters in the void behind the cafe.

There are other important ways in which Naylor's work reflects a moral and spiritual sensibility undoubtedly influenced, although probably not created, by her religious background. Primary among these is her tendency to create fictional worlds so corrupt that her characters must find some sort of sanctuary in which they can be safe. For the Jehovah's Witness believer, as I discussed in the opening chapter, the history of the world is the history of the clashes between Jesus and Satan; Jehovah's Witnesses similarly see themselves in opposition to "the world," which is evil and therefore in need of the destruction that Armageddon will bring. To protect themselves from the corruption of the world, the Jehovah's Witnesses form small communities within which their members can find safety.

This conception of the world and the forms of behavior it prompts are also, of course, consistent with the actual experiences of and the strategies for survival employed by black Americans. The physical, spiritual, and psychological brutalities both of slavery and of racism have required black Americans to deploy a set of defensive maneuvers designed to ensure survival and wholeness. Through their art (such as the spiritual sung at the end of *Bailey's Cafe*), black Americans have insisted that the realities of life imposed by a white hegemonic society are morally and spiritually wrong, inconsistent both with God's will and any meaningful system of human justice. And through the bonds and values of their communities, black Americans—like the Jehovah's Witnesses—have created spaces that are at once safe and nurturing.

Naylor's fiction similarly tends to present spaces (either actual or symbolic) that function as necessary sanctuaries for her characters, who most often find themselves in a hostile and corrupt universe. Because the majority of Naylor's characters are black women, the dangers posed by the white, capitalistic, patriarchal power structures of the world they inhabit are legion. We may recall, for example, the life-threatening beating received by Mattie Michael from her irate father and the similar treatment meted Eve by Godfather; the sexual assaults inflicted on Lorraine, on Sadie, on Sweet Esther, on Mariam; the erasure of selfhood experienced by each generation of Nedeed wives; the inescapable poverty that stifles the dreams of the many women of Brewster Place and Bailey's Cafe.

Set against these horrifying and threatening fictional worlds are the sanctuaries Naylor creates for her characters. Generally these are small spaces within which clusters of individuals can find protection from the evil of the outside world. Brewster Place is itself an impoverished and threatening street; only within their individual apartments and through bonding with each other do the various women find refuge. Lorraine is vulnerable to rape not simply because she is in the alley but also because she has been excluded from Brewster's community of women. All of Linden Hills is a dangerous place from which Willie and Lester flee each evening to the safety offered by their individual rooms. Only in *Mama Day* is the sanctuary conceived as more than a refuge—indeed, as powerful enough to challenge the hegemony of the mainland world. Even Willow Springs, however, must be protected from the threats of intrusion and appropriation posed by the larger world of the mainland. In *Bailey's Cafe*, we are made to feel very keenly both the fragility and the impermanence of the sanctuaries provided by the cafe and Eve's boardinghouse. Rarely in the novels does Naylor suggest that the world beyond the sanctuary can be safely negotiated; more often, in fact, her characters seek sanctuary because of the battering they have received as a consequence of their efforts to live in that world, which is characteristically depicted as a sexist and racist place, the aggressive, materialistic, and generally inhumane values of which have rendered its people soulless.

With the exception of *Linden Hills*, Naylor's focus, as we have seen, is typically on characters in flight from the corruption and evil of the world. Usually these characters have been horribly damaged by their experiences in the world, and Naylor possesses an extraordinary ability to delineate the forces that have crippled them and often brought them to a point of spiritual or moral crisis. Repeatedly in her fiction, sanctuary is created through her characters' willingness to forge human bonds with each other. Such bonds sometimes generate hope and provide healing, enabling her characters, in the words of Mama Day's father, to "just live on" (*MD*, 266).

Neither *Brewster Place*'s celebration of black women and the bonds they create with each other nor the affirmation and sense of hope symbolized by the black matriarchy of *Mama Day* are evident in either *Linden Hills* or *Bailey's Cafe*. *Mama Day* remains, in fact, Naylor's only novel to date in which the sanctuary she creates actually becomes an alternative world, with values and ways of living that can to some extent be transported to and used in the actual world. Significantly, *Mama Day* is also the single novel in which Naylor's characters can live in the actual world without being seriously crippled by it. In *Bailey's Cafe*, only the invocation of the blues provides relief from the collective horror of the women's lives. Eve assures Daddy Jim that she can return his daughter to him whole, but the novel offers no convincing evidence that wholeness is actually possible for the shattered women whose stories we hear.

Outside the safety of the sanctuary, the world in Naylor's fiction is menacing and corrupt, both morally and spiritually. The possibilities for wholeness and restoration of peace that are so powerfully rendered in *Mama Day* are absent from the other novels. But those possibilities are generated by the economically independent, Afrocentric, female-centric world of Willow Springs—in short, by a utopian universe bearing no resemblance to the actual world. Elsewhere in Naylor's fiction, only sanctuary, not an alternative world, can offer refuge from the nightmarish landscape of American society.

Appendix: A Conversation with Gloria Naylor

The following interview took place between Gloria Naylor and Virginia Fowler in Virginia Fowler's home on 6 September 1993.

Gloria, to what extent do you see yourself as being a political writer?
I don't. I used to call myself a cultural nationalist. People have commented that for some reason racism doesn't really exist in my work, that I seem so very centered on the black community itself. That's simply because the white world is not important to me. I know how it shapes me, how it shapes my family and my community, but it is never uppermost in my mind because self-determination is the most important thing for a community. And taking two steps backward, that is a sort of political statement. Now, had I been of age to be involved in the politics of the sixties, I would not have been an integrationist, I realize that now. I would have been a separatist, although neither of those is the answer. But sitting next to you or going to your school is not what will "better" me as a human being, or even solve my problems. The other way wouldn't have either. So I think my work probably evidences *that*. That's not political writing in the sense that I was taught political writing, you know, the protest novel. If you want to call my work political, I'm willing to live with that definition of its being political. It is just very ethnocentric. And that springs from my own politics.

Do you see yourself as having some sort of prophetic role as an artist?
I see myself more as a filter than I do as a prophet. I see myself—I call myself within my own head a wordsmith. I'm a storyteller, I really am.

That's an interesting shift, then, that I guess has been made possible for you as a black writer by the people who have come before you.
You have to be aware that there is even a problem before you can say to yourself, I will use another strategy at addressing the problem. The problem has to be evoked. When I was in the beginning stages of

143

becoming a feminist, I had to first be made aware that there was a separate entity called *woman*. Period. Then, *black woman*. And then how do I place myself in that whole ideological range. If the women had not come before me to say, hey, you have a different experience, a different history than men, then I could not have even thought of being a feminist. The same thing was true of my coming into consciousness as a black American: people had to have come before to say, there is a voice here. There are things that need to be said. So I could indeed read something like "Ego Tripping" [Nikki Giovanni, 1970] and say, yes, so this is being said.

I asked you whether your writing is political, and it seems to me that it does have very strong feminist impulses.
Yes, it's very female-centered, has been from day one. I've been real clear about that.

Female-centered and feminist? Do you see a difference?
Well, now comes the inevitable question, Ginney, what is my definition of feminism? It is inevitable, because they are not one thing.

There are so many feminisms.
Exactly. Feminism is for me the simple belief that all human beings, regardless of gender, are equal. I believe that there is nothing that should be denied me on this planet that isn't denied any other human being. And I am not determined by an accident of my biology. Feminism to me is political, social, economic equality for all human beings. That's part one. Part two, I must as a feminist celebrate that which is female and love that which is female.

It seems that in a lot of women's texts, biology becomes the determinant.
Because you're writing about women, yes. You're writing about the situation as is. There is an ideal and there is reality. What I would like to believe is that you take two steps back from the work, then perhaps there is a "statement" being made about what I feel about women, although I have just told their stories. But let's face it, it's being told my way. It is.

And they are your women.
And they're filtered through me and everything I do, everything I ate that morning—that whole thing.

Do you think you see women as victims primarily?
Interesting. No. I do see them as powerless to a degree. I see them as
more reactive than active. I would hope I don't see them as victims. I
personally see them as capable of self-determination and perhaps not
always utilizing that capability. Margaret Atwood said that people without hope do not write books. So therefore . . . no, there's always for me
at least some sort of redemption involved. When I think of *Brewster
Place*, which is probably where the best argument could be made for the
idea that my women are victims, even there I saw a little tiny victory in
each of those lives. And to me a victim is someone who is stomped on,
who stays stomped on, who believes she should have been stomped on.
Victims don't fight back. There's no resistance. And I've always seen my
characters—even if they're driven, like the woman in the basement in
Linden Hills, to insanity—as somehow resisting in some way, if the resistance is only then to resort to insanity. I couldn't write otherwise, I
couldn't just leave it like that. It would be too depressing. It's depressing enough.

Yes, you have a lot of horrifying stories to tell about women.
I think we live a lot of horrifying lives.

*In your work, do women have a certain moral superiority—they are not equal to
men, but better?*
I don't know. I would have to think about that. In every book, I've
always had a few women who are heavies. Who are bigots. Or just cruel.
There are a couple in *Brewster Place*—that woman Sophie—who victimize, literally victimize Lorraine and Theresa. And there was Ben's wife.
And those were women who were doing things to women. With *Bailey's
Cafe*, if you want to talk about changes in my perspective, I will grant
you this: it is quite true that in the early days of my coming into feminism, I fell into that school that thought, if we only had a chance we
would do it better because we have known what it's like to be oppressed.
Slowly, with maturity, I have changed; I have seen that when women
have assumed positions of power, they have not handled it better. If anything, they often have attempted to prove that they are better than men
at being hard-nosed and pragmatic.

They become honorary men.
Yes, and that disillusioned me somewhat. And I have been further disillusioned by observing the various ways that children can be abused and

by understanding that often older women are accomplices to that. *Bailey's Cafe* became the work for me where I began to see that women are probably the handmaidens of the oppression. And I think if I were critiquing that book I would see in each of those cases that it is not a man at all—they are not involved at all. It all culminates in that story with "No man has ever touched me." So at one point I did think women were morally superior. I no longer feel that.

Women have certainly participated in the socialization into gender roles of their daughters, their granddaughters, the children around them.
And they have often benefited, you know, from that. When I was looking at the whole concept of "whore," I realized that most women benefit from the fact that we have a delineation for "whore." And sometimes they are conscious that this is going on and they play into it, perpetuate it for their own ends. They are not unknowing accomplices.

To some extent, isn't it about survival? Not only their survival but the survival of the child?
But I feel this way: unless someone has a knife to your throat and your life is at stake, then it's not about survival. And I think there are payoffs, for wives, and women who regard others as whores. That's all. So I'm still a feminist, but I'm a more realistic one now—about the limitations. It's probably more akin to my whole philosophy that all human beings are equal, which means that women are just as capable of being venal as anyone else [*laughter*]. But as a matter of fact, I'm just watching the different ethnic groups in the city in which I live, and you would think that the history of one ethnic group going through oppression would somehow make them more sensitive, and it does not, because that is human nature.

That's something you make so clear in the very first book, with Lorraine and Theresa and the community's response. So suffering does not necessarily give you greater sensitivity to other people who are being abused. You talked about celebrating women, and to me there's a great celebration of woman, of women, of the female, in Mama Day, *but not so in the other novels.*
I don't know. *Bailey's Cafe* is another ball game. But I think in the first one, that was what I set out to do in the first one . . .

to celebrate them?
. . . yes, to celebrate their spirit. You know, I didn't want to paint a fairy tale, but I did want to show them with a spark of hope. Remember

[Langston Hughes's] *Montage of a Dream Deferred*? Well, each of the stories in *The Women of Brewster Place* is about a dream deferred in some way, which means that it gets pretty brutal. However, the women still continue to dream. You know, that's why I end the book the way I do, with the dream and then the little codicil of "Dusk," where the street is still waiting to die. You know, it wasn't to be about anything spectacular. I was trying to celebrate common lives and common love, and the way most women live. For me at that point, the philosophy was, if you do manage to survive, you have committed a victory. So that was all I was trying to do with *Brewster Place* in that regard.

I'm interested in what you see as being religious impulses in your work. Does a religious vision inform your work?
Because religion played such a huge part in my life in my formative years, it would be impossible, I think, for that not to be there, so if people found that there, I would not quibble with it; it does not offend me that it's there. I know there are times when I consciously will use biblical allusions, from *Brewster Place* on—that business about the rain for 40 days is a biblical allusion. This last book [*Bailey's Cafe*], I did nothing but rewrite biblical women, rewrite their lives. I've used it because I think it's a part of me. I find the Bible interesting.

But using the Bible, I mean . . .
That's different from religion?

From having a kind of . . .
But that goes back to a question, I think, Ginney, of do I see myself as some sort of prophet? And I don't. I don't think that I am on a mission.

Do you have a moral vision? Don't you see your fiction as very moral?
Other critics have said that, too. That I ask certain questions in my work, and that they are moral questions. I'm a moral woman, I think.

Do you believe that human nature is essentially corrupt?
No, I believe that within human nature, side by side and intertwined, are the potential for incredible corruption and the potential for incredible heights. But I don't believe that the essential material of human nature is corruption and evil and that we always strive away from that. I don't believe that. I believe that human nature is a mixed suit, that both are there, and that it just simply depends on how you dip into it. That's

what I think. I think that I am capable right now of the most degrading, the most heinous acts that have ever been perpetrated on this earth. I, Gloria Naylor, am capable of doing what Hitler did, of doing what Idi Amin did, I am capable of that.

You, Gloria Naylor?
I, Gloria Naylor, am capable of that, because that is part and parcel of being a human being. That's what I believe. And I believe that I, Gloria Naylor, am capable of what Mother Theresa has done, and what Martin Luther King has done, that that's part and parcel of being a human being. And what we all do, those of us who are not either those demons or those gods, is something that's a mixture in between. But I think it is all there. And why we don't do it, ah. . . . That's what I think is essential human nature. Pure evil and pure good. Truly. I am fascinated by serial killers—people they call the voids, the ones who run around just simply approximating human emotion because they have none. I think those people are the closest to having perhaps 99 percent of their nature being made up of evil. It just fascinates me, that's all. Purity fascinates me. Of whatever sort.

You've talked a lot about the impact that Toni Morrison's The Bluest Eye *had on you. Are there other writers who have been an influence on your writing?*
I aspire to do what James Baldwin did with his career, when all is said and done. Which is to leave behind a moral vision, right or wrong, and a very long and prolific career, and a courageous one. I aspire to do that. It'll be a different set of politics, because indeed it's a different era.

Not to mention the fact that you're a woman and he was a man.
Yes, that too as well. But I wasn't really thinking of that, but that's true. Among writers who affected my work, yes, definitely, direct influences where I have even written against them in my work, would be Faulkner, his whole depiction of the Dilsey character, and the fact that she's based on Caroline Norton. Caroline Norton, he said, was under five feet tall and wouldn't be 99 pounds soaking wet. And he loved this woman, he really did. She was his mother. And the process, the whole social process that turned her into a Dilsey. I wrote against that with Mattie Michael in *Brewster Place*. He has affected me.

Zora Neale Hurston—I have used her spirit for things and her politics about the celebration of the speech of the folk. I did that in *Mama Day*. I have used writers sometimes when I've had a problem, a creative problem, I have gone to them. When I was becoming a feminist, Ntozake Shange and Nikki Giovanni were very important to me, because I started out as a poet. But the very strong black women—these women may not call themselves feminists, but I conceived of them as being so in those years. I identified those as black feminist voices in those years. Now that helped me just with establishing a separate entity in my mind as the black woman. Because remember I told you I built from nothing in the late seventies, I literally built from nothing. So those writers have been important.

What would make a writer decide consciously to rewrite a Dante? Or why do you continue to invoke Shakespeare, and what does he mean to you?
With Dante, it was simply because when I was a sophomore and I read *The Inferno*, there was something about the grotesqueness of those lives that just simply called to me. They were some of the most vivid images that I had read in literature to that date, and I think even to this date. And I think also because it was a whole new spin on hell, and I had dealt with different concepts of hell, and here was a new spin on it that called to me for some reason. Just intellectually, I saw that it would be a perfect fit for what I wanted to say about the black middle class, and to say about life in America for the black middle class. Here was the quintessential mirror image—for some odd reason, mirrors are always important in my work. So when I take it apart I think those are probably the reasons why.

Shakespeare? I had to be 13, because I remember it was the house in Queens and I'd memorize sections of *Romeo and Juliet* and I would be at the bottom to be Romeo and I'd run up the steps to be Juliet. And it was the first play I'd seen, which was before I was 13, because they used to bring "Shakespeare in the Park" to New York. My mom took us over because we lived at 119th Street, and Morningside Park was just two blocks up. My mom took us over to see "Shakespeare in the Park" and the play was *A Midsummer Night's Dream*. Then once in junior high school I saw *Macbeth* performed, and just something about the way in which Shakespeare used language resonated within me. I loved tragedies. I loved the idea that everybody died. And now, in later years, I simply look at that career and I admire it. I've always hoped to be prolific, I never wanted to be just a one-novel person, or even a writer of one type of work. So I admire the span of his career, the things he attempted—not always successfully—and the courage of his vision. He got beyond his little world. Now I grant you, his Romans are like

Elizabethans and his Caribbeans are like Elizabethans and his Norwegians are like Elizabethans and everybody's like Elizabethans—however, he had the courage to dream different worlds. And like I said, with this new book, for some reason Bascombe Wade possesses those original folios. So he's probably about as close as I will get to the source of whatever it is that resonates in Shakespeare.

Perhaps that's a tie-in too to the scenic quality of your work.
Well, the Victorian novels were also important; I read the Brontës at a formative age. I loved the size of those triple-deckers, and also the whole sweep and passion of the stories. I'm always dealing with cataclysmic events, and I walk a thin line. And one day I know I'm going to fall on my face with that—I walk a thin line between drama and melodrama. And often it's just skill that has kept it from tipping over to the edge. My last book is a more mature work; I have learned to evoke emotion quietly. And I see that happening—well, at least *I* see it happening—in *Bailey's Cafe*, where there are quiet moments that are still powerful moments. I'm an old-fashioned writer in that I think novels should tell a story first and foremost.

Why do you give Miss Maple such an important placement in Bailey's Cafe?
Because he and Bailey are bookends to a story that I'm telling about sexuality and sexual identity. The core of the work is indeed the way in which the word *whore* has been used against women or to manipulate female sexual identity. That's the core of the work. However, in order to talk about what is female sexuality and female sexual identity necessitates talking about what is male sexuality and male sexual identity, because you cannot have one without the other. The same way we could not have white people without black people here in America. So that's what Bailey and Miss Maple will do, and Bailey and Miss Maple—if you take them apart, experience by experience—they are antithetical to each other. You know, Bailey went to war, Miss Maple didn't. Bailey was the typical—what would you call him?—man about town, preyer on women. Miss Maple was not. Their classes were different. Their take on history was very different. That's why Miss Maple served what he served to do. He was to say, all right now, hopefully you've subliminal-ly gone through women who would be classified as whores, and the writer's taken you into that word, all around the edges of that word, and even, if I did my job right, in the case of Sadie made that word sing for you, sing beauty for you. Now you will look at what's been going

on: what she's been attempting to do all the way through is to upset your assumptions about what is male or female, what is purity, what is whoredom.

Is Bascombe at all related to a Miss Maple kind of character?
Don't know yet, Ginney. It's too early. I don't know yet how to analyze him because he's being born. I know that I'm fascinated with him, I know that I feel for him. I think it's very sad to be such a gentle, gentle soul in the world in which he must move. That's all I know yet about Bascombe. We have to get to know each other more. I have to show him that I mean him no harm.

He's your first major white character.
He will be the white character that I will give the most space to, yes, to date. That's true. Except that "white" wasn't around then, so he is a Norwegian. See, we had not yet invented white in America.

What kind of audience do you write for?
I don't (and to this date I still haven't, although with each book it gets more difficult) think about who is going to be reading my books. I think that you cannot control popularity. Just from being inside of publishing proper, part of my job is to attempt to predict what people are going to buy, and we spend time arguing about what will people buy and why. It's a crapshoot with any book. The tastes of the public are indeed fickle. So from a commercial standpoint, I think it would be foolish. For a writer—and there are writers who write to sell, and there are writers who write because they feel they are fulfilling something—if I talk about the latter group, I think it would be suicide a little bit to try to write for popular success. But if you want to know what I'm working for, about my ambitions—I have wanted to last. You want to know where my ego is? Yes. I have wanted and desired and prayed and fantasized about being here a hundred years after I am gone. I have wanted my work to last. And I know that that's something I can't control. Politics and publishing, I can't control those. Only time will tell.

And the politics of the people who make canons. I don't think that the best necessarily survives. I don't think that merit alone does it.
I kind of started saying that that's my ambition. To write work that will resonate for many years to come. If I have an ambition, it is that. And my ambition is to be excellent. It truly is. I'm driven that way.

How do you achieve excellence?
By keeping myself as uncorrupted as possible. And maybe that's what I—if I fear anything, I fear that as, indeed, prominence grows. And that's why I kept one editor and followed this editor, because he is an honest man. And because he also cares about my work, he would not let me embarrass myself. I keep this man. Because I was afraid, because success came early, and people will not tell you the truth, and sometimes they don't know the truth themselves, they're blinded by certain things. I will always try to have someone who cares about me, cares about the quality of the work I produce, and will be honest enough to look me in the face.

Let's shift gears for a moment. What kind of narrative structure will "Sapphira Wade" have?
I think the next novel is going to be from two different perspectives, if not three, you know, because there will be Miss Ophelia. I know that their voices will emerge through the elements to her because there are no written documents. I know I will have two distinct voices, if not three, because Sapphira—you know Sapphira is Scheherazade, you've probably already figured that out. I see somewhat that there will be different voices in "Sapphira Wade," but for different reasons than *Mama Day*. *Mama Day* had to have those voices because I was making a commentary about reality and truth, among other things. When this interview lives in our minds, it will live in two totally different worlds, two totally different perspectives, and what is the truth? None of it and all of it. And that's what I was attempting to do with that. One of the things I was attempting to do—I was doing a lot of stuff. Faulkner was in that, in the structure of that. *As I Lay Dying*.

Yes, I remember you've said that.
It's true, it's literally what I had to read to get over the hump. Because I was trying to write that book in third-person past tense. Trying to do it. And it was not coming. But I could have, I know how to write third-person past tense. I could have pushed out this story third-person past tense.

But it wouldn't have been the same book.
There you go, there you go! It was a living resistance, and I had to say, there's something here greater than me, there's something I am not doing. I'm not doing it. What's wrong? And so you stop, you stop and

say, well, I don't know what's wrong. I was in Guadalajara visiting my girlfriend Andrea. I was depressed, and so I went walking. I knew that each embassy has a library, I knew that from being stranded in places all over the world. And I went shuffling through books to get something to read. And I said, oh, I've never read *As I Lay Dying,* and I'd heard that that was sort of his six-week wonder. And then it was like, *aha.*

Gloria, could you talk about One Way Productions *and the projects you're trying to do there?*
One Way Productions is basically about self-determination and being able to control the production of images to a larger audience. The intent is to reach as many people as possible with these images. I realized that so often we are just the producers of things and we rarely control our own talents. So now I do. I just legally control anything that happens to my own personal work beyond its being in book form, because it belongs to my company. I want to present positive images of the black community to as many people in America and the world as possible. That's the goal. It is an extension of what I do when I write except that it's a public business so you get as many people as possible involved.

So that's where your political activism comes in.
Maybe in a way—it's cultural activism. But with my novels, that's a whole other area—maybe it *is* sacred. If you want to know about religion, my novel-writing is sacred territory. It's another place, you see, because I know how my sanity was saved that way. And I'm going to protect that. I know how I remain sane, and no one touches that. I do what I can to preserve that. But yes, with One Way Productions, it's to reach people. And make lots of money! [laughter]

I wanted to ask a question about Brewster Place. *You seem to suggest, with your treatment of Mattie and her relationship to Basil, that somehow the mothers have to answer for the punks that we're getting. And does Basil have a relation to Eugene or C. C. Baker?*
I think that Eugene and Basil might be closer to each other in my mind than they are to C. C. Baker, because they perpetuated a certain violence against people who loved them, who had made them, in a sense, what they were. I'm not saying that single mothers are responsible for crime in the streets. But I do believe this: that they are responsible for how their sons perceive women. And perceive of themselves as men. Mattie,

I held her accountable for the monster that she had created. There were warnings that she was given.

Yes, Eva tries to tell her.
Yes. Even the child's father in a dream—the whole business of the sugar cane was about that—he's saying, let go, you can't get all that sweetness. I was making a comment about, in a sense, bad mothering, but that was part of what I told you about writing against Faulkner and Dilsey. I created an Earth Mother, and I wanted an anti–Earth Mother in that regard, so by the time Mattie serves her Dilsey function on Brewster Place, she's been given the things Faulkner never gave his Dilsey. She's been given a sexuality, she's been given a sort of ulterior motive for mothering, and it's selfishness on her part. She wanted to *keep* him.

C. C. Baker was a different case. I remember deliberately taking the narrative risk with that rape to stop the action (now that's Victorian), to stop the action—it's two paragraphs long—and to explain why that young man is raping her and to point the finger toward society and their definition of manhood. It was real clear to me. Because today I would not do that. If I were writing that scene today, I would just write it. But I remember consciously saying—now here's where I undercut my own statement—because that's a place where I remember consciously saying, I don't want anyone to read this and think—because, see, I had a problem with Susan Brownmiller's book *Against Our Wills* (that was the sort of hot book at that point), a real problem with how she treated black men in that work. And I said, I don't want anyone to read this and think that black men rape, that they just rape because of whatever. I wanted them to see that what's raping this woman, among other things, is society's conception of manhood, and their low evaluation of women. And no, I don't connect that at all to mothering, to how C. C. Baker was mothered. It was how he was taught he could be a man by society.

Yes, you make that very clear.
Yes, and outside of that novel, in my own politics, I don't think that single mothers are the reason why we have so much crime. But I *do* think that mothers, either single or married, are part of the reason why women are not thought of better by young men, I really do. And I'm not going to back off from that.

You're right that you do give it a very clear social causal analysis. And yet—and maybe it's just my failure as a reader—when I meet C. C. Baker, to me he is a

more extreme form of Eugene and of Basil, and so maybe I'm making the mistake
of seeing those three as having similarities.
I would not see them as the same because Mattie's son, and I knew him
fairly well, he could not rape. He was just selfish, he was spoiled. He
didn't hate women. Rape is an act of hatred. He loved his mother. Basil
loved his mother. He loved her in the way he had been taught to love
her, to love her as a provider of his needs. To love her as a something that
would empty itself to his ends. She was loved for the function that she
provided, and that was his total cushioning and gratification. He did
love her. He would not have raped a woman. I don't know what C. C.
Baker's parents were like. The life of a C. C. Baker—he could not have
had Mattie for a mother. Those people trouble me. Eugene—I don't
know about Eugene. Eugene was not a well-drawn character. That was
my first, my very first story. I could have given him, I think, with perhaps more skill and more empathy a bit more depth than he has.

Were you too hard on the men in The Women of Brewster Place*?*
That's an early work. I think if you want to know how I feel about that
subject, the last work is probably more telling of my present feelings on
the whole subject. There the men, if they do fail, they are well meaning
in their failures. Bailey, even though you call him a sexist, he's the only
one who will not judge what's going on at Eve's.

I like Bailey.
I think my attitude toward men would probably be closer to what I did
in *Bailey's Cafe*, as well as my attitude toward women.

Do you believe that readers get from your work what you hope they will?
Well, what surprised me with *Linden Hills* is that no one quite got it. I
don't think most people did. But then again, I haven't been analyzed
that much. But as far as I'm concerned, that was my masterwork.

Linden Hills?
Yes. It really was. And I'm really waiting for people to go to *The Inferno*
and go to my work and see what I did as far as images and the terza
rima. No one has gotten it yet. Granted, I bobble the terza rima just a
tiny bit toward the end of the book, but for a good seven-eighths of it, I
have re-created through images what he did through rhyme schemes.
And no one has seen it. And the colors, and how I play with colors, no
one has gotten it yet.

I'll tell you the kind of kid I was. Before my parents discovered that I
was as bright as I was, I used to love to watch adults play out their lives,
and I would know more than I let on that I knew and then proceed into
their fantasy of what was actually going on, and I would like that feeling
of going "ahh." That's why I love irony. A feeling of superiority. Or a
feeling even that you don't control me. I've hated always to be controlled. You don't control me, and childhood is by definition a helpless
position. Anyway. So a little bit of my watching what's happened with
Linden Hills and hasn't happened with *Linden Hills* has been that kind of
thing, like, "You don't know what I really did with that work." I think
that maybe in time—if I'm still around—in time someone will figure
out what happened with that book and Dante's *Inferno*. Besides what's
really obvious. In general, people have never gotten it, as far as what I
do with colors. And I don't think that they're so obscure—you know,
some symbols can be self-serving—but that they are actually an integral
part. I was on tour with *Mama Day*, I think, and this woman said, "I
read *Linden Hills*, and you didn't have a lot of editorial help, did you?"
[*laughter*]. But just for the record, I've never rewritten a book, or an ending, or whatever, because of editorial intrusion. What readers have from
me is truly my own vision.

Do you show the manuscript in process?
I wait until I'm through. I did that once. I took a contract on *Linden
Hills* mid-book because of my insecurity. I said, I wonder if this is any
good. And then my editor left Viking Press, and the contract was with
Viking Press. *Linden Hills* was finally published by Ticknor & Fields, but
I had to go through all kinds of permutations—got rid of an agent
because of that whole mess—to have this book with this man at the new
house, which was Ticknor & Fields. So after that I said, unless I am literally starving and cannot get another switchboard job, they're never seeing anything from me until I'm ready to have it published. I'll *read* from
a work in progress, I enjoy doing that, because you never know. I think
it's funny—do they think it's funny? I think this is riveting—do they
think it's riveting? That I will share. That comes from the old habit
when I was in college of reading your poetry and stuff to people. The
times I enjoy the most reading my work is when it's in progress. For
example, with *Bailey's Cafe*, because it is now in paperback, I'll have to
do a little small mini-tour again with it. That will be the least pleasurable reading of the work—after it's old. What I'm eager now to do is to
read new work to people.

What do you read from Bailey's Cafe?
I will read Esther's story and then go on to read Jesse's story. Because one is so intense, and one is kind of funny and revealing.

Notes and References

Chapter 1

1. Gloria Naylor, "Telling Tales and Mississippi Sunsets," in *Grand Mothers: Poems, Reminiscences, and Short Stories about the Keepers of Our Traditions*, ed. Nikki Giovanni (New York: Henry Holt, 1994), 59; hereafter cited in text as "Telling."

2. From a conversation with the author, 5 September 1993.

3. Gloria Naylor, "Reflections," in *Centennial*, ed. Michael Rosenthal (New York: Pindar Press, 1986), 68; hereafter cited in text as "Reflections."

4. Gloria Naylor, "Of Fathers and Sons: A Daughter Remembers," in *In Their Footsteps*, ed. Henry Chase (New York: Henry Holt, 1994), 5.

5. Mateo Bellinelli, dir., RTSJ-Swiss Television, prod., *A Conversation with Gloria Naylor* (videotape), California Newsreel, 1992; hereafter cited in text as Bellinelli.

6. Angels Carabi, [Interview with Gloria Naylor], *Belles Lettres* 7 (Spring 1992): 36; hereafter cited in text.

7. From a conversation with the author, 5 September 1993.

8. Gloria Naylor, [untitled "Hers" column], *New York Times*, 20 February 1986.

9. Gloria Naylor, [untitled], in *Writers Dreaming*, ed. Naomi Epel (New York: Carol Southern Books, 1993), 176; hereafter cited in text as *Dreaming*.

10. Mickey Pearlman and Katherine Usher Henderson, *A Voice of One's Own: Conversations with America's Writing Women* (Boston: Houghton Mifflin, 1990), 32; hereafter cited in text.

11. Kay Bonetti, "An Interview with Gloria Naylor" (New York: American Prose Library, 1988), audiotape; hereafter cited in text.

12. From a conversation with the author, 5 September 1993.

13. Heather Botting and Gary Botting, *The Orwellian World of Jehovah's Witnesses* (Toronto: University of Toronto Press, 1984), xxxiv; hereafter cited in text.

14. Milton G. Henschel, "Who Are Jehovah's Witnesses?" in *Religions of America*, ed. Leo Rosten (New York: Simon & Schuster, 1975), 132; hereafter cited in text.

15. Barbara Grizzuti Harrison, *Visions of Glory: A History and a Memory of Jehovah's Witnesses* (New York: Simon & Schuster, 1978), 13; hereafter cited in text.

16. Kimberly Rae Connor, *Conversions and Visions in the Writings of African-American Women* (Knoxville: University of Tennessee Press, 1994), 18.

17. From a conversation with the author, 5 September 1993.

18. "Gloria Naylor and Toni Morrison: A Conversation," *Southern Review* 21 (1985): 567; hereafter cited in text as "Conversation."

19. From a conversation with the author, 5 September 1993.

20. Ibid.

21. Naylor's marriage lasted only a short time. In my conversation with her of 5 September 1993, she stated that she does not believe in marriage.

22. Henry Louis Gates, Jr., preface to *Gloria Naylor: Critical Perspectives Past and Present*, ed. Henry Louis Gates, Jr., and K. A. Appiah (New York: Amistad, 1993), ix.

23. Gloria Naylor, "Love and Sex in the Afro-American Novel," *Yale Review* 78 (1988): 20; hereafter cited in text as "Love."

24. Deborah E. McDowell, "'The Changing Same': Generational Connections and Black Women Novelists," *New Literary History* 18 (1987): 297; hereafter cited in text.

25. Barbara Christian, "Trajectories of Self-definition: Placing Contemporary Afro-American Women's Fiction," in *Conjuring: Black Women, Fiction, and Literary Tradition*, ed. Marjorie Pryse and Hortense J. Spillers (Bloomington: Indiana University Press, 1985), 237; hereafter cited in text.

26. Mary Helen Washington, foreword to *Their Eyes Were Watching God* by Zora Neale Hurston (New York: Harper & Row, 1990), x.

27. Toni Cade, preface to *The Black Woman: An Anthology* (New York: New American Library, 1970), 9.

28. Deborah E. McDowell, "Boundaries; or, Distant Relations and Close Kin," in *Afro-American Literary Study in the 1990s*, ed. Houston A. Baker, Jr., and Patricia Redmond (Chicago: University of Chicago Press, 1989), 53; hereafter cited in text.

29. Sarah Blackburn, [review of *Sula* by Toni Morrison], *New York Times Book Review*, December 30, 1973, reprinted in *Toni Morrison: Critical Perspectives Past and Present*, ed. Henry Louis Gates, Jr., and K. A. Appiah (New York: Amistad, 1993), 8.

30. Deborah E. McDowell, "Reading Family Matters," in *Changing Our Own Words: Essays on Criticism, Theory, and Writing by Black Women*, ed. Cheryl A. Wall (New Brunswick, N.J.: Rutgers University Press, 1989), 77; hereafter cited in text.

31. In his review of Giovanni's *My House* (1972), Kalamu Ya Salaam (Val Ferdinand) deplored the new directions Giovanni was taking in her poetry and attributed the problem to her inability to find a man: "I betcha Nikki wanted to be married." See review of *My House* and *Like a Ripple on a Pond*, *Black World* (July 1974): 65.

32. Robert Staples, "The Myth of Black Macho: A Response to Angry Black Feminists," *Black Scholar* (March/April 1979): 26.

33. Mel Watkins, "Sexism, Racism, and Black Women Writers," *New*

York Times Book Review, 15 June 1986, 35–36; hereafter cited in text.

34. Langston Hughes, "The Negro Artist and the Racial Mountain," in *The Portable Harlem Renaissance Reader*, ed. David Levering Lewis (New York: Viking/Penguin, 1994), 95.

35. Barbara Smith, "Black Feminist Criticism," in *All the Women Are White, All the Blacks Are Men, But Some of Us Are Brave*, ed. Gloria T. Hull, Patricia Bell Scott, and Barbara Smith (New York: Feminist Press, 1982), 159.

Chapter 2

1. Naylor stated in her interview with Bonetti that "I was a great starter but I never finished; I was one of those people who had a very low threshold for pain. So when the going got rough in anything, I would just get going. I had begun a career as a minister, which I didn't finish. I had begun a marriage, which I didn't finish. I had started school . . . I didn't know whether or not I would finish *that*."

2. According to Jacqueline Bobo and Ellen Seiter, "approximately forty-seven million viewers watched the programme the first night and approximately forty-nine million the second. The share numbers indicate that more than one-third of the viewing audience was tuned into *The Women of Brewster Place*." See their "Black Feminism and Media Criticism: *The Women of Brewster Place*," *Screen* 32, no. 3 (Autumn 1991): 293, n. 22.

3. For a discussion of the relation of the novel to *The Bluest Eye* and *Cane*, see Michael Awkward, *Inspiriting Influences: Tradition, Revision, and Afro-American Women's Novels* (New York: Columbia University Press, 1989), 97–134; hereafter cited in text. For connections to *The Street*, see James Robert Saunders, "The Ornamentation of Old Ideas: Gloria Naylor's First Three Novels," *Hollins Critic* 27, no. 2 (April 1990): 1–11.

4. From a conversation with the author, 5 September 1993.

5. Awkward (100) argues that Naylor's opening sentence echoes the first sentence of *Cane*'s "Seventh Street": "Seventh Street is a bastard of Prohibition and War."

6. Gloria Naylor, *The Women of Brewster Place: A Novel in Seven Stories* (New York: Penguin, 1983), 1; all references are to the Penguin edition, hereafter cited in text as *BP*.

7. Kathryn Palumbo, "The Uses of Female Imagery in Naylor's *The Women of Brewster Place*," *Notes on Contemporary Literature* 15 (May 1985): 6.

8. Toni Morrison, "City Limits, Village Values: Concepts of the Neighborhood in Black Fiction," in *Literature and the Urban Experience*, ed. Michael C. Jaye and Ann Chalmers Watts (New Brunswick, N.J.: Rutgers University Press, 1981), 37.

9. Awkward (124–27) discusses Naylor's departure in this regard from such precursor texts as *The Bluest Eye* and *Their Eyes Were Watching God*.

10. Susan Meisenhelder, "'Eating Cane' in Gloria Naylor's *The Women of Brewster Place* and Zora Neale Hurston's 'Sweat,'" *Notes on Contemporary Literature* 23, no. 2 (March 1993): 6. Meisenhelder's argument seems to be further undercut by Naylor's use of similar imagery in relation to Miranda on the closing page of *Mama Day*.

11. Barbara Christian reaches a similar conclusion in "Naylor's Geography: Community, Class, and Patriarchy in *The Women of Brewster Place* and *Linden Hills*," in *Reading Black, Reading Feminist*, ed. Henry Louis Gates, Jr. (New York: Meridian/Penguin, 1990), 355; hereafter cited in text.

12. Naylor has said that, since she has never been a mother, she "worried about whether I could write about a mother. So I talked to several friends, one of them being Amanda, a single parent who has two children. I could tell that the boy was her heart. It's not that she loved one child more than the other, but she had that attraction for her son. I never forgot what she told me: 'I think the boy is so special to you because you know that's the one man that could never leave you.' This is how Mattie's story got structured. She lost her father, and Butch, her lover, but she could keep this boy" (Carabi, 38).

13. Ebele Eko makes a similar point in her "Beyond the Myth of Confrontation: A Comparative Study of African and African-American Female Protagonists," *Ariel* 17 (October 1986): 147; hereafter cited in text.

14. Ciel's splitting as a way of avoiding responsibility for the abortion is similar to the web of lies constructed by the nameless narrator of Margaret Atwood's *Surfacing* (1972). Atwood's narrator rewrites the history of her abortion in order, like Ciel, to avoid responsibility for it.

15. See, for example, Awkward (116–19), and Larry R. Andrews, "Black Sisterhood in Gloria Naylor's Novels," *CLA Journal* 33 (1989): 5–6; hereafter cited in text.

16. Celeste Fraser, "Stealing B(l)ack Voices: The Myth of the Black Matriarchy and *The Women of Brewster Place*," *Critical Matrix* 5 (Fall/Winter 1989), reprinted in Gates and Appiah, *Gloria Naylor*, 96; hereafter cited in text.

17. Peter Erickson, "'Shakespeare's Black?': The Role of Shakespeare in Naylor's Novels," in his *Rewriting Shakespeare, Rewriting Ourselves* (Berkeley: University of California Press, 1991), reprinted in Gates and Appiah, *Gloria Naylor*, 233; hereafter cited in text.

18. Jill L. Matus, "Dream, Deferral, and Closure in *The Women of Brewster Place*," *Black American Literature Forum* 24 (1990): 56; hereafter cited in text.

19. Charles Johnson, *Being and Race: Black Writing since 1970* (Bloomington: Indiana University Press, 1988), 110.

20. Barbara Christian, in her discussion of "The Two," points out that "Naylor captures in one succinct utterance the community's evaluation of the right kind of woman as *nice*, as *girl*. She emphasizes how *nice* for single women means appearing nonsexual." Barbara Christian, *Black Feminist Criticism* (New

York: Pergamon Press, 1985), 191; hereafter cited in text.

21.   Barbara Smith, "The Truth That Never Hurts: Lesbians in Fiction in the 1980s," in *Wild Women in the Whirlwind: Afra-American Culture and the Contemporary Literary Renaissance*, ed. Joanne M. Braxton and Andrée Nicola McLaughlin (New Brunswick, N.J.: Rutgers University Press, 1990), 225; hereafter cited in text.

22.   Helen Fiddyment Levy, *Fiction of the Home Place: Jewett, Cather, Glasgow, Porter, Welty, and Naylor* (Jackson: University Press of Mississippi, 1992), 199; hereafter cited in text.

Chapter 3

1.   The connection between *Linden Hills* and *Mama Day* is through Willa Prescott Nedeed, whose great-aunt is Miranda Day. The connection between *Mama Day* and *Bailey's Cafe* is through George, one of the main characters in *Mama Day*: his birth is recorded in *Bailey's Cafe*, and his place of birth, referred to in *Mama Day*, gives *Bailey's Cafe* its title. Irene Jackson, who directs the boys' home in which George grows up, also appears in both *Mama Day* and *Bailey's Cafe*.

2.   Naylor remarked in her interview with Bonetti that she "liked Mrs. Browne so much after her appearance in *Brewster Place* that I couldn't put her too far down in hell. The Brownes are sort of in that place that corresponds to Dante's place of unbaptized pagans."

3.   Gloria Naylor, letter to the author, 5 August 1994.

4.   Dante Alighieri, *Inferno*, in *The Divine Comedy*, trans. Thomas G. Bergin (New York: Appleton-Century-Crofts, 1955), 3.35, 38; hereafter cited in text.

5.   Gloria Naylor, *Linden Hills* (New York: Penguin, 1986), 1; all references are to the Penguin edition, hereafter cited in text as *LH*.

6.   This point is also made by Catherine C. Ward in her useful analysis of Naylor's use of Dante, "Gloria Naylor's *Linden Hills*: A Modern Inferno," *Contemporary Literature* 28 (1987): 72; hereafter cited in text.

7.   Naylor makes this equation in an interview with Cromie, cited in Ward (70n).

8.   Willie and Lester both have nicknames derived from their skin color. Willie is ironically dubbed "White" because he is "so black that the kids said if he turned just a shade darker, there was nothing he could do but start going the other way" (*LH*, 24). Lester's nickname of "Shit" derives from "the milky-yellow tone in his skin," which a ninth-grader says looks like "Baby Shit" (*LH*, 24).

9.   Quoted in Thomas G. Bergin, *Dante* (Boston: Houghton Mifflin, 1965), 251; hereafter cited in text.

10.   The roman numerals distinguishing the Nedeed men are my designations, not Naylor's.

11. Luke Bouvier, "Reading in Black and White: Space and Race in *Linden Hills*," in Gates and Appiah, *Gloria Naylor*, 142; hereafter cited in text.

12. See Hans Biedermann, *Dictionary of Symbolism: Cultural Icons and the Meanings behind Them*, trans. James Hulbert (New York: Facts on File, 1992), 58; hereafter cited in text.

13. Teresa Goddu, "Reconstructing History in *Linden Hills*," in Gates and Appiah, *Gloria Naylor*, 216; hereafter cited in text.

14. Luther and Willa's son's name is concealed until the end of the novel, when we learn that "his father had said that he didn't care what she called him, so she had taught him to spell Sinclair" (*LH*, 294). It is not the case, as Bouvier claims (150), that Willa *names* the child at the end of the novel.

15. Henry Louis Gates, Jr., "Significant Others," *Contemporary Literature* 29 (1988): 609.

16. See *Juba to Jive: A Dictionary of African-American Slang*, ed. Clarence Major (New York: Penguin, 1994), 351.

17. A similar point is made by Missy Dehn Kubitschek in *Claiming the Heritage: African American Women Novelists and History* (Jackson: University Press of Mississippi, 1991), 124.

18. I am grateful to Professor John N. Moore for sharing his insightful working paper on this scene with me.

19. Alice Walker, *In Search of Our Mothers' Gardens* (New York: Harcourt Brace & Co., 1983), 250–51.

20. An entire essay could be devoted to Naylor's use of numbers in this novel. I note here that Luwana's 665 cuts on her body correspond to the 665 poems Willie has memorized (some of them his own). The biblical sign of the beast is 666. Luwana's conclusion that "there can be no God" appears to be simultaneous with the 666th cut she makes. Willie creates the first line of the 666th poem of his repertoire near the end of the novel: "There is a man in a house at the bottom of a hill. And his wife has no name."

21. Significantly, this passage is followed by the funeral of Lycentia Parker, a scene in which we see Luther carefully making last-minute touches to the corpse (*LH*, 175, 184–85). Luther's perversity is further suggested by Willie's horrified shudder when he glimpses Luther bending over Lycentia's coffin (*LH*, 186).

22. Willa's experience of seeking her reflection in the pot of water—and the ensuing peace it brings her—recalls the experience of Shadrack in Morrison's *Sula*: "He had been harboring a skittish apprehension that he was not real—that he didn't exist at all. But when the blackness greeted him with its indisputable presence, he wanted nothing more." Toni Morrison, *Sula* (New York: Alfred A. Knopf, 1973), 13.

23. Margaret Homans, "The Woman in the Cave: Recent Feminist Fictions and the Classical Underworld," *Contemporary Literature* 29 (1988): 396. Homans adds that "it is striking that the novel institutes no countertradition of strong womanhood to oppose the destructive legacy of patriarchy" (396).

24. I disagree with Ward's claim that Willie "becomes, as his name implies, a decisive builder" (69). At the end of the novel, Willie is in flight from the horrors he has witnessed, and there is no suggestion that he goes forth to create a different kind of space.

25. Naylor herself has said that she was dismayed that Willa reclaimed her roles of wife and mother: "When I put Willa in that basement my overall idea was to have this very conservative upper-middle class black woman through her discovery of all those remnants from the past wives who'd lived in that house, just get up, walk out of there and say, 'No, this is shallow. This is not for me.' I wanted her to learn from those lessons in history. But what eventually evolved through all the pain that she went through was the discovery that she liked being where she was—a conventional housewife. . . . That was a real surprise to me; I hadn't planned on the character doing that" ("Conversation," 572–73).

Chapter 4

1. Gloria Naylor, *Mama Day* (New York: Vintage/Random House, 1989), 311; all references are to the Vintage edition, hereafter cited in text as *MD*.

2. Naylor also commented in the Bonetti interview that Gabriel García Márquez's *One Hundred Years of Solitude* (1967) "influenced just a tiny bit the opening of *Linden Hills*."

3. Lindsey Tucker, "Recovering the Conjure Woman: Texts and Contexts in Gloria Naylor's *Mama Day*," *African-American Review* 28 (Summer 1994): 180; hereafter cited in text.

4. Elaine Showalter, *Sister's Choice: Tradition and Change in American Women's Writing* (New York: Clarendon/Oxford, 1991), 28; hereafter cited in text.

5. Valerie Traub, "Rainbows of Darkness: Deconstructing Shakespeare in the Work of Gloria Naylor and Zora Neale Hurston," in *Cross-cultural Performances: Differences in Women's Re-Visions of Shakespeare*, ed. Marianne Novy (Urbana and Chicago: University of Illinois Press, 1993), 154; hereafter cited in text.

6. Naylor said in her interview with me (see appendix) that Sapphira also invokes the figure of Scheherazade, an association also remarked by Showalter (40).

7. For discussions of the African belief systems at work in the novel, see Tucker, "Conjure Woman," and Ralph Reckley, Sr., "Science, Faith, and Religion in Gloria Naylor's *Mama Day*," in *Twentieth-Century Black American Women in Print: Essays by Ralph Reckley, Sr.*, ed. Lola E. Jones (Acton, Mass.: Copley Publishing Group, 1991), 87–95.

8. One of Naylor's jokes in the novel is her extensive use of Reema's children, usually either to mitigate the idyllic quality of life on the island or to suggest the corruptive power of the mainland. For example, Ruby is believed

to have killed her first husband because "he kept messing with that little loose gal of Reema's" (*MD*, 69). Dr. Smithfield's receptionist, who has forgotten "how to talk to folks," is Sue Henry, "the runt of Reema's litter" (*MD*, 77). Carmen Rae, the neglectful mother whose baby suffers from croup, is "Reema's oldest gal" (*MD*, 192). And Carmen Rae's husband, Rickshaw, is "a pitiful specimen of a man" who spends the money Reema gives his family playing cards with Dr. Buzzard (*MD*, 192, 209). The breech birth of Reema's oldest boy was the occasion of one of Mama Day's two surgeries; although "them stitches on Reema's stomach was neat as a pin and she never set up a fever" (*MD*, 84), we might wonder whether this oldest boy is the ethnographer "with the pear-shaped head."

     9.   Suzanne Juhasz, *Reading from the Heart: Women, Literature, and the Search for True Love* (New York: Viking/Penguin, 1994), 184; hereafter cited in text.

     10.   Margot Anne Kelley, "Sisters' Choices: Quilting Aesthetics in Contemporary African American Women's Fiction," in *Quilt Culture: Tracing the Pattern*, ed. Cheryl B. Torsney and Judith Elsley (Columbia: University of Missouri Press, 1994), 66, 53.

     11.   Houston A. Baker, Jr., and Charlotte Pierce-Baker, "Patches: Quilts and Community in Alice Walker's 'Everyday Use,'" in *"Everyday Use": Alice Walker*, ed. Barbara T. Christian (New Brunswick, N.J.: Rutgers University Press, 1994), 149.

     12.   Toni Morrison, *Tar Baby* (New York: New American Library, 1981), 269; hereafter cited in text as *Tar Baby*.

     13.   One might further speculate that Naylor's creation of the Days is on one level a response to Morrison's *Song of Solomon*, in particular to the Seven Days in that novel. Morrison's Seven Days is an all-male group that avenges white killings of black people through the random murder of whites.

     14.   Gloria Naylor, "Sexual Ease," *Essence* (December 1988): 108.

     15.   Tea Cake's death, at Janie's hand, is necessitated by the madness that overtakes him as a result of the rabies he contracts saving Janie's life. If she does not kill him, he will kill her. This plot contrivance may be interpreted as Hurston's oblique method of dealing with Tea Cake's beating of Janie, about which Janie is curiously silent. See Mary Helen Washington, "'I Love the Way Janie Crawford Left Her Husbands': Zora Neale Hurston's Emergent Female Hero," in her *Invented Lives: Narratives of Black Women 1860–1960* (New York: Doubleday, 1987), 237–54.

     16.   Susan Meisenhelder, "'The Whole Picture' in Gloria Naylor's *Mama Day*," *African-American Review* 27 (1993): 405; hereafter cited in text.

     17.   In *Bailey's Cafe*, we learn that George was misinformed about his mother.

     18.   Traub severely criticizes George's sensitivity, which she examines from the perspective of his identification with Edmund. Although Traub's analysis of Naylor's re-visioning of Shakespeare's *King Lear* is valuable, she is

perhaps harsher than Naylor herself on this point: "In the novel and in the world at this time, blackness has a political basis for oppression, resistance, and community in a way that being a father-rejected child does not" (Traub, 160). Traub overlooks—as does George—the historical realities that make "legitimacy" an important political aspect of black oppression.

19.   In light of the novel's extensive use of the image of hands, which I discuss at the end of the chapter, this description of George is one of many that make his death a genuine loss.

20.   Naylor's repeated use of the phrase "cross over" to describe passage from the mainland to Willow Springs resonates with meaning. Its roots lie in such spirituals as "Deep River," in which it expresses the slaves' yearning to return again to their African home across the Atlantic Ocean. More recently, the term is used by African Americans to refer to enduring "the secret ritual that initiates one into a fraternity or sorority"; George's failed initiation into the world of Willow Springs seems to invoke this meaning of the phrase. For current usage, see Geneva Smitherman, *Black Talk: Words and Phrases from the Hood to the Amen Corner* (Boston: Houghton Mifflin, 1994), 127.

21.   As Cocoa explains to George, owing to "some kind of crazy clause in our deed," the land is "always owned two generations down. That's to keep any Day from selling it." Even though Cocoa is "two generations down," the land automatically passed to her children when she was born. When George wonders what would happen if Cocoa never has children, Cocoa says, "I guess it reverts back to the original owner" (*MD*, 219). Mama Day's protracted life is due in part to her desire to make sure Cocoa has children.

22.   Naylor makes yet another connection between her novels through the "peace" that eludes the Days. In *Linden Hills*, Willa Nedeed also finds peace after she has come to terms with history and acknowledged to herself who she is. Willa is Cocoa's cousin; in her job interview with George, Cocoa tells him about the fire that killed Willa and Luther.

23.   Bonnie Winsbro, *Supernatural Forces: Belief, Difference, and Power in Contemporary Works by Ethnic Women* (Amherst: University of Massachusetts Press, 1993), 21.

24.   Mary E. Young, *Mules and Dragons: Popular Culture Images in the Selected Writings of African-American and Chinese-American Women Writers* (Westport, Conn.: Greenwood Press, 1993), 39.

25.   bell hooks, *Black Looks: Race and Representation* (Boston: South End Press, 1992), 120.

26.   Gloria Naylor, [untitled], in *I Know What the Red Clay Looks Like: The Voice and Vision of Black Women Writers*, ed. Rebecca Carroll (New York: Crown Trade Paperbacks, 1994), 161.

27.   Naylor's use of this image in the novel parallels in many ways the celebration of women's hands in Nikki Giovanni's poem "Hands: For Mother's Day," in her *Those Who Ride the Night Winds* (New York: Morrow, 1983), 16–18.

Chapter 5

1. David Streitfield, "A Writer at Last," *Washington Post Book World*, October 11, 1992, 15.

2. Gloria Naylor, *Bailey's Cafe* (New York: Vintage/Random House, 1993), 143; all references are to the Vintage edition, hereafter cited in text as *BC*.

3. In the program notes to the stage production of *Bailey's Cafe*, Naylor explicitly describes Bailey's Cafe as "more of an experience than a place. It exists in the space where the human heart makes the ultimate decision to either die— or dream." *Bailey's Cafe: Hartford Stage Program* (Hartford, Conn.: Parker Media, 1994), 7.

4. From the taped workshop offered by Gloria Naylor and Novella Nelson at the Hartford Stage Company on 24 April 1994.

5. J. C. J. Metford, *Dictionary of Christian Lore and Legend* (London: Thames and Hudson, 1983), 96.

6. I am excluding the supporting characters, Nadine and Sister Carrie, who, like Sadie, do not seem to be based on biblical women; nor are they, of course, among Eve's boarders.

7. The novel suggests that Sadie continues to live but that Iceman Jones does not. Bailey begins Sadie's story by saying that he has not seen "her any this summer, but she was a regular here for a while" (*BC*, 39). At the end of the story, Sadie leaves Iceman Jones "standing in the middle of the pier" behind the cafe, while she herself "retrieved her satchel" and left (*BC*, 78). Since Iceman Jones was greatly affected by Sadie, his death may be what the text is suggesting; this interpretation would also explain Bailey's statement that "the story really gets sad" when Iceman Jones enters it (*BC*, 68). Naylor may also intend a connection to Eugene O'Neill's "Iceman" of death. In the stage version, Sadie and Iceman Jones dance away into the void and do not return.

8. There are many obvious ways in which Bailey and Miss Maple counterpoint each other: Bailey has only a high school education, Miss Maple has a Ph.D.; Bailey fought in the war, Miss Maple was a conscientious objector; Bailey is a native New Yorker, Miss Maple is from California; Bailey's parents were working-class, Miss Maple's parents were wealthy landowners. Interestingly, we do not know Bailey's real name, nor do we know Miss Maple's surname, although we know his real first and many middle names: Stanley Beckwourth Booker T. Washington Carver.

9. Miss Maple may have been inspired by the character of Carl in Richard Wright's "Man of All Work" (in his collection *Eight Men* [1961]). In the story, Carl, who has lost his job and cannot find another, decides to wear his wife's clothes and apply for a position as a housekeeper. Naylor refers explicitly to Carl in her essay "The Myth of the Matriarch," *Life* 11 (Spring 1988): 65.

10. Jesse Bell and Esther are, to a small extent, exceptions. Jesse draws attention to the class distinctions between her family and the Kings; she notes,

for example, that the King family objected to the "slave food" eaten by the Bell family. Esther's fondness for white roses seems to be related to the fact that "they show up in the dark," whereas she does not because she is "the black gal. Monkey face. Tar. Coal. Ugly. Soot. Unspeakable. Pitch" (*BC*, 95).

11. Peter Erickson, [review of *Bailey's Café*], *Kenyon Review* 15 (Summer 1993), reprinted in Gates and Appiah, *Gloria Naylor*, 34.

12. Ralph Ellison, "Richard Wright's Blues," in his *Shadow and Act* (New York: Vintage/Random House, 1972), 78–79; hereafter cited in text.

13. Barry Kernfeld, ed., *The New Grove Dictionary of Jazz* (New York: St. Martin's Press, 1994), 1238.

14. Sherley Anne Williams, "The Blues Roots of Contemporary Afro-American Poetry," *Massachusetts Review* 18 (1977): 542–43; hereafter cited in text.

15. James H. Cone, *The Spirituals and the Blues* (New York: Seabury Press, 1972), 35; hereafter cited in text.

Selected Bibliography

PRIMARY WORKS

Novels

Bailey's Cafe. New York: Harcourt, Brace, Jovanovich, 1992. Paperback reprint, New York: Vintage/Random House, 1993.

Linden Hills. New York: Ticknor & Fields, 1985. Paperback reprint, New York: Penguin, 1986.

Mama Day. New York: Ticknor & Fields, 1988. Paperback reprint, New York: Vintage, 1989.

The Women of Brewster Place: A Novel in Seven Stories. New York: Viking, 1982. Paperback reprint, New York: Penguin, 1983.

Essays, Notes, Poems, and "Conversations" (a chronological listing)

"Famous First Words." *New York Times Book Review*, 2 June 1985, 52. Comments on the opening paragraph of Toni Morrison's *The Bluest Eye.*

"Gloria Naylor and Toni Morrison: A Conversation." *Southern Review* 21 (1985): 567–93. Important comments on Morrison's influence and on the art of writing fiction.

"Reflections." In *Centennial*, edited by Michael Rosenthal, 68–71. New York: Pindar Press, 1986. Biographical information about Naylor's parents.

[Untitled "Hers" column]. *New York Times*, 20 February 1986. Essay about the word *nigger.*

"The Myth of the Matriarch." *Life* 11 (Spring 1988): 65. An essay debunking the myths about relationships between black men and black women.

"Power: Rx for Good Health." *Ms.* (May 1989): 58–60. Essay on Byllye Avery's activism for black women's health.

"Love and Sex in the Afro-American Novel." *Yale Review* 78 (1988): 19–31. In Naylor's only major essay of literary criticism, she defends black women writers' depiction of relationships between black men and women.

"Sexual Ease." *Essence* (December 1988): 108. Short note.

"African-American or Black: What's in a Name?" *Ebony* (July 1989): 80. Short note.

"Graceful Passages." *Essence* (May 1990): 134. Short note on turning 40.

[Untitled]. In *Writers Dreaming*, edited by Naomi Epel, 167–77. New York: Carol Southern Books, 1993. Important reflections on the process of writing the novels.

"Hidden Wealth?" In *First Words: Earliest Writing from Favorite Contemporary Authors*, edited by Paul Mandelbaum, 364. Chapel Hill, N.C.: Algonquin

Books, 1993. A nature poem, originally published in Naylor's high school literary magazine.

"Of Fathers and Sons: A Daughter Remembers." In *In Their Footsteps*, edited by Henry Chase, 5–7. New York: Henry Holt, 1994. Naylor's reflections about her father, written shortly before his death.

"Telling Tales and Mississippi Sunsets." In *Grand Mothers: Poems, Reminiscences, and Short Stories about the Keepers of Our Traditions*, edited by Nikki Giovanni, 59–62. New York: Henry Holt, 1994. Naylor's recollections of her grandmothers.

[Untitled]. In *I Know What the Red Clay Looks Like: The Voice and Vision of Black Women Writers*, edited by Rebecca Carroll, 160–65. New York: Crown Trade Paperbacks, 1994. Naylor's reflections about spirituality.

Interviews

Bellinelli, Mateo, dir. *A Conversation with Gloria Naylor* (videotape). Produced by RTSJ-Swiss Television. California Newsreel, 1992. Naylor talks about her family, politics, and literature.

Bonetti, Kay. "An Interview with Gloria Naylor" (audiotape). New York: American Prose Library, 1988. An important interview in which Naylor talks at length about her background and her writing.

Carabi, Angels. [Interview with Gloria Naylor]. *Belles Lettres* 7 (Spring 1992): 36–42. Naylor comments on her family and on her novels.

Pearlman, Mickey, and Katherine Usher Henderson. *A Voice of One's Own: Conversations with America's Writing Women*, 27–34. Boston: Houghton Mifflin, 1990. Naylor comments about her development as a writer.

SECONDARY SOURCES

Andrews, Larry. "Black Sisterhood in Gloria Naylor's Novels." *CLA Journal* 33 (1989): 1–25. Analysis of the theme of female bonding in the first three novels.

Awkward, Michael. "Authorial Dreams of Wholeness: (Dis)Unity, (Literary) Parentage, and *The Women of Brewster Place*." In his *Inspiriting Influences: Tradition, Revision and Afro-American Women's Novels*, 97–134. New York: Columbia University Press, 1989. Reprinted in Gates and Appiah, *Gloria Naylor*, 37–70. Extended analysis of the relationship of Naylor's first novel to two important precursor texts, Jean Toomer's *Cane* and Toni Morrison's *The Bluest Eye*.

Bobo, Jacqueline, and Ellen Seiter. "Black Feminism and Media Criticism: *The Women of Brewster Place*." *Screen* 32 (Autumn 1991): 286–302. Feminist analysis of the novel and the made-for-television movie.

Bouvier, Luke. "Reading in Black and White: Space and Race in *Linden Hills*." In Gates and Appiah, *Gloria Naylor*, 140–51. Analysis of interconnections between class, race, and place in the novel.

Branzburg, Judith V. "Seven Women and a Wall." *Callaloo* 7 (Spring/Summer 1984): 116–19. Overview of Naylor's community of women in *The Women of Brewster Place*.

Christian, Barbara. "Naylor's Geography: Community, Class, and Patriarchy in *The Women of Brewster Place* and *Linden Hills*." In *Reading Black, Reading Feminist*, edited by Henry Louis Gates, Jr., 348–73. New York: Meridian/Penguin, 1990. Reprinted in Gates and Appiah, *Gloria Naylor*, 106–25. Analysis of Naylor's use of setting and of the intersection of gender, race, and class in the first two novels.

————. "No More Buried Lives: The Theme of Lesbianism in Audre Lorde's *Zami*, Gloria Naylor's *The Women of Brewster Place*, Ntozake Shange's *Sassafras, Cypress and Indigo*, and Alice Walker's *The Color Purple*." In her *Black Feminist Criticism*, 187–204. New York: Pergamon Press, 1985. Analysis of the impact of homophobia on Lorraine and Theresa in Naylor's first novel.

Collins, Grace E. "Narrative Structure in *Linden Hills*." *CLA Journal* 34 (1991): 290–300. Analysis of the parallels between Willie and Willa's respective journeys.

Eko, Ebele. "Beyond the Myth of Confrontation: A Comparative Study of African and African-American Female Protagonists." *Ariel* 17 (October 1986): 139–52. Comparative study of mother-daughter relationships; focuses on Kiswana Browne and her mother in *The Women of Brewster Place*.

Erickson, Peter. [Review of *Bailey's Cafe*]. *Kenyon Review* 15 (Summer 1993). Reprinted in Gates and Appiah, *Gloria Naylor*, 32–34. Brief but useful analysis of the male characters in *Bailey's Cafe*, with special attention to the relationship of Miss Maple and his father.

————. "'Shakespeare's Black?' The Role of Shakespeare in Naylor's Novels." In his *Rewriting Shakespeare, Rewriting Ourselves*. Berkeley: University of California Press, 1991. Reprinted in Gates and Appiah, *Gloria Naylor*, 231–48. Analysis of Naylor's re-visioning of Shakespeare in *The Women of Brewster Place* and *Mama Day*; extended discussion of parallels between *Mama Day* and Paule Marshall's *Praisesong for the Widow* (1983).

Fraser, Celeste. "Stealing B(l)ack Voices: The Myth of the Black Matriarchy and *The Women of Brewster Place*." *Critical Matrix* 5 (Fall/Winter 1989). Reprinted in Gates and Appiah, *Gloria Naylor*, 90–105. Excellent analysis of Naylor's deconstruction of the myth of the black matriarch, especially as that myth was codified in the Moynihan Report.

Gates, Henry Louis, Jr. "Significant Others." *Contemporary Literature* 29 (1988): 606–23. Brief discussion of the relationship between Willie and Lester in

Linden Hills; Gates claims that Willie "functions as a sexual cynosure in the novel" (610).

————, and K. A. Appiah, eds. *Gloria Naylor: Critical Perspectives Past and Present*. New York: Amistad, 1993. A valuable collection of 14 critical essays and 13 reviews.

Goddu, Teresa. "Reconstructing History in *Linden Hills*." In Gates and Appiah, *Gloria Naylor*, 215–30. Analysis of the conflicting models of history represented by Luther Nedeed, Daniel Braithwaite, Willie Mason, and Willa Nedeed in Naylor's second novel.

Haralson, Eric L. "Gloria Naylor." In *African American Writers: Profiles of Their Lives and Works*, edited by Valerie Smith, Lea Baechler, and A. Walton Litz, 267–78. New York: Macmillan/Collier, 1991. Useful overview of Naylor's first three novels.

Holloway, Karla F. C. *Moorings and Metaphors: Figures of Culture and Gender in Black Women's Literature*. New Brunswick, N.J.: Rutgers University Press, 1992. Places Naylor within a tradition of contemporary black women writers whose work has figurative, cultural, and spiritual connections to West African writers.

Homans, Margaret. "The Woman in the Cave: Recent Feminist Fictions and the Classical Underworld." *Contemporary Literature* 29 (1988): 369–402. Reprinted in Gates and Appiah, *Gloria Naylor*, 152–81. Analysis of the allegorical structure of *Linden Hills* and of Naylor's feminist rewriting of both Dante and Virgil.

Juhasz, Suzanne. *Reading from the Heart: Women, Literature, and the Search for True Love*. New York: Viking/Penguin, 1994. Reads *Mama Day* as a novel about the magic circle of mother love into which the male hero cannot be admitted.

Kelley, Margot Anne. "Sisters' Choices: Quilting Aesthetics in Contemporary African American Women's Fiction." In *Quilt Culture: Tracing the Pattern*, edited by Cheryl B. Torsney and Judith Elsley, 49–67. Columbia: University of Missouri Press, 1994. Analysis of Naylor's use in *Mama Day* of an aesthetics taken from African American quilting.

Kelly, Lori Duin. "The Dream Sequence in *The Women of Brewster Place*." *Notes on Contemporary Literature* 21 (September 1991): 8–10. Discussion of Mattie's dream at the end of the novel.

Kubitschek, Missy Dehn. *Claiming the Heritage: African American Women Novelists and History*. Jackson: University Press of Mississippi, 1991. Discussion of the parallels between Willie Mason and the women of *Linden Hills*.

Levy, Helen Fiddyment. "Lead on with Light." In her *Fiction of the Home Place: Jewett, Cather, Glasgow, Porter, Welty, and Naylor*, 196–222. Jackson: University Press of Mississippi, 1992. Reprinted in Gates and Appiah, *Gloria Naylor*, 263–84. Traces the development of Naylor's female characters and the values associated with them in her first three novels; connects Naylor to the traditions of women's domestic and introspective novels.

Matus, Jill L. "Dream, Deferral, and Closure in *The Women of Brewster Place.*" *Black American Literature Forum* 24 (1990): 49–64. Reprinted in Gates and Appiah, *Gloria Naylor*, 126–39. Excellent analysis of the connections between the novel's structure and the theme of dreams and dreaming.

Meisenhelder, Susan. "'Eating Cane' in Gloria Naylor's *The Women of Brewster Place* and Zora Neale Hurston's 'Sweat.'" *Notes on Contemporary Literature* 23, no. 2 (March 1993): 5–7. Analysis of Butch Fuller's philosophy of life, which she interprets as misogynistic.

————. "'The Whole Picture' in Gloria Naylor's *Mama Day.*" *African American Review* 27 (1993): 405–19. Excellent analysis of the contrasting worlds and values in the novel.

Montgomery, Maxine L. "The Fathomless Dream: Gloria Naylor's Use of the Descent Motif in *The Women of Brewster Place.*" *CLA Journal* 36 (1992): 1–11. Uses Northrop Frye's concept of the romantic mode of literature to analyze the "journeys" taken by each of the characters in the novel.

Novy, Marianne. *Engaging with Shakespeare: Responses of George Eliot and Other Women Novelists.* Athens: University of Georgia Press, 1994. Brief discussion of Naylor's use of Shakespeare in *Mama Day.*

Palumbo, Kathryn. "The Uses of Female Imagery in Naylor's *The Women of Brewster Place.*" *Notes on Contemporary Literature* 15 (May 1985): 6–7. Brief analysis of womb imagery in the novel.

Reckley, Ralph, Sr. "Science, Faith, and Religion in Gloria Naylor's *Mama Day.*" In *Twentieth-Century Black American Women in Print: Essays by Ralph Reckley, Sr.*, edited by Lola E. Jones, 87–95. Acton, Mass.: Copley Publishing Group, 1991. Discussion of the novel's delineation of the conflict between an "African" worldview (Willow Springs) and a "rationalist" worldview (George).

Russell, Sandi. *Render Me My Song: African-American Women Writers from Slavery to the Present.* New York: St. Martin's Press, 1990. Draws attention to the similarity of *The Women of Brewster Place* to the British *Union Street* (1982) by Pat Barker.

Sandiford, Keith. "Gothic and Intertextual Constructions in *Linden Hills.*" *Arizona Quarterly* 47 (1991): 117–39. Reprinted in Gates and Appiah, *Gloria Naylor*, 195–214. Uses Mikhail Bakhtin's concept of multiple, competing voices; reads *Linden Hills* as a gothic novel.

Saunders, James Robert. "The Ornamentation of Old Ideas: Gloria Naylor's First Three Novels." *Hollins Critic* 27, no. 2 (April 1990): 1–11. Reprinted in Gates and Appiah, *Gloria Naylor*, 249–62. Sees Naylor as a "borrower" whose first three novels draw upon Petry, Dante, and Shakespeare.

Showalter, Elaine. *Sister's Choice: Tradition and Change in American Women's Writing.* New York: Clarendon/Oxford, 1991. Connects Naylor's *Mama*

Day to other American texts that have reworked Shakespeare's *The Tempest*.

Sisney, Mary F. "The View from the Outside: Black Novels of Manners." In *Reading and Writing Women's Lives: A Study of the Novel of Manners*, edited by Bege K. Bowers and Barbara Brothers, 171–85. Ann Arbor: UMI Research Press, 1990. Reads *Linden Hills* as a new kind of novel of manners.

Smith, Barbara. "The Truth That Never Hurts: Lesbians in Fiction in the 1980s." In *Wild Women in the Whirlwind: Afra-American Culture and the Contemporary Literary Renaissance*, edited by Joanne M. Braxton and Andrée Nicola McLaughlin, 213–45. New Brunswick, N.J.: Rutgers University Press, 1990. Sharply critical analysis of Naylor's depiction of lesbianism in *The Women of Brewster Place*.

Tanner, Laura E. "Reading Rape: *Sanctuary* and *The Women of Brewster Place*." *American Literature* 62 (1990): 559–82. Reprinted in Gates and Appiah, *Gloria Naylor*, 71–89. Contrasts the rape scenes in these two novels to demonstrate Naylor's disruption of the "'eroticized' response to rape seemingly authorized by literary convention."

Toombs, Charles P. "The Confluence of Food and Identity in Gloria Naylor's *Linden Hills*: 'What We Eat Is Who We Is.'" *CLA Journal* 37 (1993): 1–18. Analysis of the food and eating rituals associated with various characters in the novel.

Traub, Valerie. "Rainbows of Darkness: Deconstructing Shakespeare in the Work of Gloria Naylor and Zora Neale Hurston." In *Cross-cultural Performances: Differences in Women's Re-Visions of Shakespeare*, edited by Marianne Novy, 150–64. Urbana and Chicago: University of Illinois Press, 1993. Excellent extended analysis of Naylor's complex use of *King Lear*, *Hamlet*, and *The Tempest* in *Mama Day*.

Tucker, Lindsey. "Recovering the Conjure Woman: Texts and Contexts in Gloria Naylor's *Mama Day*." *African American Review* 28 (Summer 1994): 173–88. Valuable analysis of Naylor's "restitution" and use of the conjure woman; extensive discussion of historical conjure women and of African beliefs and medicinal practices.

Wagner-Martin, Linda. "Quilting in Gloria Naylor's *Mama Day*." *Notes on Contemporary Literature* 18 (May 1988): 6–7. This brief note first drew attention to Naylor's figurative use of the quilt.

Ward, Catherine C. "Gloria Naylor's *Linden Hills*: A Modern Inferno." *Contemporary Literature* 28 (1987): 67–81. Reprinted in Gates and Appiah, *Gloria Naylor*, 182–94. Extended analysis of Naylor's use of Dante.

Winsbro, Bonnie. "Modern Rationality and the Supernatural: Bridging Two Worlds in Gloria Naylor's *Mama Day*." In her *Supernatural Forces: Belief, Difference, and Power in Contemporary Works by Ethnic Women*, 109–28. Amherst: University of Massachusetts Press, 1993. Analysis of the two worlds in *Mama Day*, with useful attention to Cocoa's illness.

Index

The Author

An associate professor of English at Virginia Tech, Virginia Fowler received her B.A. from the University of Kentucky and her M.A. and Ph.D. degrees from the University of Pittsburgh. Her teaching and research interests are in African American literature, with special focus on African American women writers. Professor Fowler has previously published *Henry James's American Girl: The Embroidery on the Canvas* (University of Wisconsin Press, 1984), *Nikki Giovanni* (Twayne, 1992), and *Conversations with Nikki Giovanni* (University Press of Mississippi, 1992).

The Editor

Frank Day is a professor of English and head of the English Department at Clemson University. He is the author of *Sir William Empson: An Annotated Bibliography* (1984) and *Arthur Koestler: A Guide to Research* (1985). He was a Fulbright lecturer in American literature in Romania (1980–81) and in Bangladesh (1986–87).